We Were Here First

Other *Baby Blues*® Books from Andrews McMeel Publishing

Guess Who Didn't Take a Nap?
I Thought Labor Ended When the Baby Was Born
We Are Experiencing Parental Difficulties . . . Please Stand By
Night of the Living Dad
I Saw Elvis in My Ultrasound
One More and We're Outnumbered!
Check, Please . . .
threats, bribes & videotape
If I'm a Stay-at-Home Mom, Why Am I Always in the Car?
Lift and Separate
I Shouldn't Have to Scream More Than Once!
Motherhood Is Not for Wimps
Baby Blues®: Unplugged
Dad to the Bone
Never a Dry Moment
Two Plus One Is Enough
Playdate: Category 5
Our Server Is Down
Something Chocolate This Way Comes
Briefcase Full of Baby Blues®
Night Shift
The Day Phonics Kicked In
My Space
The Natural Disorder of Things

Treasuries

The Super-Absorbent Biodegradable Family-Size Baby Blues®
Baby Blues®: Ten Years and Still in Diapers
Butt-Naked Baby Blues®
Wall-to-Wall Baby Blues®
Driving Under the Influence of Children
Framed!
X-Treme Parenting

We Were Here First

Baby Blues® Looks at Couplehood with Kids

by Rick Kirkman & Jerry Scott

**Andrews McMeel
Publishing, LLC**

Kansas City · Sydney · London

Baby Blues® is syndicated internationally by King Features Syndicate, Inc. For information, write King Features Syndicate, Inc., 300 West Fifty-Seventh Street, New York, New York 10019.

10 11 12 13 14 RR2 10 9 8 7 6 5 4 3 2 1

ISBN-13: 978-0-7407-9111-6
ISBN-10: 0-7407-9111-7

Library of Congress Catalog Number: 2009943091

www.andrewsmcmeel.com

Find *Baby Blues*® on the Web at
www.babyblues.com.

Our special thanks to Nancy Evans for her help on the design and production of this book.

For Carrie Lane, Superteacher.
—J.S.

To Sukey, my amazing partner in the ever-changing journey of parenting.
—R.K.

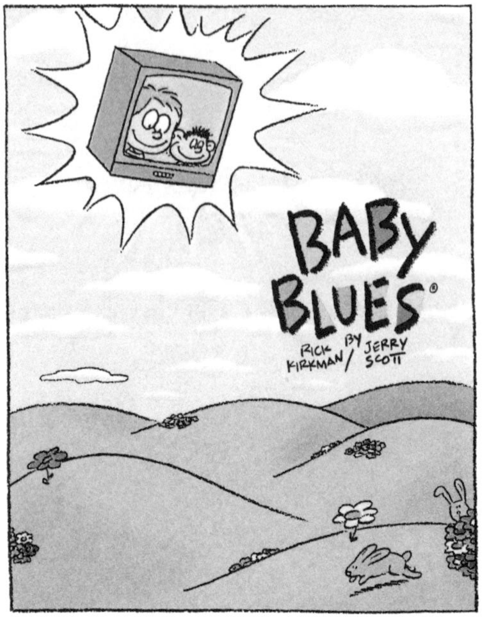
BABY BLUES®
BY RICK KIRKMAN / JERRY SCOTT

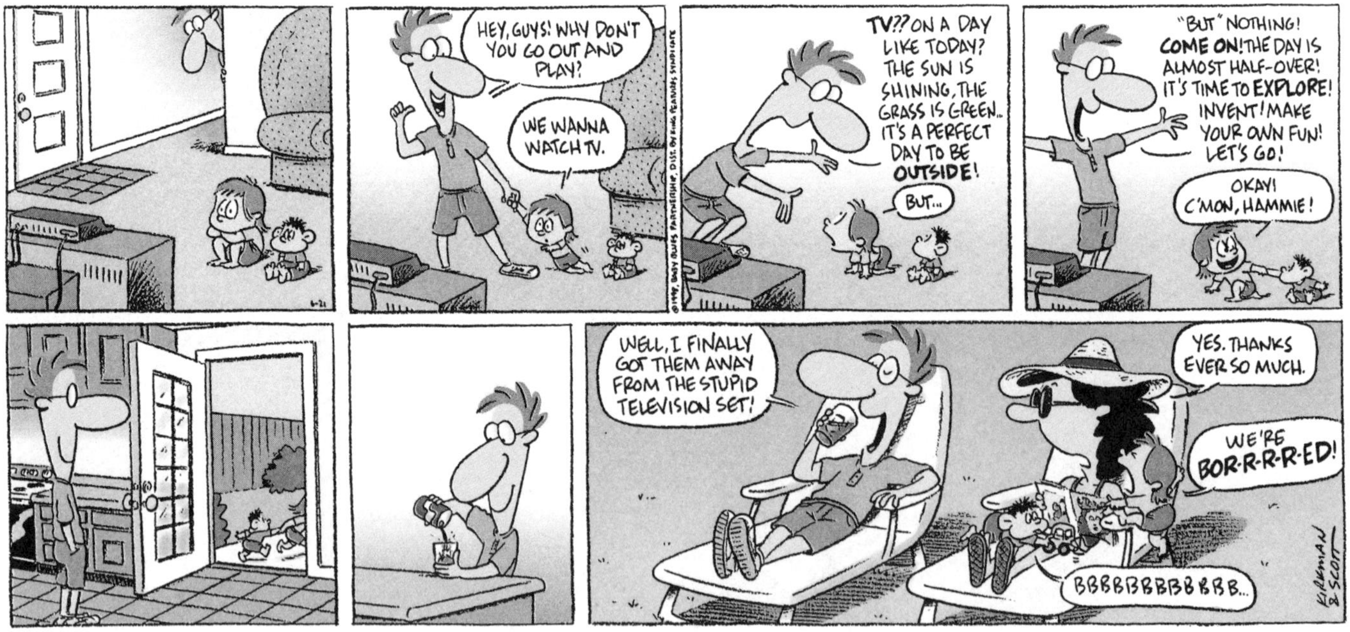
HEY, GUYS! WHY DON'T YOU GO OUT AND PLAY?
WE WANNA WATCH TV.
©1998, BABY BLUES PARTNERSHIP. DIST. BY KING FEATURES SYNDICATE
TV?? ON A DAY LIKE TODAY? THE SUN IS SHINING, THE GRASS IS GREEN... IT'S A PERFECT DAY TO BE OUTSIDE!
BUT...
"BUT" NOTHING! COME ON! THE DAY IS ALMOST HALF-OVER! IT'S TIME TO EXPLORE! INVENT! MAKE YOUR OWN FUN! LET'S GO!
OKAY! C'MON, HAMMIE!
WELL, I FINALLY GOT THEM AWAY FROM THE STUPID TELEVISION SET!
YES. THANKS EVER SO MUCH.
WE'RE BOR-R-R-R-ED!
BBBBBBBBBBBB...
KIRKMAN & SCOTT

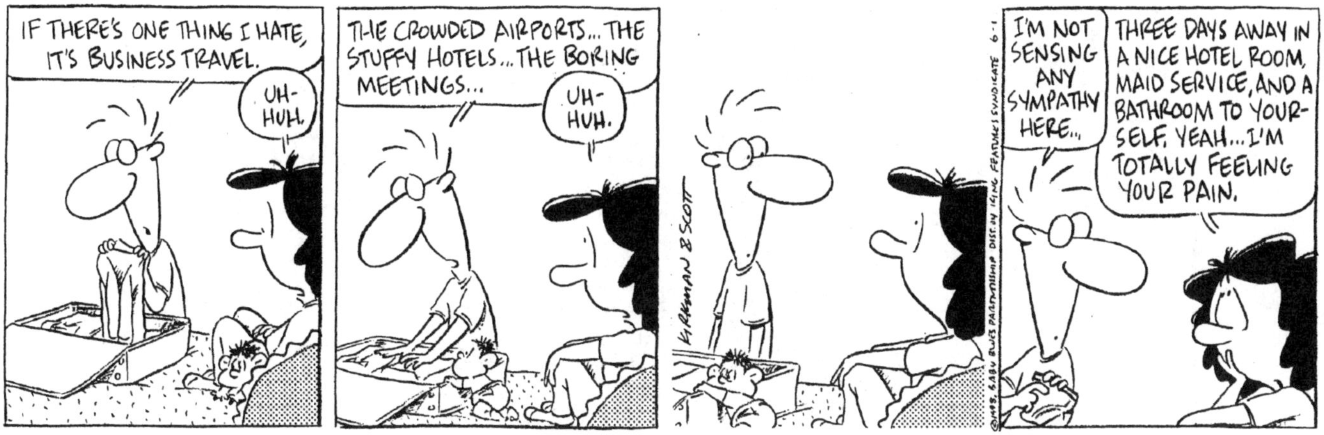
IF THERE'S ONE THING I HATE, IT'S BUSINESS TRAVEL.
UH-HUH.
THE CROWDED AIRPORTS... THE STUFFY HOTELS... THE BORING MEETINGS...
UH-HUH.
KIRKMAN & SCOTT
I'M NOT SENSING ANY SYMPATHY HERE...
THREE DAYS AWAY IN A NICE HOTEL ROOM, MAID SERVICE, AND A BATHROOM TO YOURSELF. YEAH... I'M TOTALLY FEELING YOUR PAIN.

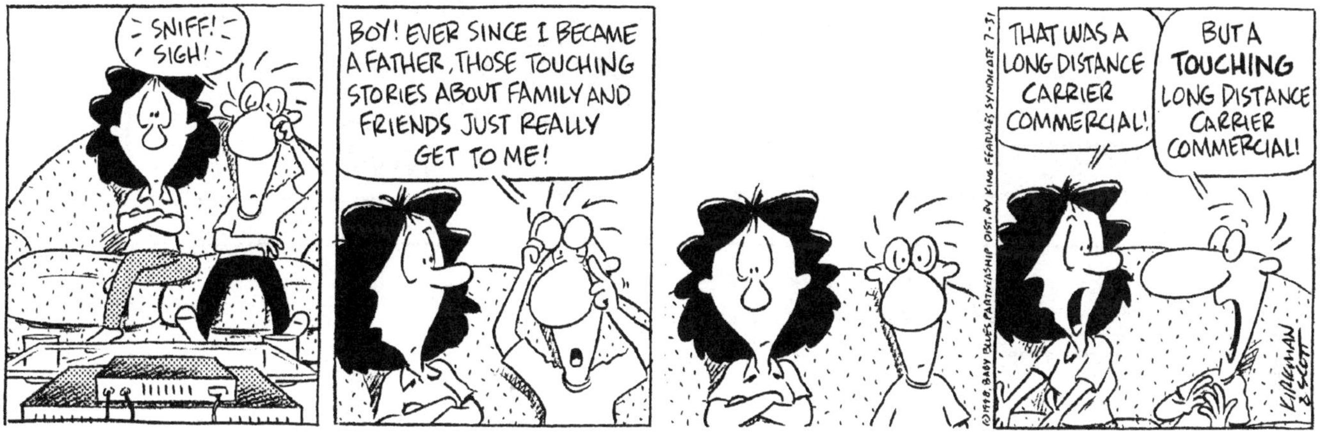
SNIFF! SIGH!
BOY! EVER SINCE I BECAME A FATHER, THOSE TOUCHING STORIES ABOUT FAMILY AND FRIENDS JUST REALLY GET TO ME!
THAT WAS A LONG DISTANCE CARRIER COMMERCIAL!
BUT A **TOUCHING** LONG DISTANCE CARRIER COMMERCIAL!
KIRKMAN & SCOTT

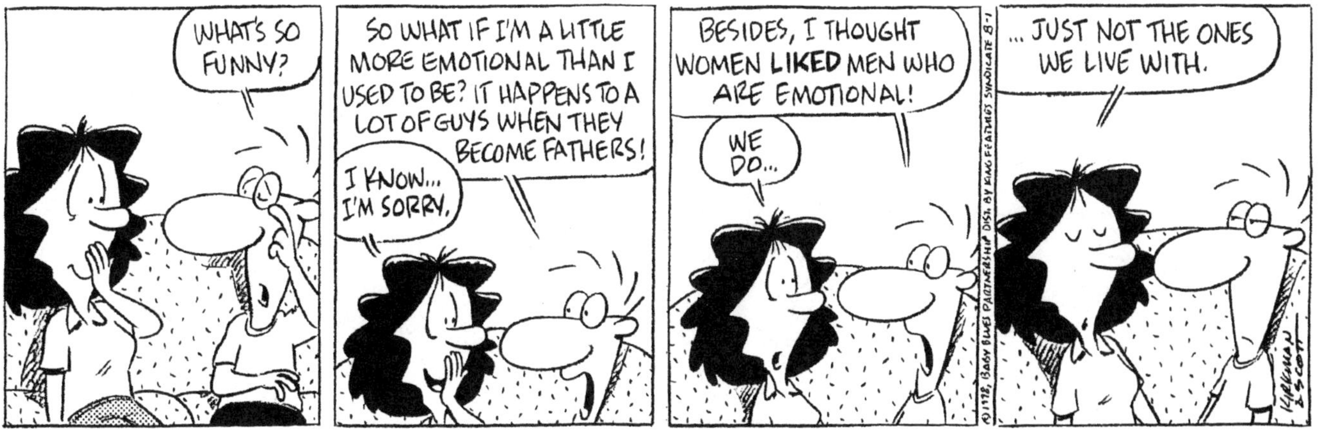
WHAT'S SO FUNNY?
SO WHAT IF I'M A LITTLE MORE EMOTIONAL THAN I USED TO BE? IT HAPPENS TO A LOT OF GUYS WHEN THEY BECOME FATHERS!
I KNOW... I'M SORRY.
BESIDES, I THOUGHT WOMEN **LIKED** MEN WHO ARE EMOTIONAL!
WE DO...
... JUST NOT THE ONES WE LIVE WITH.
KIRKMAN & SCOTT

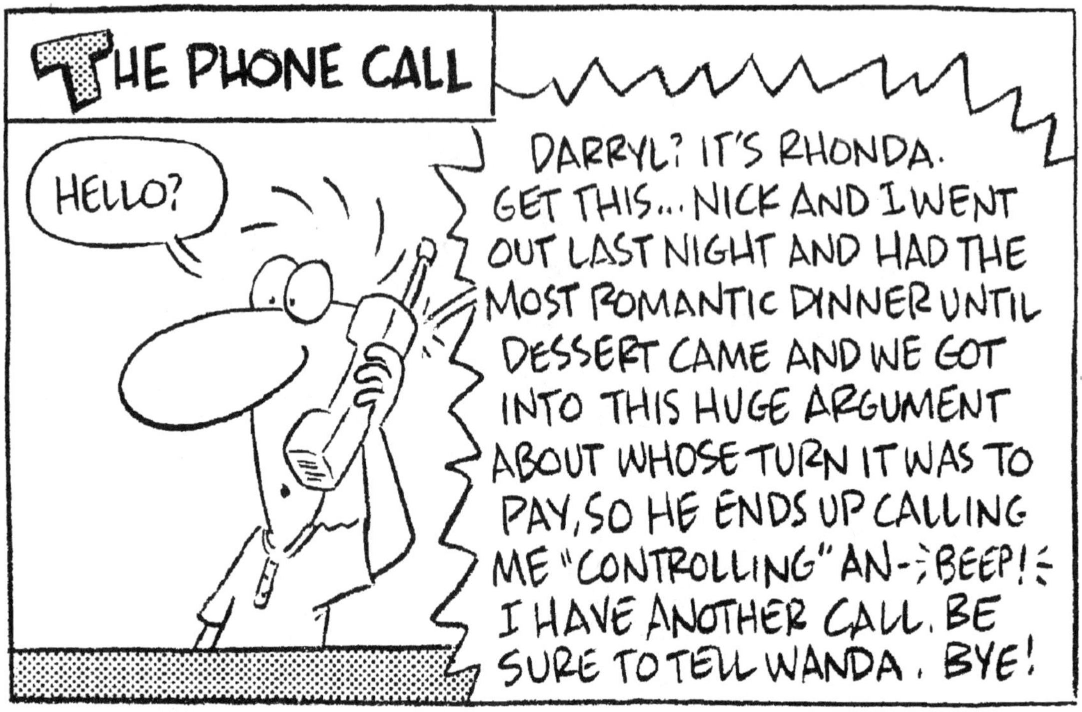
THE PHONE CALL
HELLO?
DARRYL? IT'S RHONDA. GET THIS... NICK AND I WENT OUT LAST NIGHT AND HAD THE MOST ROMANTIC DINNER UNTIL DESSERT CAME AND WE GOT INTO THIS HUGE ARGUMENT ABOUT WHOSE TURN IT WAS TO PAY, SO HE ENDS UP CALLING ME "CONTROLLING" AN- BEEP! I HAVE ANOTHER CALL. BE SURE TO TELL WANDA. BYE!

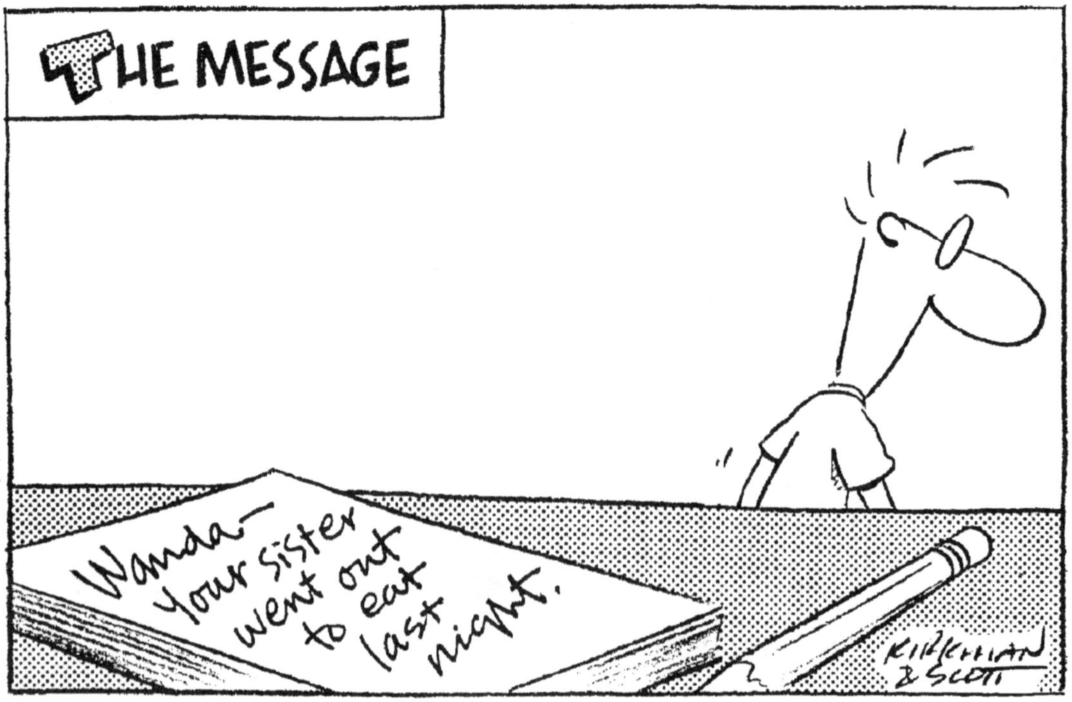
THE MESSAGE
Wanda—
Your sister went out to eat last night.
KIRKMAN & SCOTT

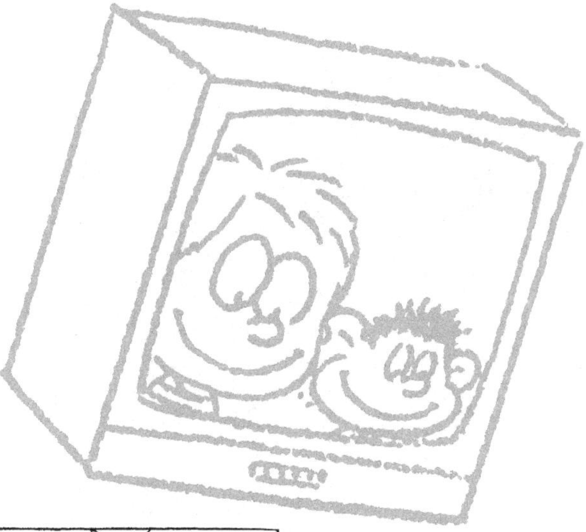

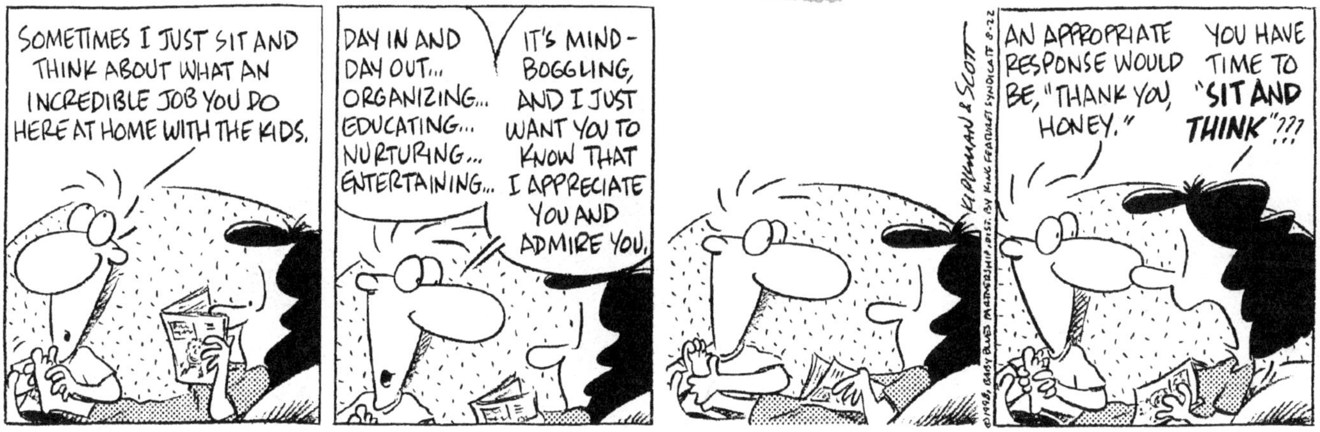

SOMETIMES I JUST SIT AND THINK ABOUT WHAT AN INCREDIBLE JOB YOU DO HERE AT HOME WITH THE KIDS.
DAY IN AND DAY OUT... ORGANIZING... EDUCATING... NURTURING... ENTERTAINING...
IT'S MIND-BOGGLING, AND I JUST WANT YOU TO KNOW THAT I APPRECIATE YOU AND ADMIRE YOU.
KIRKMAN & SCOTT
AN APPROPRIATE RESPONSE WOULD BE, "THANK YOU, HONEY."
YOU HAVE TIME TO "**SIT AND THINK**"???

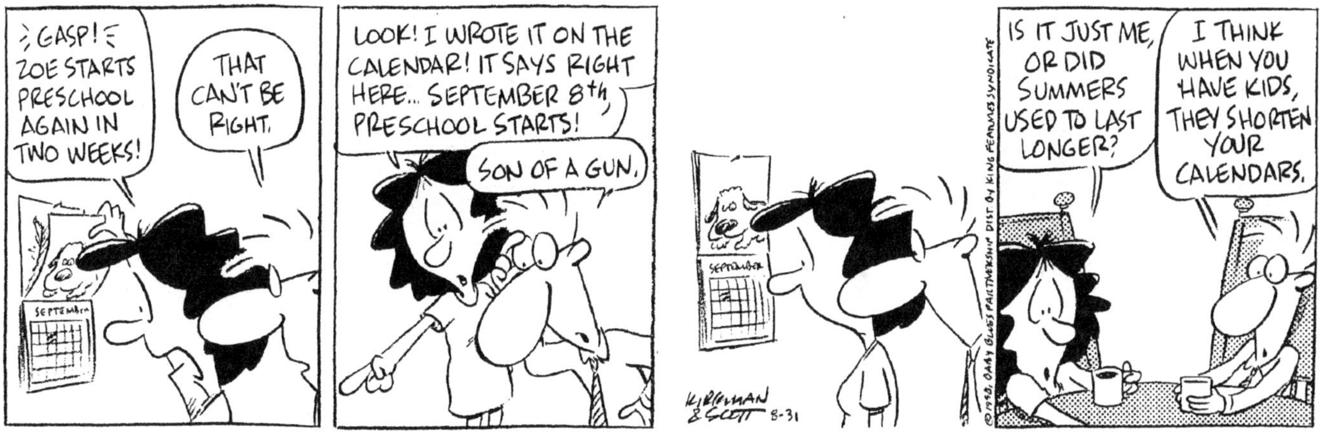

GASP! ZOE STARTS PRESCHOOL AGAIN IN TWO WEEKS!
THAT CAN'T BE RIGHT.
LOOK! I WROTE IT ON THE CALENDAR! IT SAYS RIGHT HERE... SEPTEMBER 8th, PRESCHOOL STARTS!
SON OF A GUN.
KIRKMAN & SCOTT 8-31
IS IT JUST ME, OR DID SUMMERS USED TO LAST LONGER?
I THINK WHEN YOU HAVE KIDS, THEY SHORTEN YOUR CALENDARS.

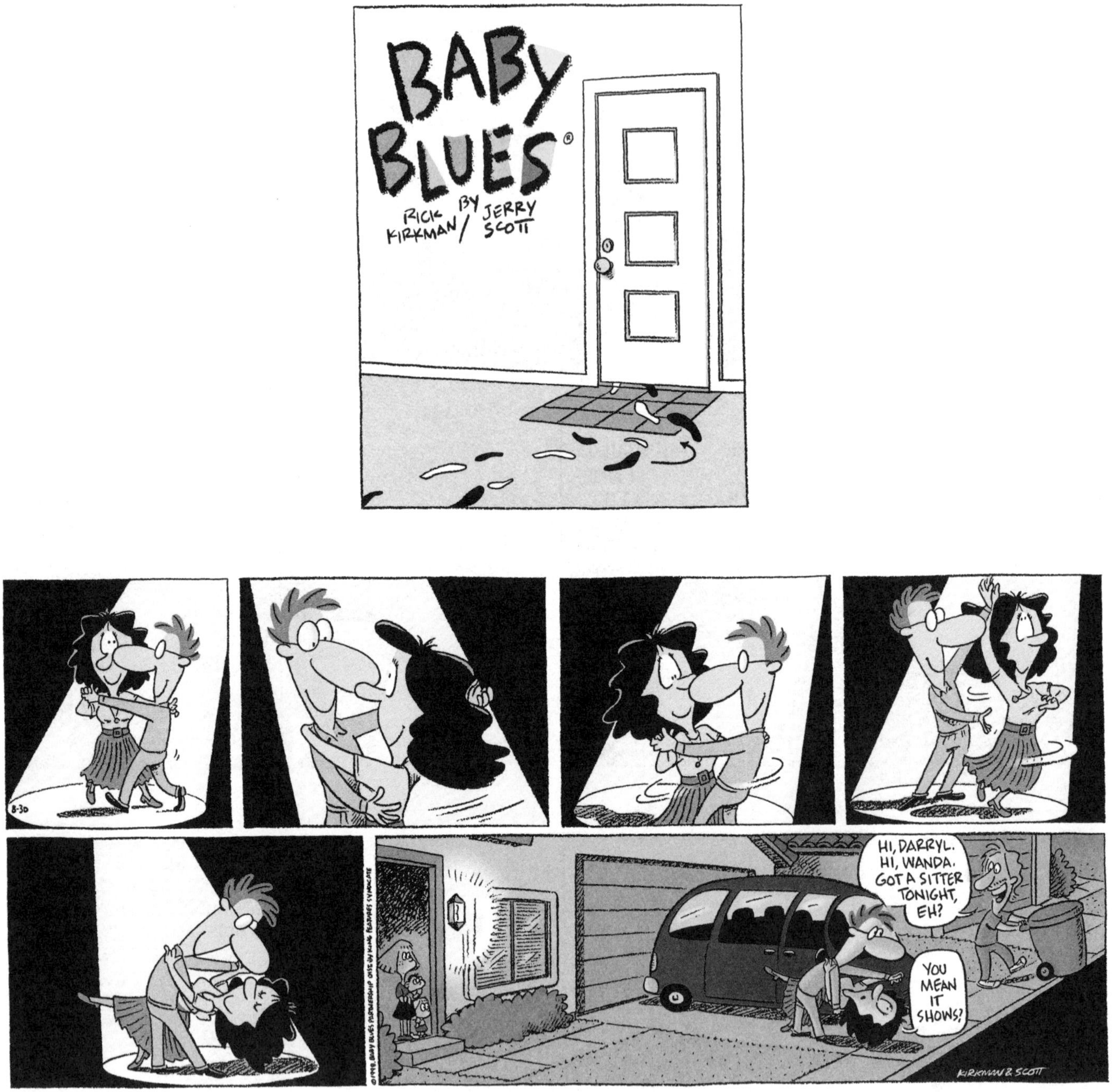
BABY BLUES®
BY RICK KIRKMAN / JERRY SCOTT
8-30
©1998, BABY BLUES PARTNERSHIP DIST. BY KING FEATURES SYNDICATE
HI, DARRYL. HI, WANDA. GOT A SITTER TONIGHT, EH?
YOU MEAN IT SHOWS?
KIRKMAN & SCOTT

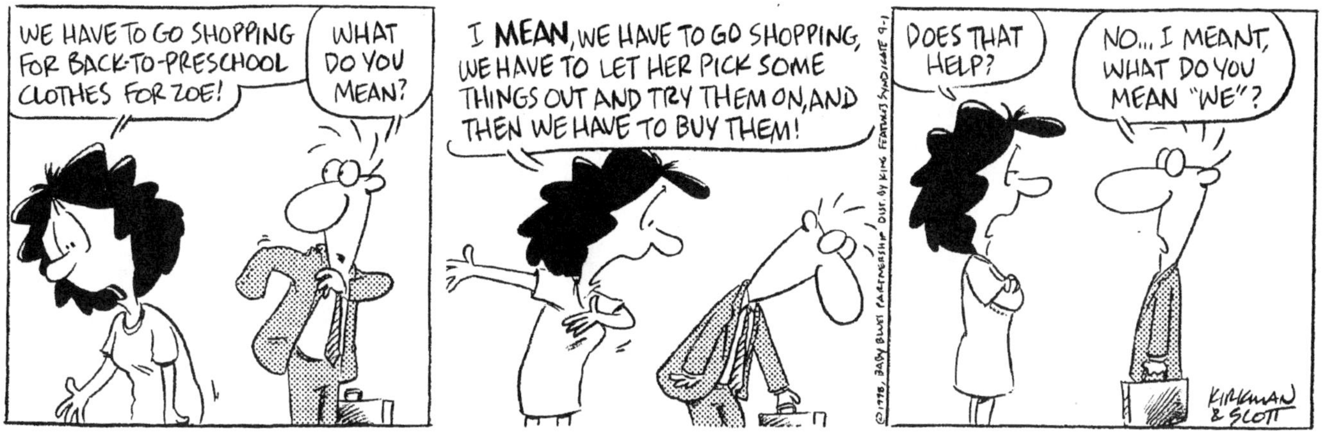
WE HAVE TO GO SHOPPING FOR BACK-TO-PRESCHOOL CLOTHES FOR ZOE!
WHAT DO YOU MEAN?
I **MEAN**, WE HAVE TO GO SHOPPING, WE HAVE TO LET HER PICK SOME THINGS OUT AND TRY THEM ON, AND THEN WE HAVE TO BUY THEM!
DOES THAT HELP?
NO... I MEANT, WHAT DO YOU MEAN "WE"?
©1998, BABY BLUES PARTNERSHIP DIST. BY KING FEATURES SYNDICATE 9-1
KIRKMAN & SCOTT

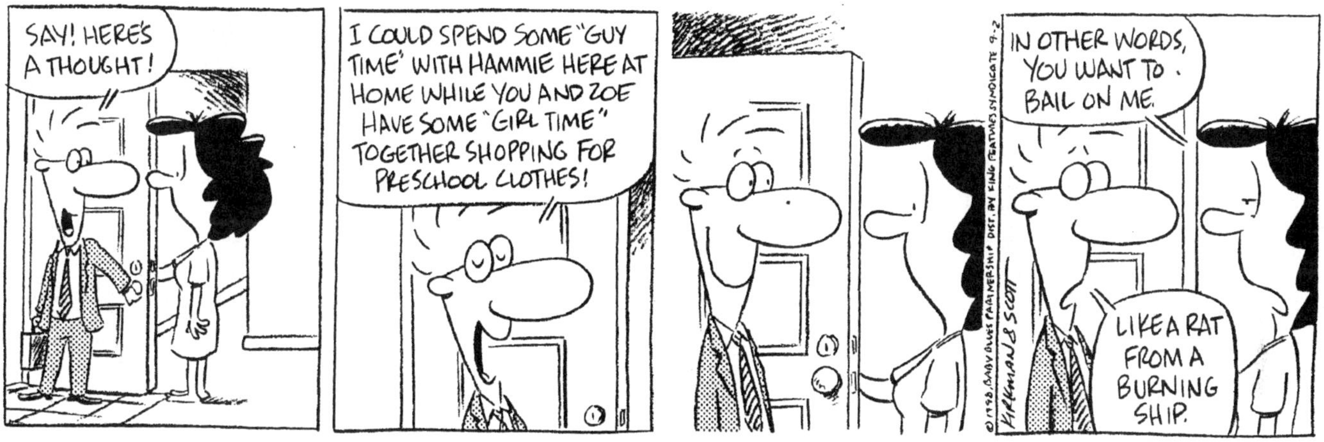
SAY! HERE'S A THOUGHT!
I COULD SPEND SOME "GUY TIME" WITH HAMMIE HERE AT HOME WHILE YOU AND ZOE HAVE SOME "GIRL TIME" TOGETHER SHOPPING FOR PRESCHOOL CLOTHES!
IN OTHER WORDS, YOU WANT TO BAIL ON ME.
LIKE A RAT FROM A BURNING SHIP.
©1998, BABY BLUES PARTNERSHIP DIST. BY KING FEATURES SYNDICATE 9-2
KIRKMAN & SCOTT

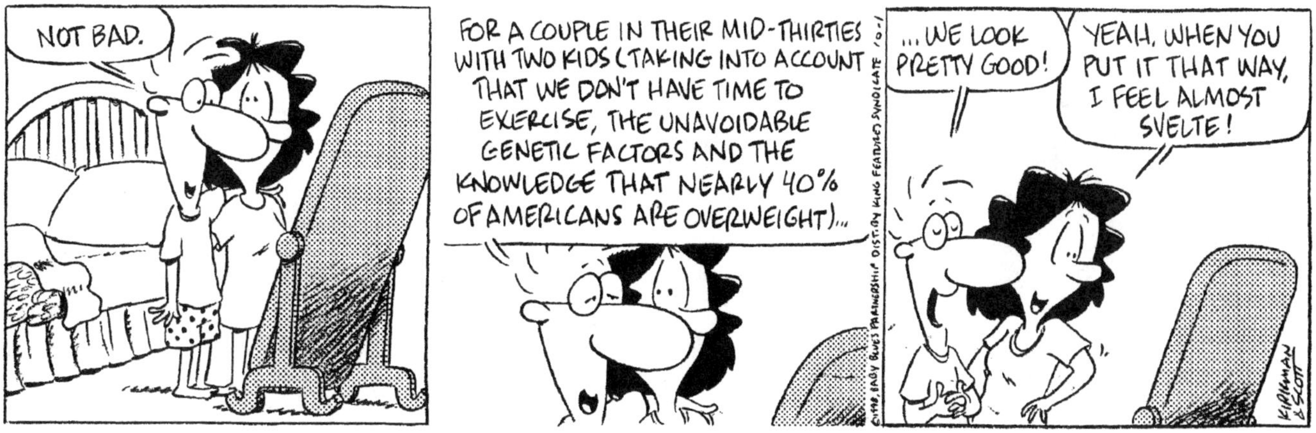
NOT BAD.
FOR A COUPLE IN THEIR MID-THIRTIES WITH TWO KIDS (TAKING INTO ACCOUNT THAT WE DON'T HAVE TIME TO EXERCISE, THE UNAVOIDABLE GENETIC FACTORS AND THE KNOWLEDGE THAT NEARLY 40% OF AMERICANS ARE OVERWEIGHT)...
...WE LOOK PRETTY GOOD!
YEAH, WHEN YOU PUT IT THAT WAY, I FEEL ALMOST SVELTE!
©1998, BABY BLUES PARTNERSHIP DIST. BY KING FEATURES SYNDICATE 10-1
KIRKMAN & SCOTT

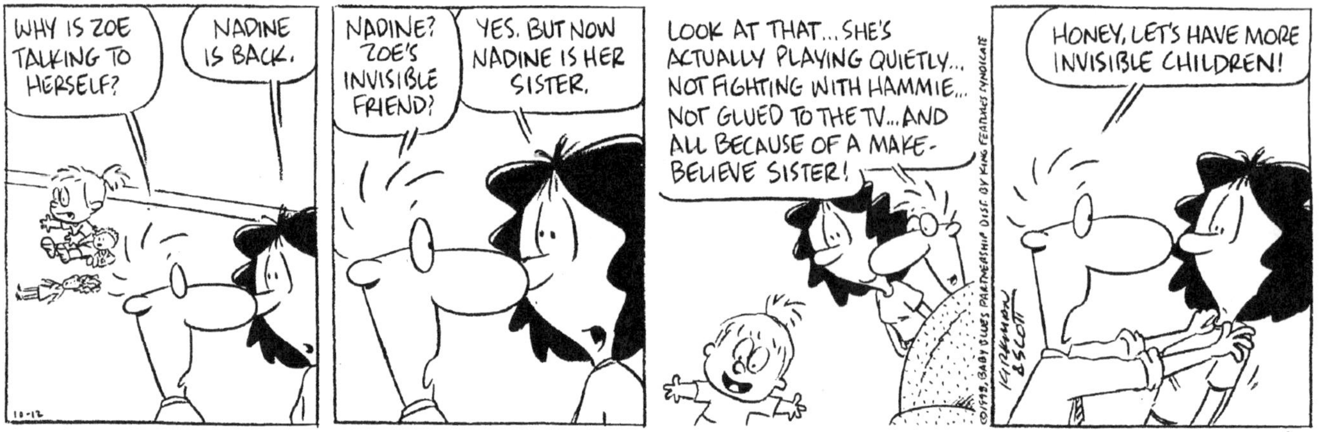
WHY IS ZOE TALKING TO HERSELF?
NADINE IS BACK.
NADINE? ZOE'S INVISIBLE FRIEND?
YES. BUT NOW NADINE IS HER SISTER.
LOOK AT THAT... SHE'S ACTUALLY PLAYING QUIETLY... NOT FIGHTING WITH HAMMIE... NOT GLUED TO THE TV... AND ALL BECAUSE OF A MAKE-BELIEVE SISTER!
HONEY, LET'S HAVE MORE INVISIBLE CHILDREN!
10-12
KIRKMAN & SCOTT

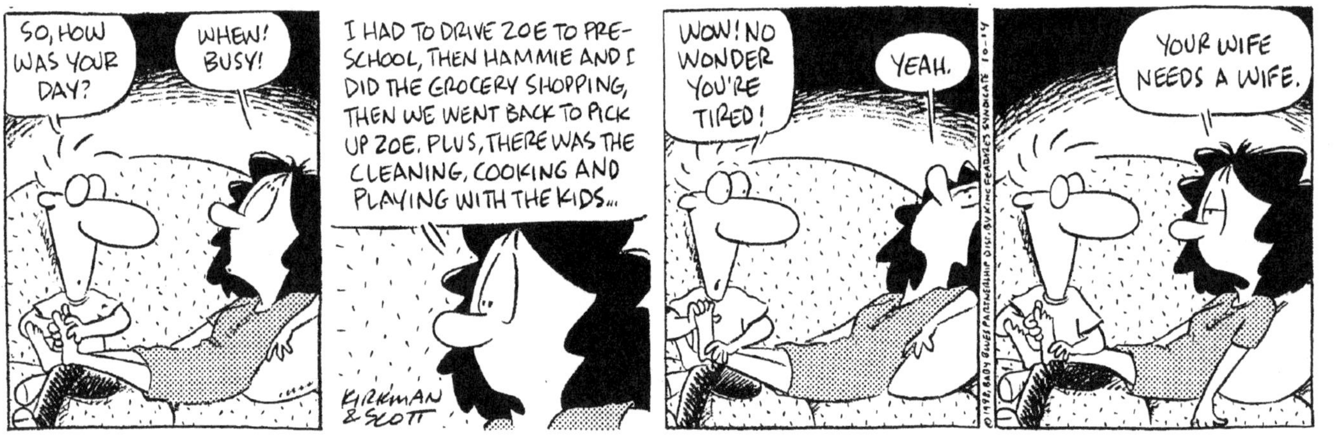
SO, HOW WAS YOUR DAY?
WHEW! BUSY!
I HAD TO DRIVE ZOE TO PRE-SCHOOL, THEN HAMMIE AND I DID THE GROCERY SHOPPING, THEN WE WENT BACK TO PICK UP ZOE. PLUS, THERE WAS THE CLEANING, COOKING AND PLAYING WITH THE KIDS...
KIRKMAN & SCOTT
WOW! NO WONDER YOU'RE TIRED!
YEAH.
YOUR WIFE NEEDS A WIFE.

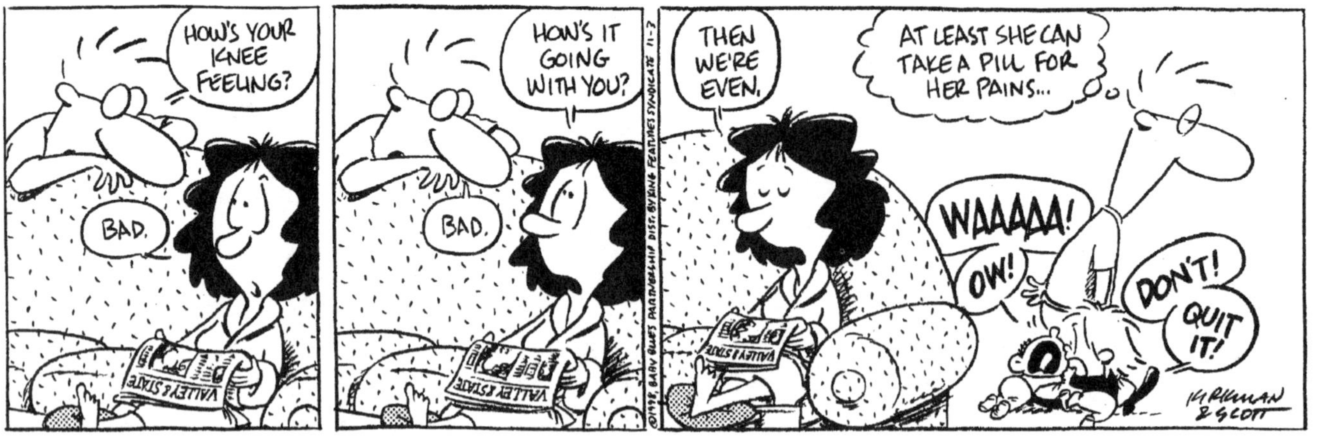
HOW'S YOUR KNEE FEELING?
BAD.
HOW'S IT GOING WITH YOU?
BAD.
THEN WE'RE EVEN.
AT LEAST SHE CAN TAKE A PILL FOR HER PAINS...
WAAAAA!
OW!
DON'T!
QUIT IT!
VALLEY STATE
KIRKMAN & SCOTT

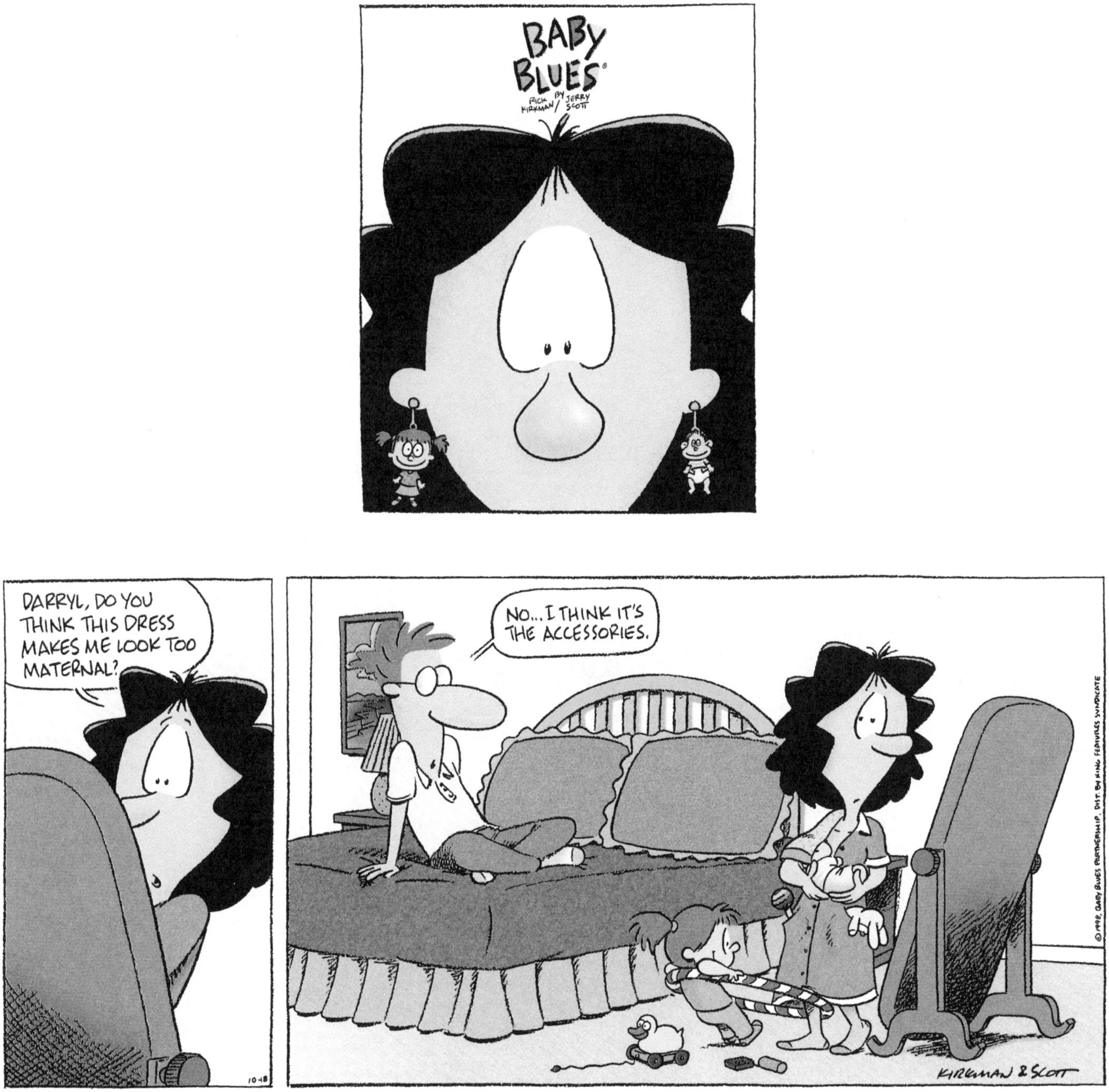
BABY BLUES®
BY RICK KIRKMAN / JERRY SCOTT
DARRYL, DO YOU THINK THIS DRESS MAKES ME LOOK TOO MATERNAL?
10-18
NO... I THINK IT'S THE ACCESSORIES.
©1998, BABY BLUES PARTNERSHIP. DIST. BY KING FEATURES SYNDICATE
KIRKMAN & SCOTT

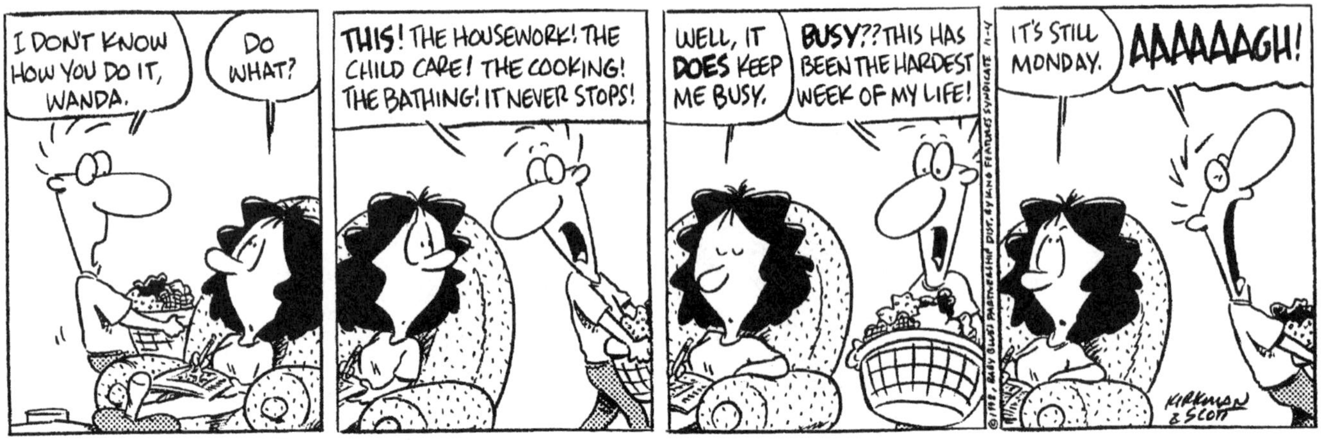
I DON'T KNOW HOW YOU DO IT, WANDA.
DO WHAT?
THIS! THE HOUSEWORK! THE CHILD CARE! THE COOKING! THE BATHING! IT NEVER STOPS!
WELL, IT DOES KEEP ME BUSY.
BUSY?? THIS HAS BEEN THE HARDEST WEEK OF MY LIFE!
IT'S STILL MONDAY.
AAAAAAGH!
KIRKMAN & SCOTT

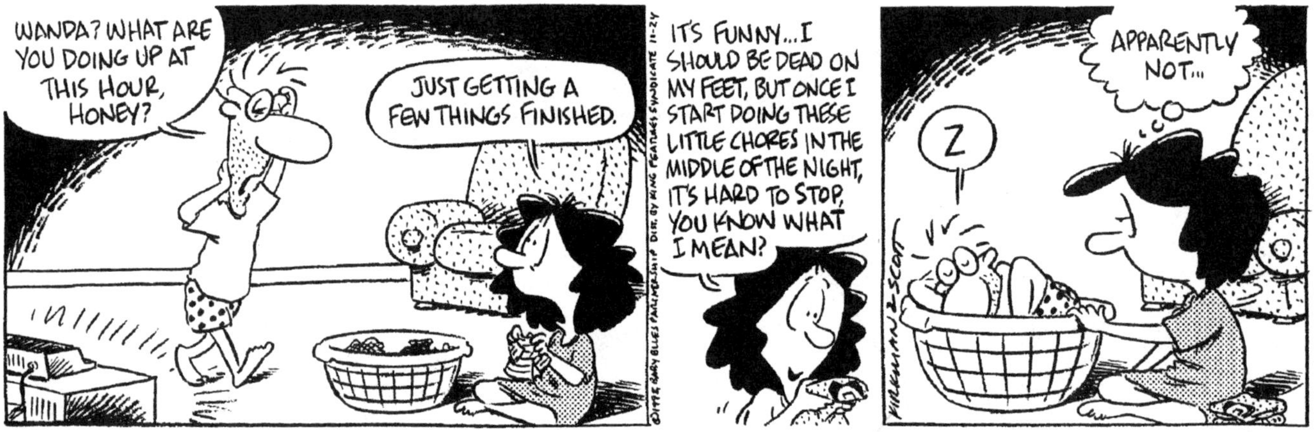
WANDA? WHAT ARE YOU DOING UP AT THIS HOUR, HONEY?
JUST GETTING A FEW THINGS FINISHED.
IT'S FUNNY... I SHOULD BE DEAD ON MY FEET, BUT ONCE I START DOING THESE LITTLE CHORES IN THE MIDDLE OF THE NIGHT, IT'S HARD TO STOP, YOU KNOW WHAT I MEAN?
Z
APPARENTLY NOT...
KIRKMAN & SCOTT

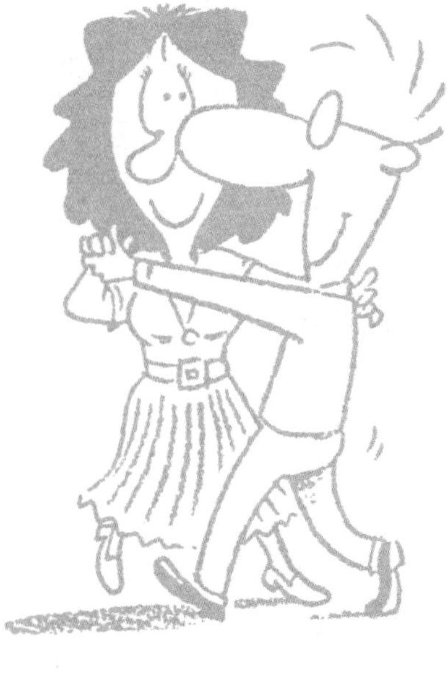

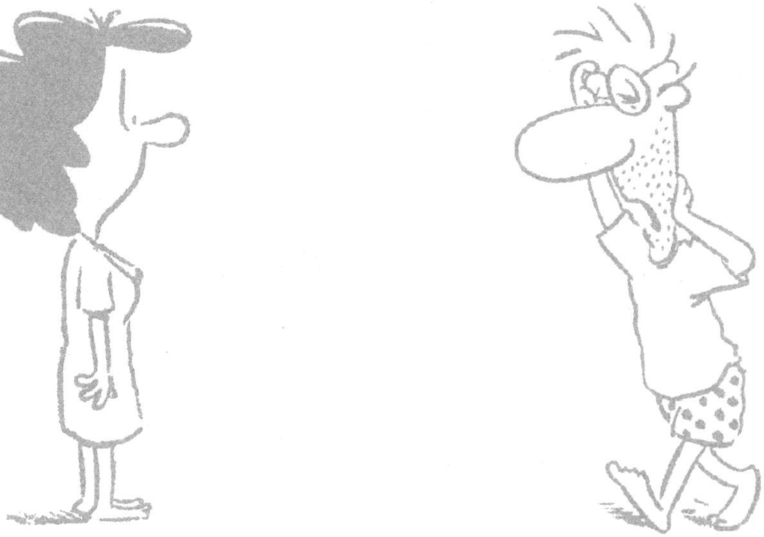

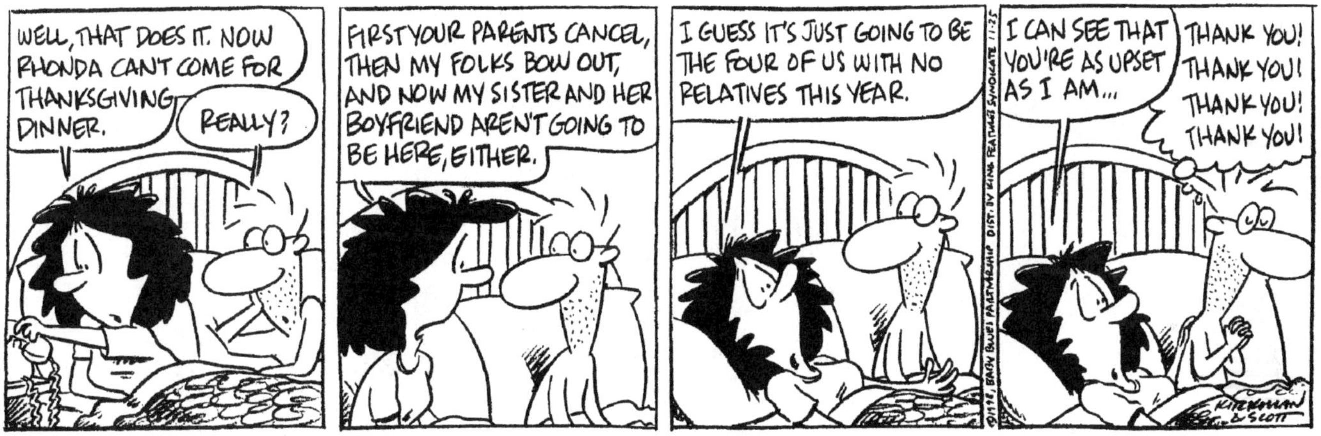
WELL, THAT DOES IT. NOW RHONDA CAN'T COME FOR THANKSGIVING DINNER.
REALLY?
FIRST YOUR PARENTS CANCEL, THEN MY FOLKS BOW OUT, AND NOW MY SISTER AND HER BOYFRIEND AREN'T GOING TO BE HERE, EITHER.
I GUESS IT'S JUST GOING TO BE THE FOUR OF US WITH NO RELATIVES THIS YEAR.
©1998, BABY BLUES PARTNERSHIP DIST. BY KING FEATURES SYNDICATE 11-25
I CAN SEE THAT YOU'RE AS UPSET AS I AM...
THANK YOU! THANK YOU! THANK YOU! THANK YOU!
KIRKMAN & SCOTT

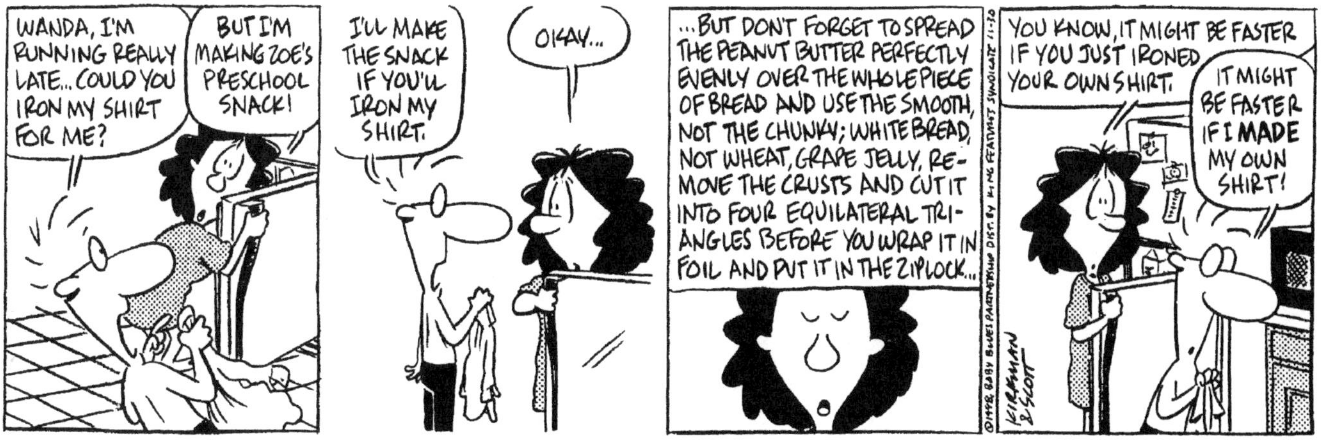
WANDA, I'M RUNNING REALLY LATE... COULD YOU IRON MY SHIRT FOR ME?
BUT I'M MAKING ZOE'S PRESCHOOL SNACK!
I'LL MAKE THE SNACK IF YOU'LL IRON MY SHIRT.
OKAY...
...BUT DON'T FORGET TO SPREAD THE PEANUT BUTTER PERFECTLY EVENLY OVER THE WHOLE PIECE OF BREAD AND USE THE SMOOTH, NOT THE CHUNKY; WHITE BREAD, NOT WHEAT, GRAPE JELLY, REMOVE THE CRUSTS AND CUT IT INTO FOUR EQUILATERAL TRIANGLES BEFORE YOU WRAP IT IN FOIL AND PUT IT IN THE ZIPLOCK...
©1998 BABY BLUES PARTNERSHIP DIST. BY KING FEATURES SYNDICATE 11-20
KIRKMAN & SCOTT
YOU KNOW, IT MIGHT BE FASTER IF YOU JUST IRONED YOUR OWN SHIRT.
IT MIGHT BE FASTER IF I **MADE** MY OWN SHIRT!

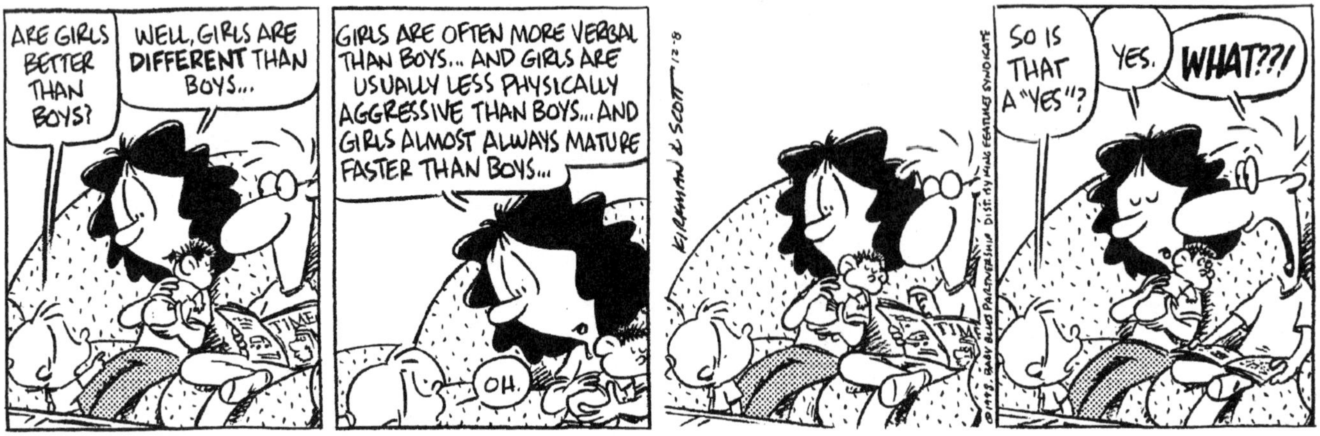
ARE GIRLS BETTER THAN BOYS?
WELL, GIRLS ARE **DIFFERENT** THAN BOYS...
GIRLS ARE OFTEN MORE VERBAL THAN BOYS... AND GIRLS ARE USUALLY LESS PHYSICALLY AGGRESSIVE THAN BOYS... AND GIRLS ALMOST ALWAYS MATURE FASTER THAN BOYS...
OH.
SO IS THAT A "YES"?
YES.
WHAT??!

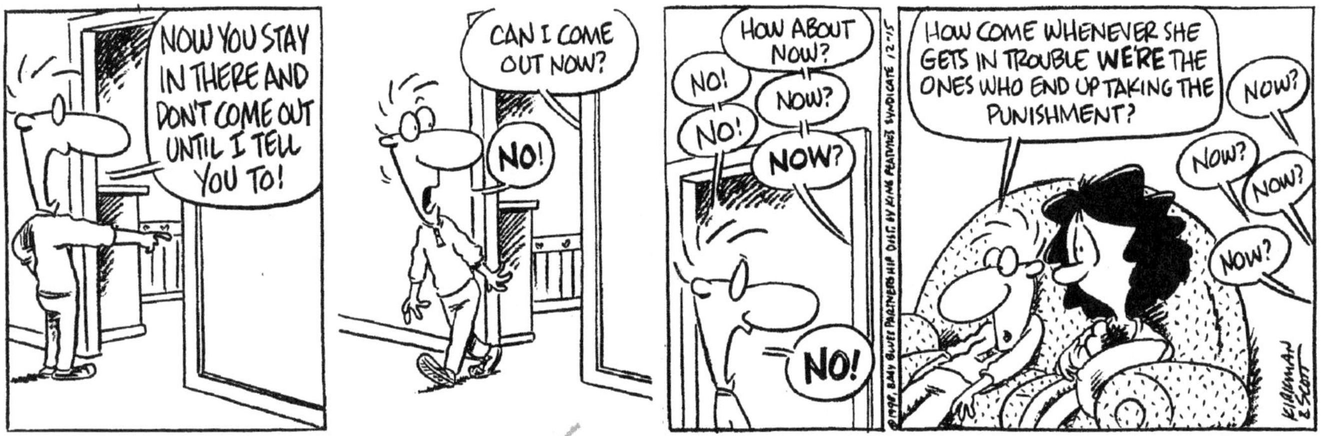
NOW YOU STAY IN THERE AND DON'T COME OUT UNTIL I TELL YOU TO!
CAN I COME OUT NOW?
NO!
NO!
HOW ABOUT NOW?
NO!
NOW?
NOW?
NO!
HOW COME WHENEVER SHE GETS IN TROUBLE **WE'RE** THE ONES WHO END UP TAKING THE PUNISHMENT?
NOW?
NOW?
NOW?
NOW?

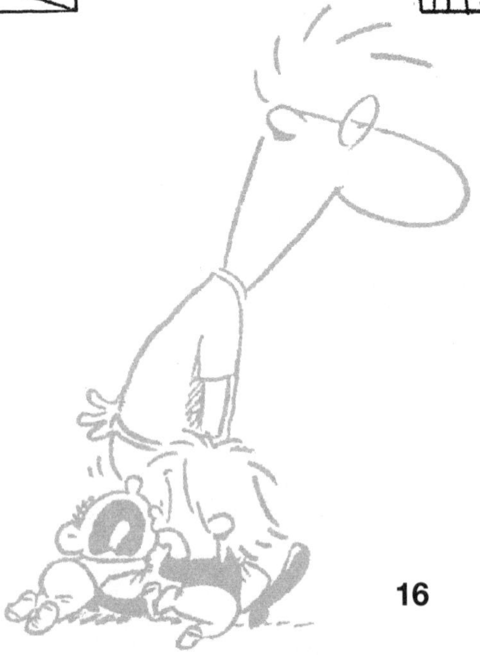

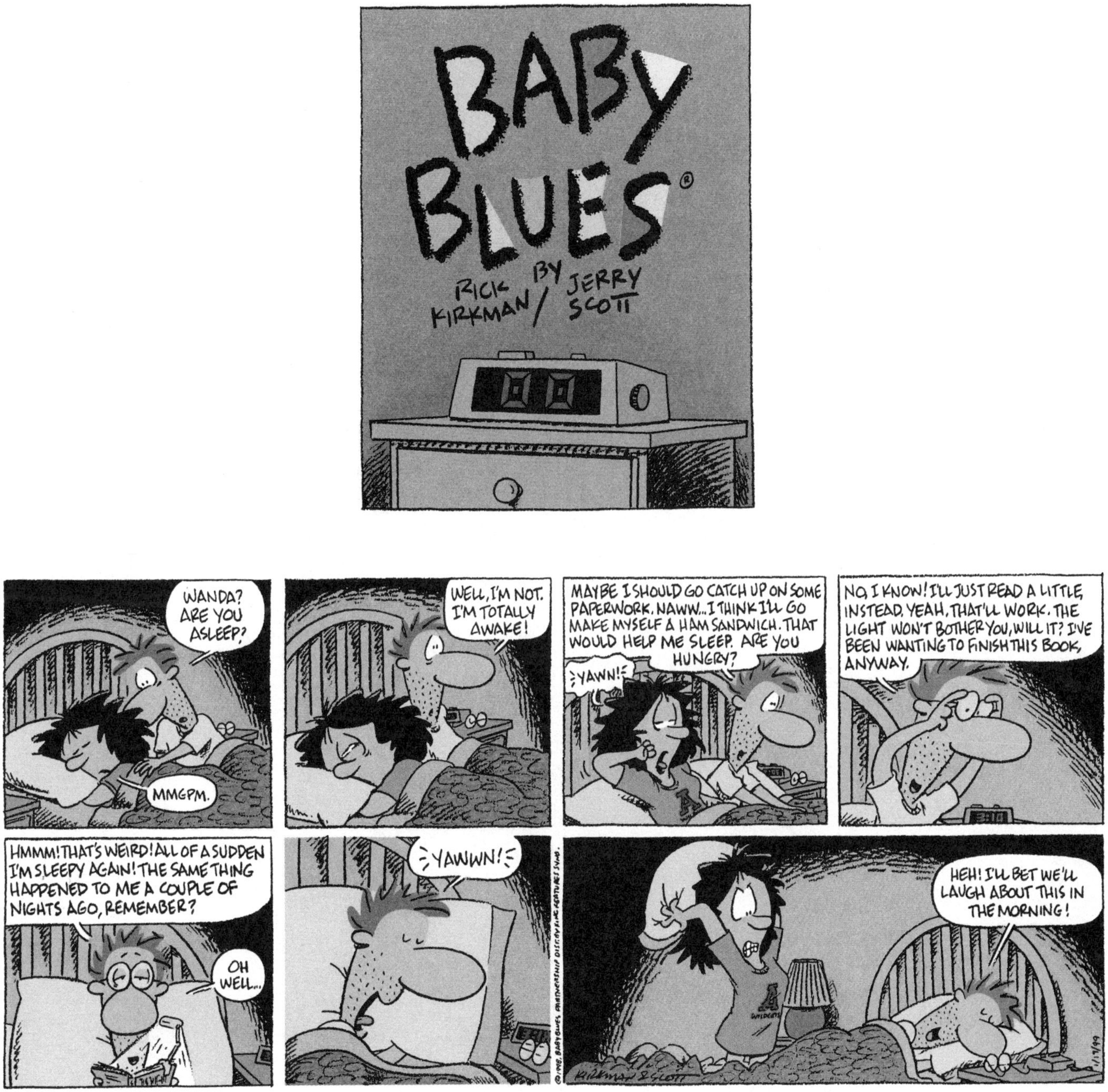
BABY BLUES®
BY RICK KIRKMAN / JERRY SCOTT
WANDA? ARE YOU ASLEEP?
MMGPM.
WELL, I'M NOT. I'M TOTALLY AWAKE!
MAYBE I SHOULD GO CATCH UP ON SOME PAPERWORK. NAWW... I THINK I'LL GO MAKE MYSELF A HAM SANDWICH. THAT WOULD HELP ME SLEEP. ARE YOU HUNGRY?
YAWN!
NO, I KNOW! I'LL JUST READ A LITTLE, INSTEAD. YEAH, THAT'LL WORK. THE LIGHT WON'T BOTHER YOU, WILL IT? I'VE BEEN WANTING TO FINISH THIS BOOK, ANYWAY.
HMMM! THAT'S WEIRD! ALL OF A SUDDEN I'M SLEEPY AGAIN! THE SAME THING HAPPENED TO ME A COUPLE OF NIGHTS AGO, REMEMBER?
OH WELL...
YAWWN!
HEH! I'LL BET WE'LL LAUGH ABOUT THIS IN THE MORNING!
KIRKMAN & SCOTT

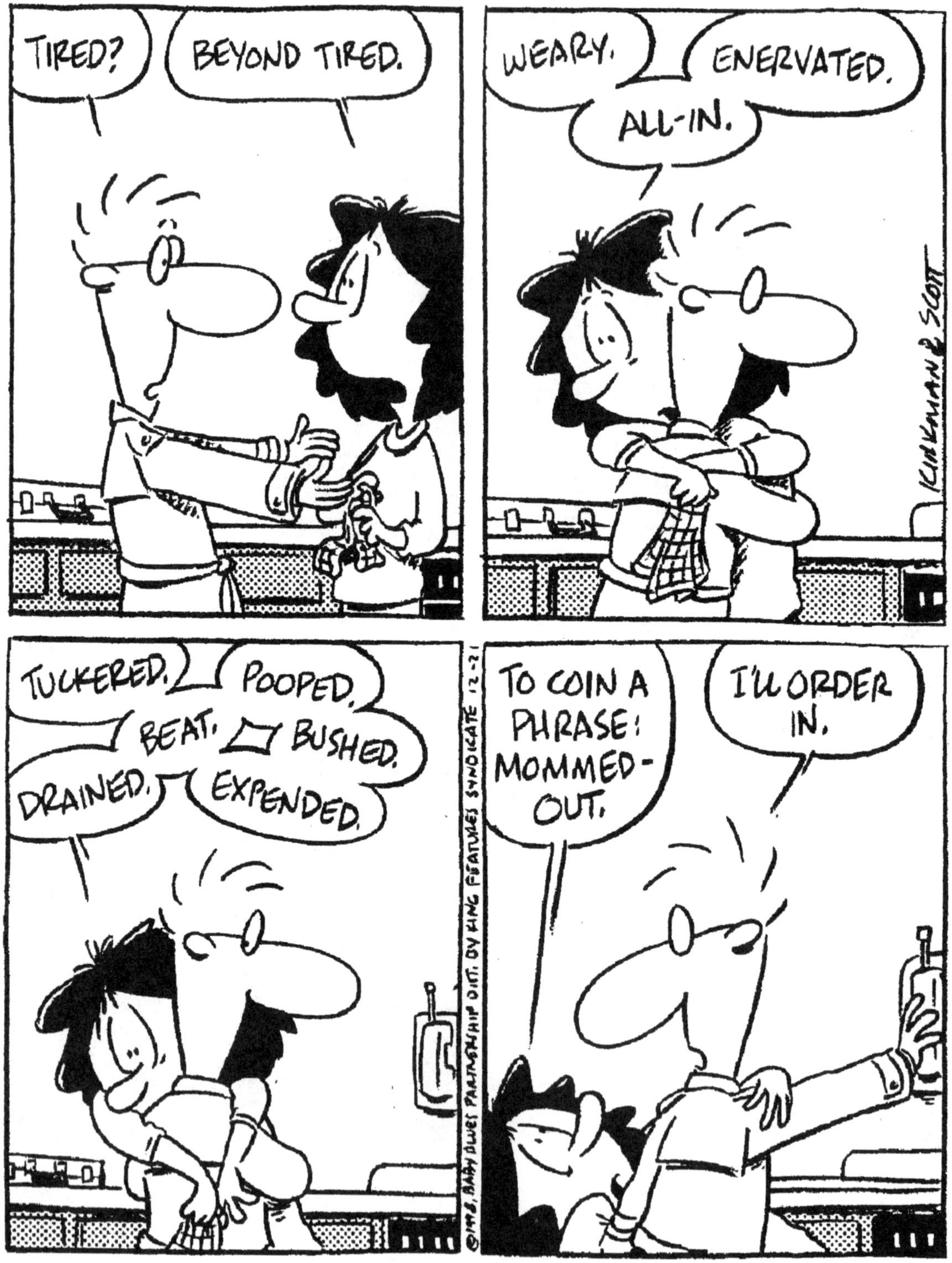
TIRED?
BEYOND TIRED.
WEARY.
ALL-IN.
ENERVATED.
KIRKMAN & SCOTT
TUCKERED.
POOPED.
BEAT.
BUSHED.
DRAINED.
EXPENDED.
©1998, BABY BLUES PARTNERSHIP DIST. BY KING FEATURES SYNDICATE 12-21
TO COIN A PHRASE: MOMMED-OUT.
I'LL ORDER IN.

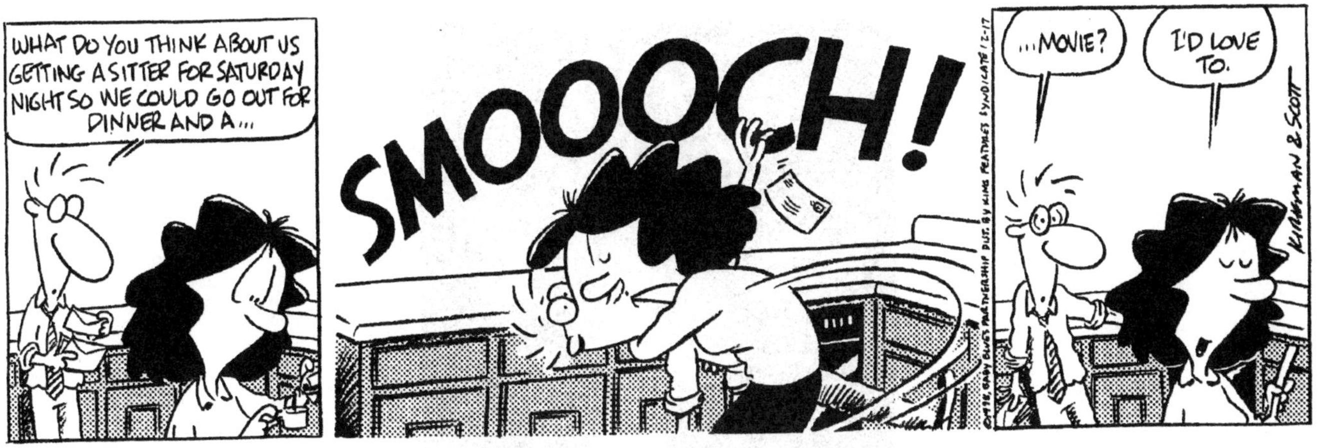
WHAT DO YOU THINK ABOUT US GETTING A SITTER FOR SATURDAY NIGHT SO WE COULD GO OUT FOR DINNER AND A...
SMOOOCH!
...MOVIE?
I'D LOVE TO.
KIRKMAN & SCOTT

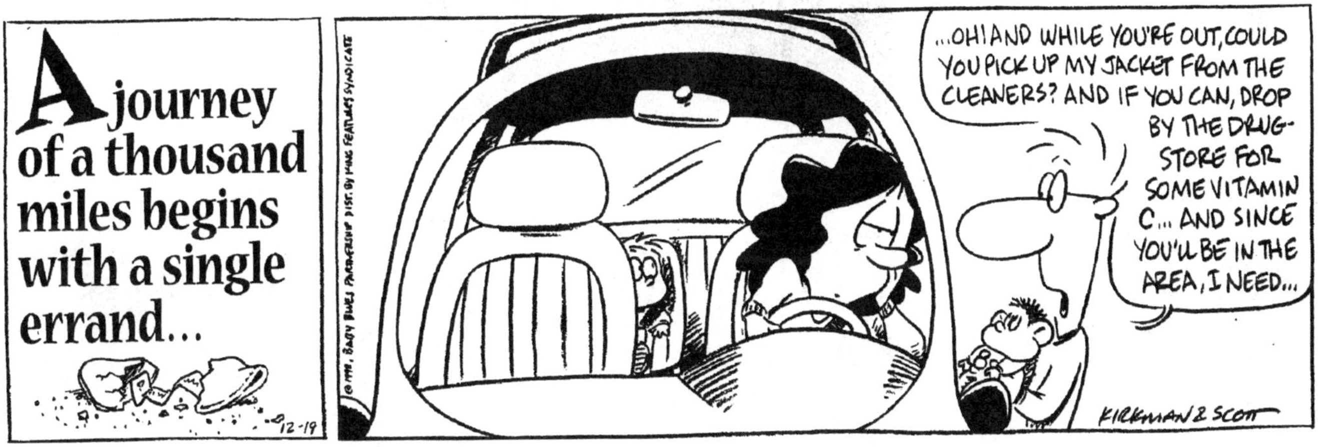
A journey of a thousand miles begins with a single errand...
...OH! AND WHILE YOU'RE OUT, COULD YOU PICK UP MY JACKET FROM THE CLEANERS? AND IF YOU CAN, DROP BY THE DRUG-STORE FOR SOME VITAMIN C... AND SINCE YOU'LL BE IN THE AREA, I NEED...
KIRKMAN & SCOTT

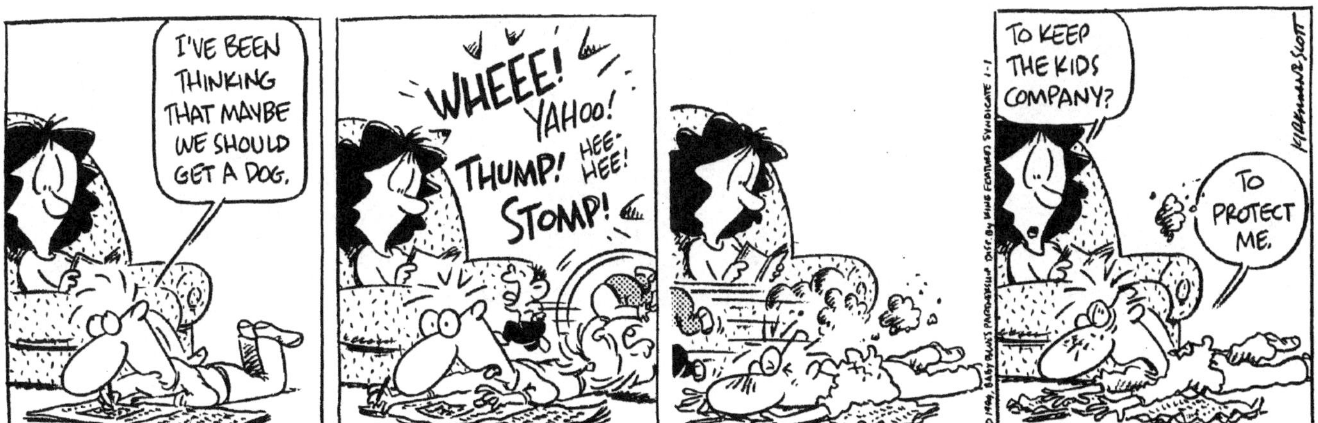
I'VE BEEN THINKING THAT MAYBE WE SHOULD GET A DOG.
WHEEEE!
YAHOO!
THUMP!
HEE-HEE!
STOMP!
TO KEEP THE KIDS COMPANY?
TO PROTECT ME.
KIRKMAN & SCOTT

BABY BLUES®
BY RICK KIRKMAN / JERRY SCOTT

JUST HOLLER IF YOU WANT ANY HELP, HONEY.
AAAAAAAAAAAAAAAAAGGGGGGHHHH!
©1998, BABY BLUES PARTNERSHIP DIST. BY KING FEATURES SYNDICATE
THAT'S JUST A FIGURE OF SPEECH, YOU KNOW.
FELT GOOD, THOUGH.
2-7-99
KIRKMAN & SCOTT

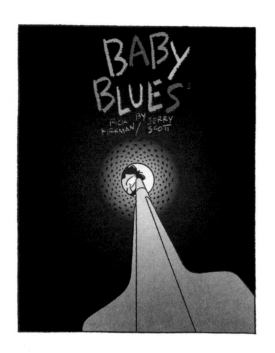

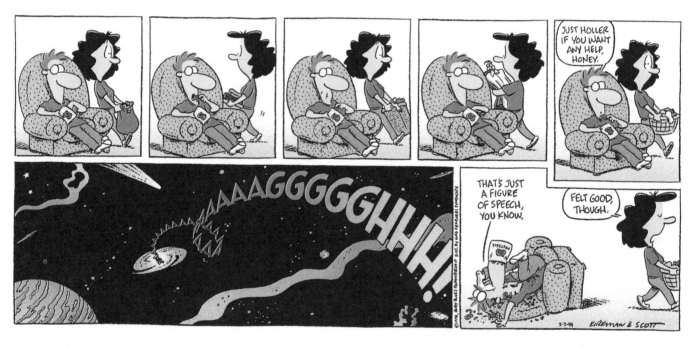

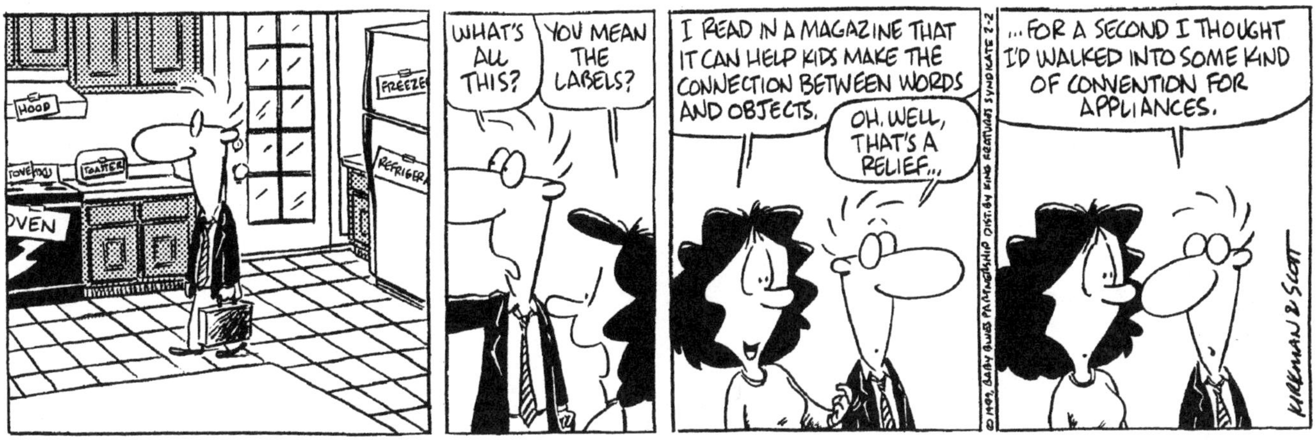
HOOD
TOASTER
OVEN
FREEZER
REFRIGERA
WHAT'S ALL THIS?
YOU MEAN THE LABELS?
I READ IN A MAGAZINE THAT IT CAN HELP KIDS MAKE THE CONNECTION BETWEEN WORDS AND OBJECTS.
OH. WELL, THAT'S A RELIEF...
...FOR A SECOND I THOUGHT I'D WALKED INTO SOME KIND OF CONVENTION FOR APPLIANCES.

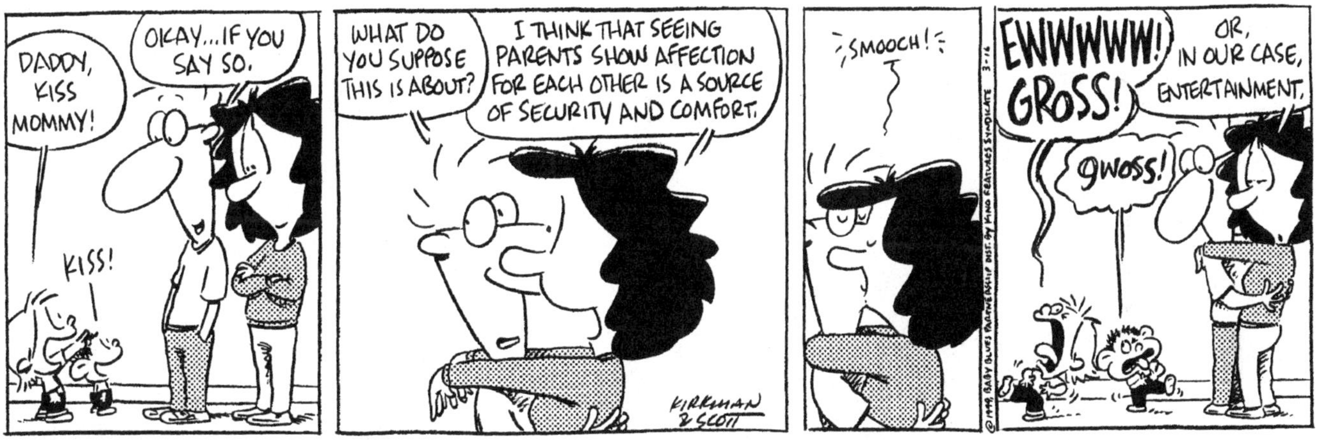
DADDY, KISS MOMMY!
OKAY...IF YOU SAY SO.
KISS!
WHAT DO YOU SUPPOSE THIS IS ABOUT?
I THINK THAT SEEING PARENTS SHOW AFFECTION FOR EACH OTHER IS A SOURCE OF SECURITY AND COMFORT.
SMOOCH!
EWWWWW! GROSS!
GWOSS!
OR, IN OUR CASE, ENTERTAINMENT.

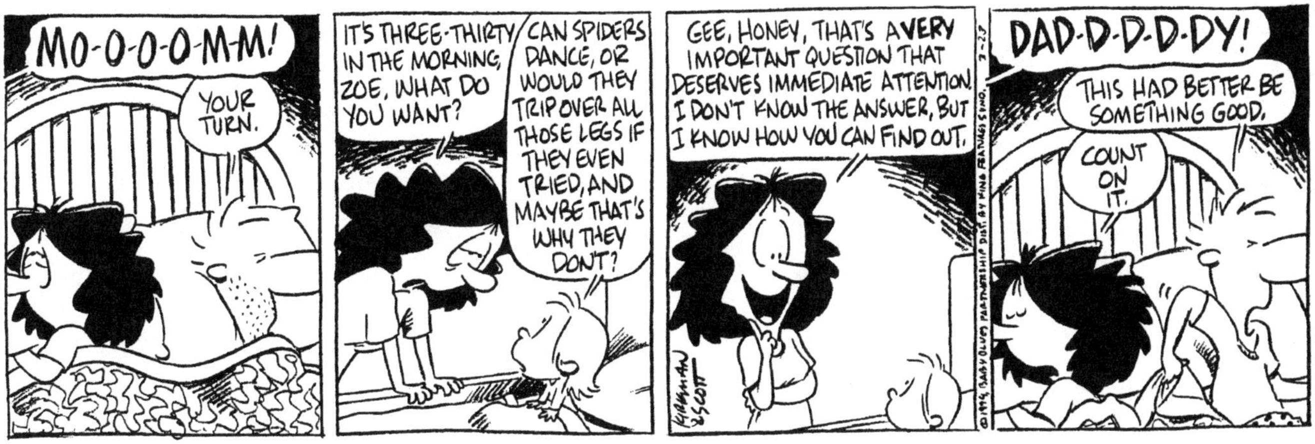
MO-O-O-O-M-M!
YOUR TURN.
IT'S THREE-THIRTY IN THE MORNING, ZOE. WHAT DO YOU WANT?
CAN SPIDERS DANCE, OR WOULD THEY TRIP OVER ALL THOSE LEGS IF THEY EVEN TRIED, AND MAYBE THAT'S WHY THEY DON'T?
GEE, HONEY, THAT'S A VERY IMPORTANT QUESTION THAT DESERVES IMMEDIATE ATTENTION. I DON'T KNOW THE ANSWER, BUT I KNOW HOW YOU CAN FIND OUT.
DAD-D-D-D-DY!
THIS HAD BETTER BE SOMETHING GOOD.
COUNT ON IT.

The Gourmet Palate
MM... NO, NO, NO... ZE CUMIN IS FIGHTING ZE GARLIC.
The DISCERNING Palate
DO I DETECT CILANTRO?
KIRKMAN & SCOTT

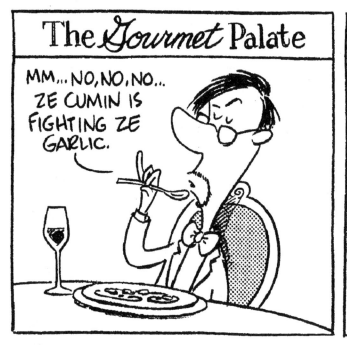

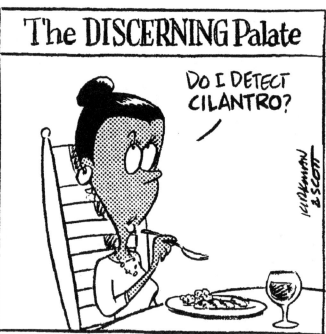

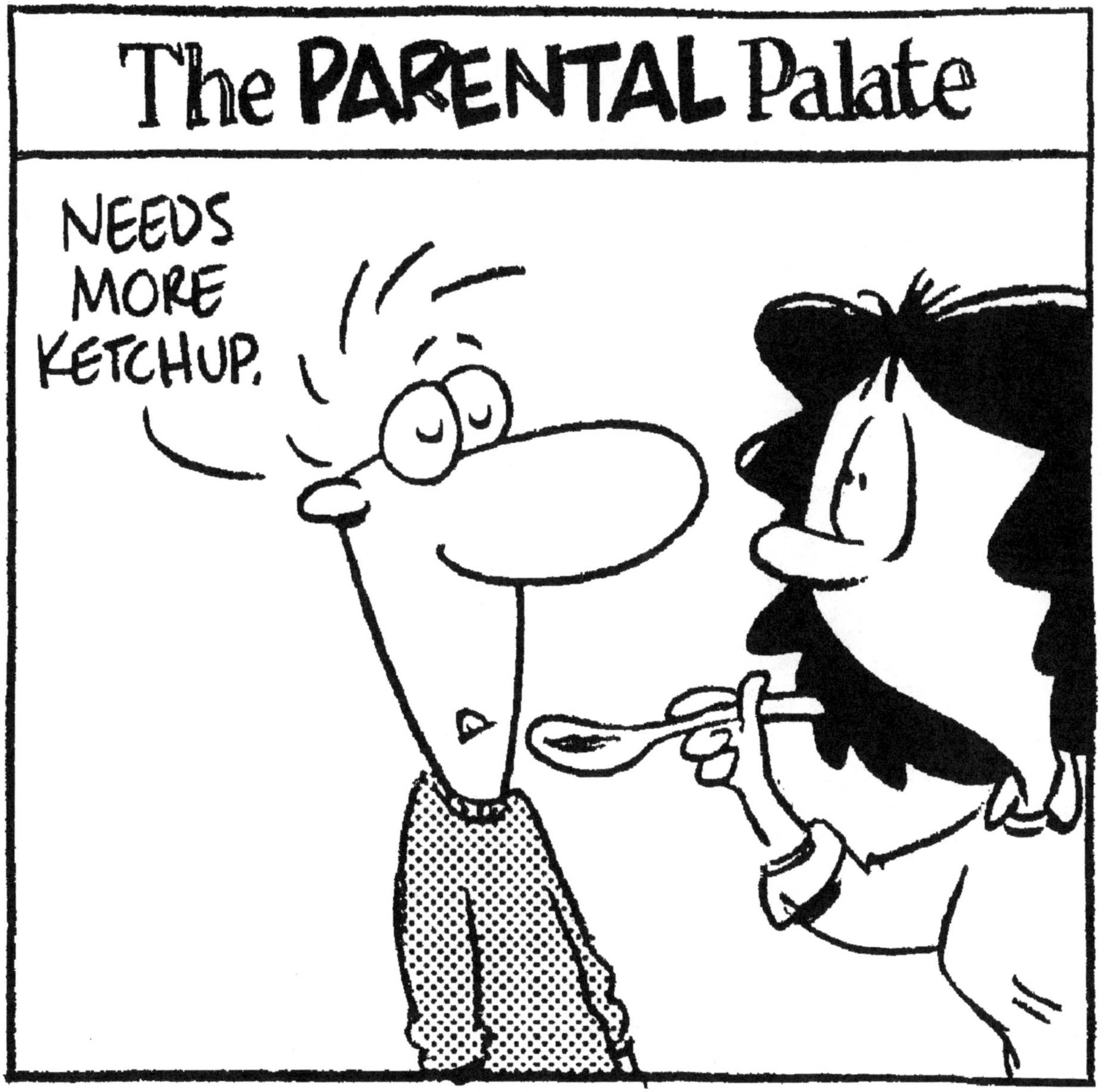
The PARENTAL Palate
NEEDS MORE KETCHUP.

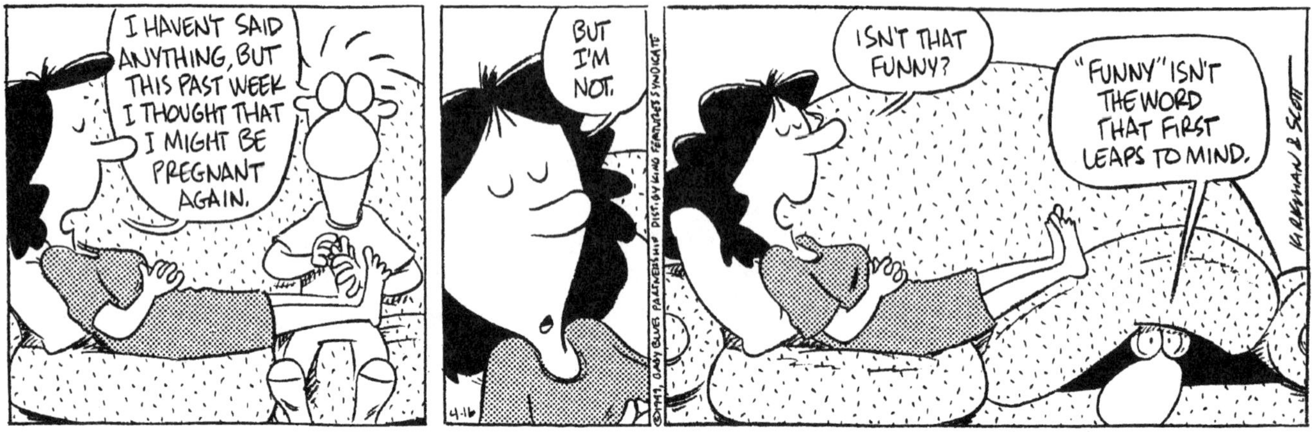
I HAVEN'T SAID ANYTHING, BUT THIS PAST WEEK I THOUGHT THAT I MIGHT BE PREGNANT AGAIN.
BUT I'M NOT.
ISN'T THAT FUNNY?
"FUNNY" ISN'T THE WORD THAT FIRST LEAPS TO MIND.
KIRKMAN & SCOTT

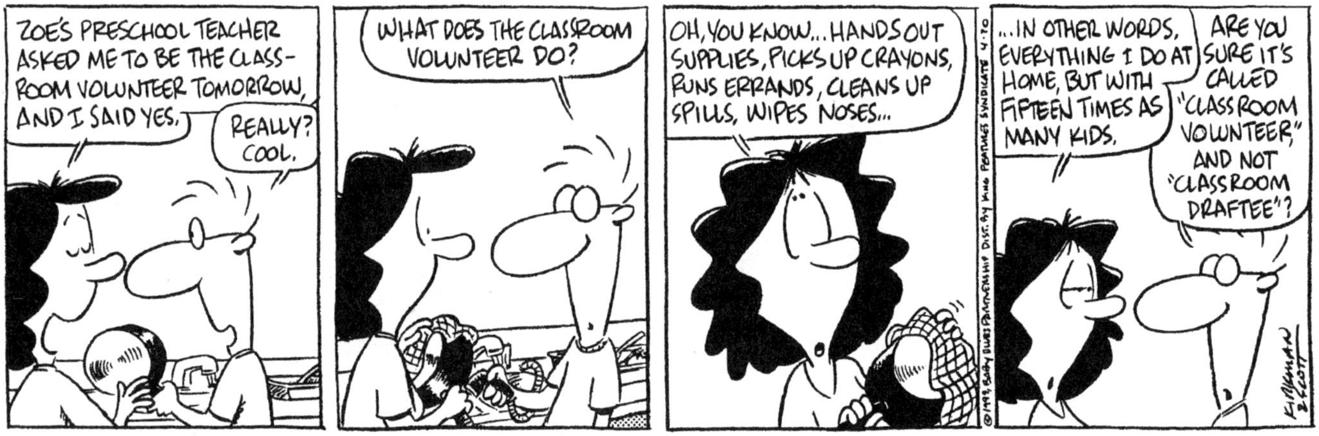
ZOE'S PRESCHOOL TEACHER ASKED ME TO BE THE CLASSROOM VOLUNTEER TOMORROW, AND I SAID YES.
REALLY? COOL.
WHAT DOES THE CLASSROOM VOLUNTEER DO?
OH, YOU KNOW... HANDS OUT SUPPLIES, PICKS UP CRAYONS, RUNS ERRANDS, CLEANS UP SPILLS, WIPES NOSES...
...IN OTHER WORDS, EVERYTHING I DO AT HOME, BUT WITH FIFTEEN TIMES AS MANY KIDS.
ARE YOU SURE IT'S CALLED "CLASSROOM VOLUNTEER," AND NOT "CLASSROOM DRAFTEE"?
KIRKMAN & SCOTT

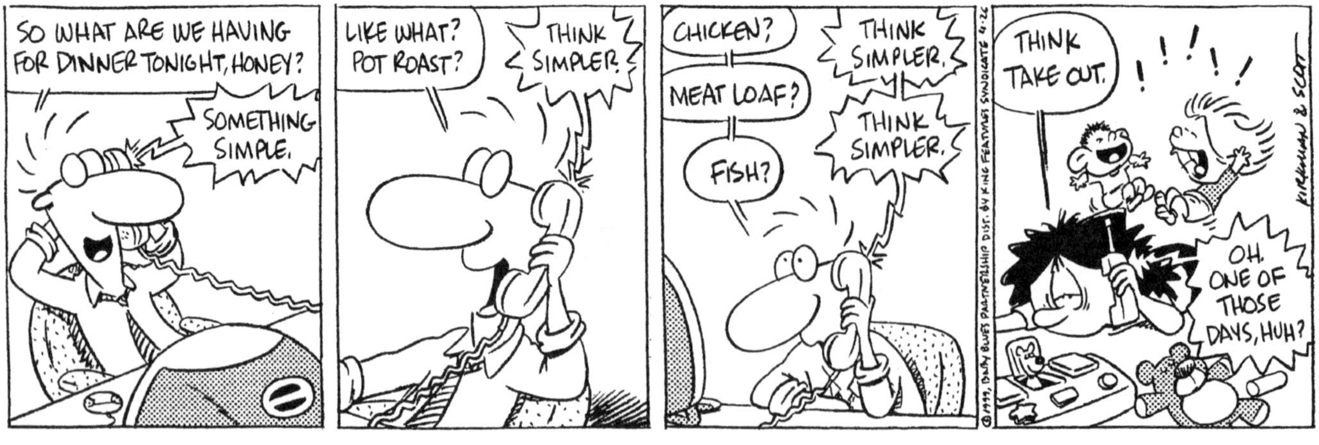
SO WHAT ARE WE HAVING FOR DINNER TONIGHT, HONEY?
SOMETHING SIMPLE.
LIKE WHAT? POT ROAST?
THINK SIMPLER.
CHICKEN?
THINK SIMPLER.
MEAT LOAF?
THINK SIMPLER.
FISH?
THINK TAKE OUT.
! ! ! ! !
OH. ONE OF THOSE DAYS, HUH?
KIRKMAN & SCOTT

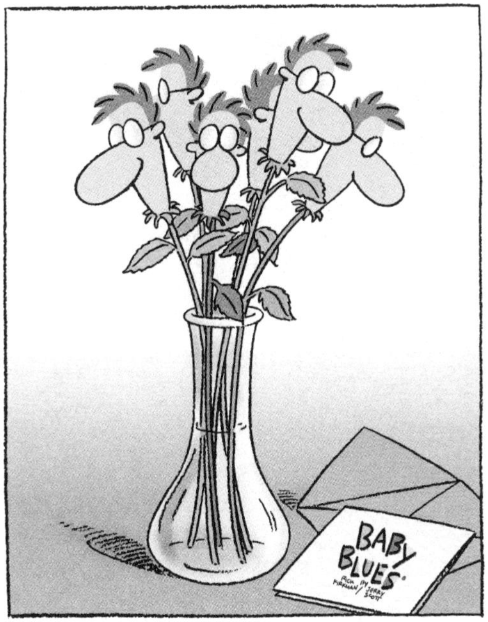
BABY BLUES®

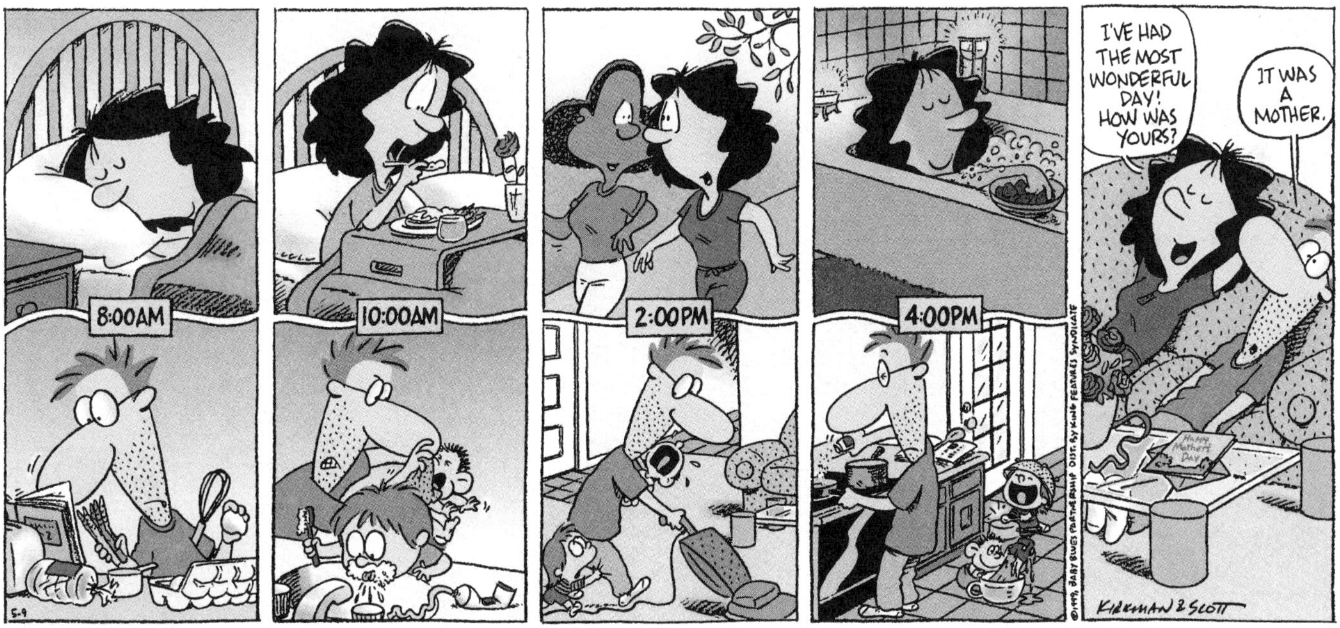
8:00AM
10:00AM
2:00PM
4:00PM
I'VE HAD THE MOST WONDERFUL DAY! HOW WAS YOURS?
IT WAS A MOTHER.
KIRKMAN & SCOTT

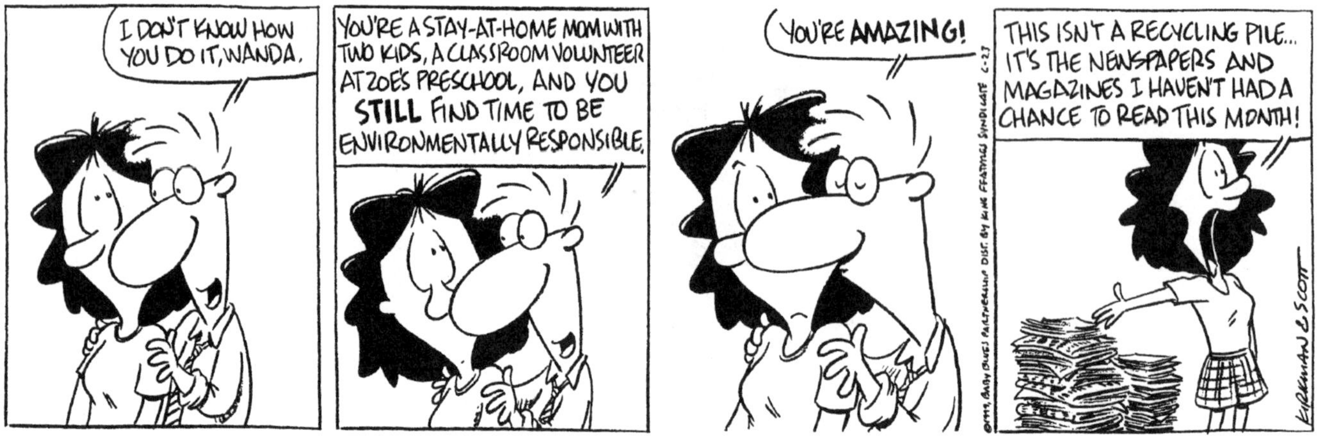
I DON'T KNOW HOW YOU DO IT, WANDA.
YOU'RE A STAY-AT-HOME MOM WITH TWO KIDS, A CLASSROOM VOLUNTEER AT ZOE'S PRESCHOOL, AND YOU STILL FIND TIME TO BE ENVIRONMENTALLY RESPONSIBLE.
YOU'RE AMAZING!
THIS ISN'T A RECYCLING PILE... IT'S THE NEWSPAPERS AND MAGAZINES I HAVEN'T HAD A CHANCE TO READ THIS MONTH!
KIRKMAN & SCOTT

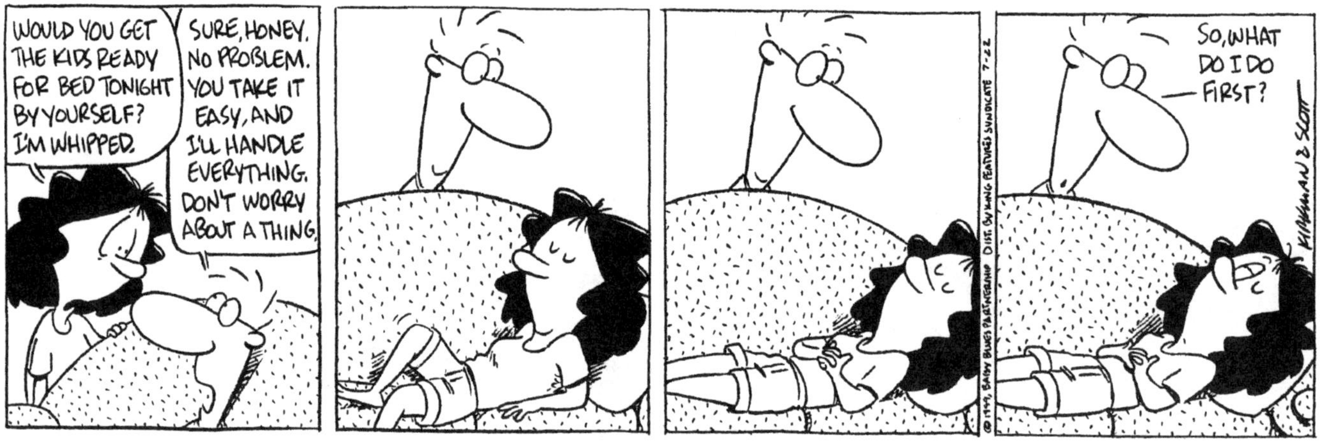
WOULD YOU GET THE KIDS READY FOR BED TONIGHT BY YOURSELF? I'M WHIPPED.
SURE, HONEY. NO PROBLEM. YOU TAKE IT EASY, AND I'LL HANDLE EVERYTHING. DON'T WORRY ABOUT A THING.
SO, WHAT DO I DO FIRST?
KIRKMAN & SCOTT

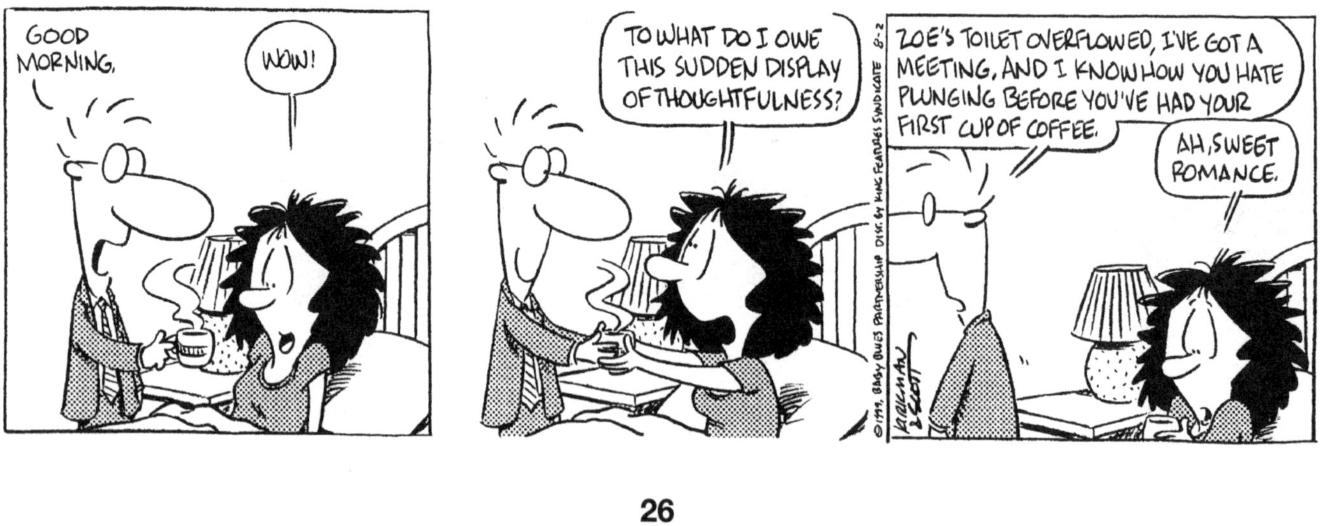
GOOD MORNING.
WOW!
TO WHAT DO I OWE THIS SUDDEN DISPLAY OF THOUGHTFULNESS?
ZOE'S TOILET OVERFLOWED, I'VE GOT A MEETING, AND I KNOW HOW YOU HATE PLUNGING BEFORE YOU'VE HAD YOUR FIRST CUP OF COFFEE.
AH, SWEET ROMANCE.
KIRKMAN & SCOTT

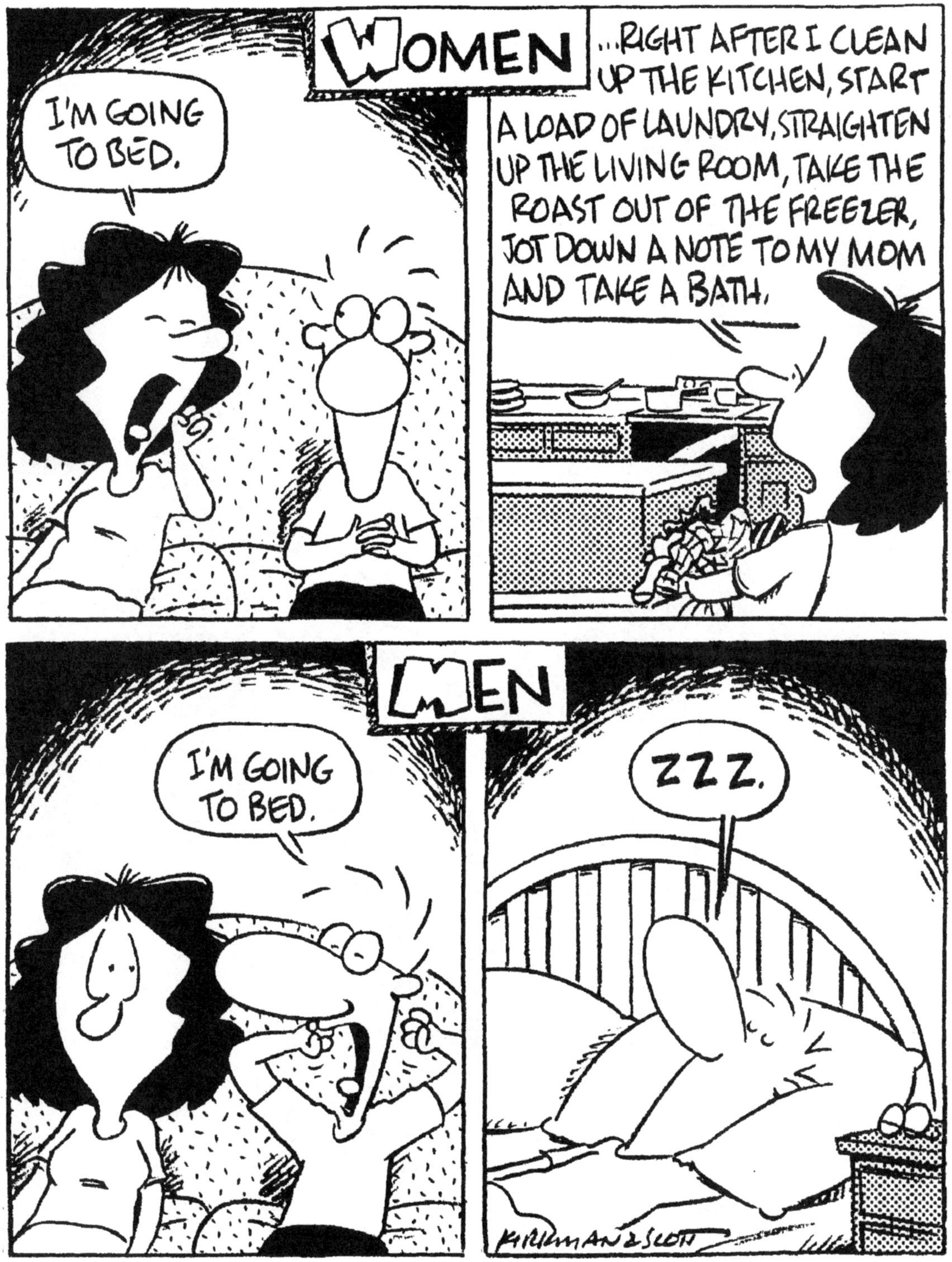
WOMEN
I'M GOING TO BED.
...RIGHT AFTER I CLEAN UP THE KITCHEN, START A LOAD OF LAUNDRY, STRAIGHTEN UP THE LIVING ROOM, TAKE THE ROAST OUT OF THE FREEZER, JOT DOWN A NOTE TO MY MOM AND TAKE A BATH.
MEN
I'M GOING TO BED.
ZZZ.
KIRKMAN & SCOTT

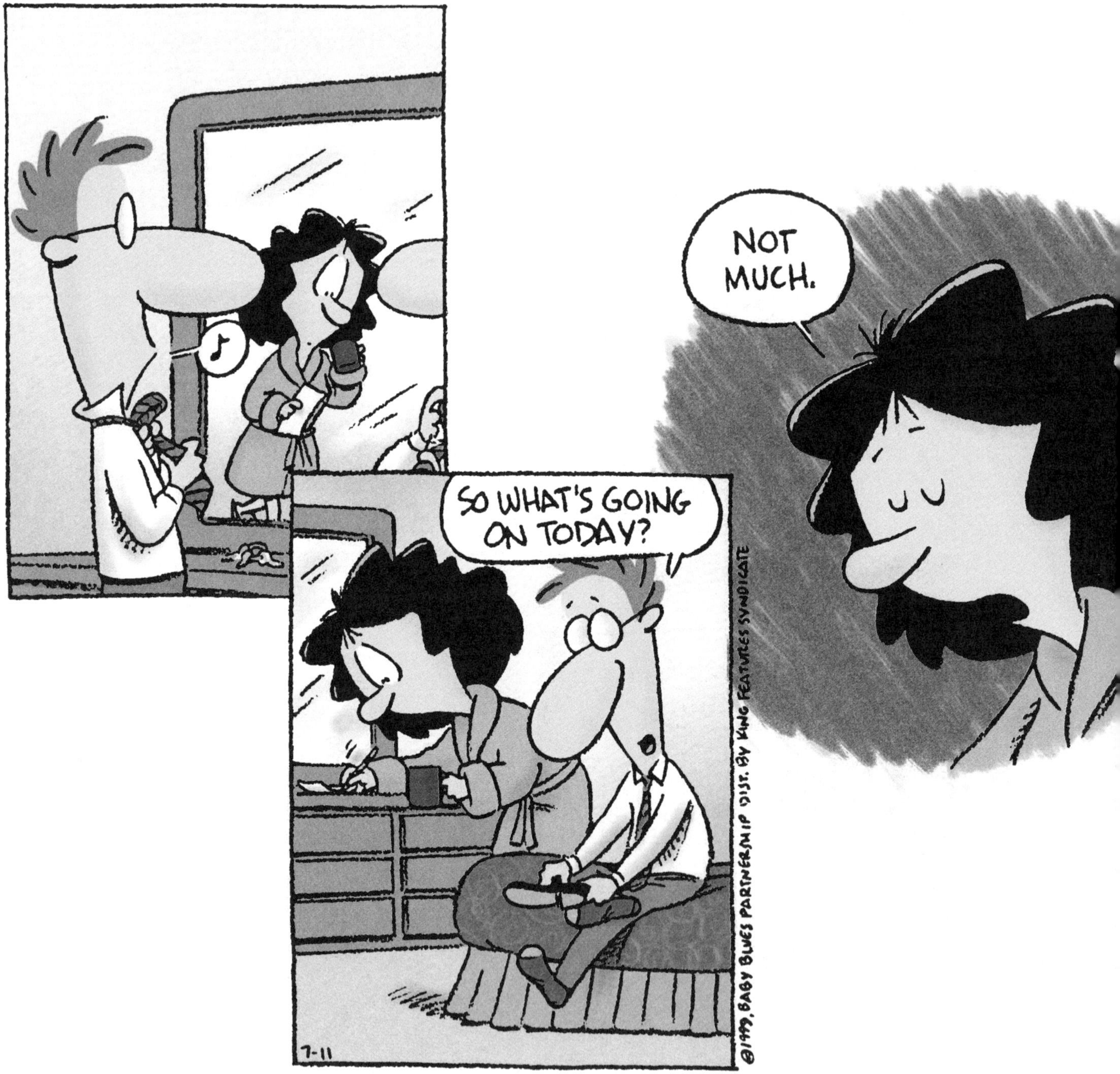
SO WHAT'S GOING ON TODAY?
NOT MUCH.
©1999, BABY BLUES PARTNERSHIP DIST. BY KING FEATURES SYNDICATE
7-11

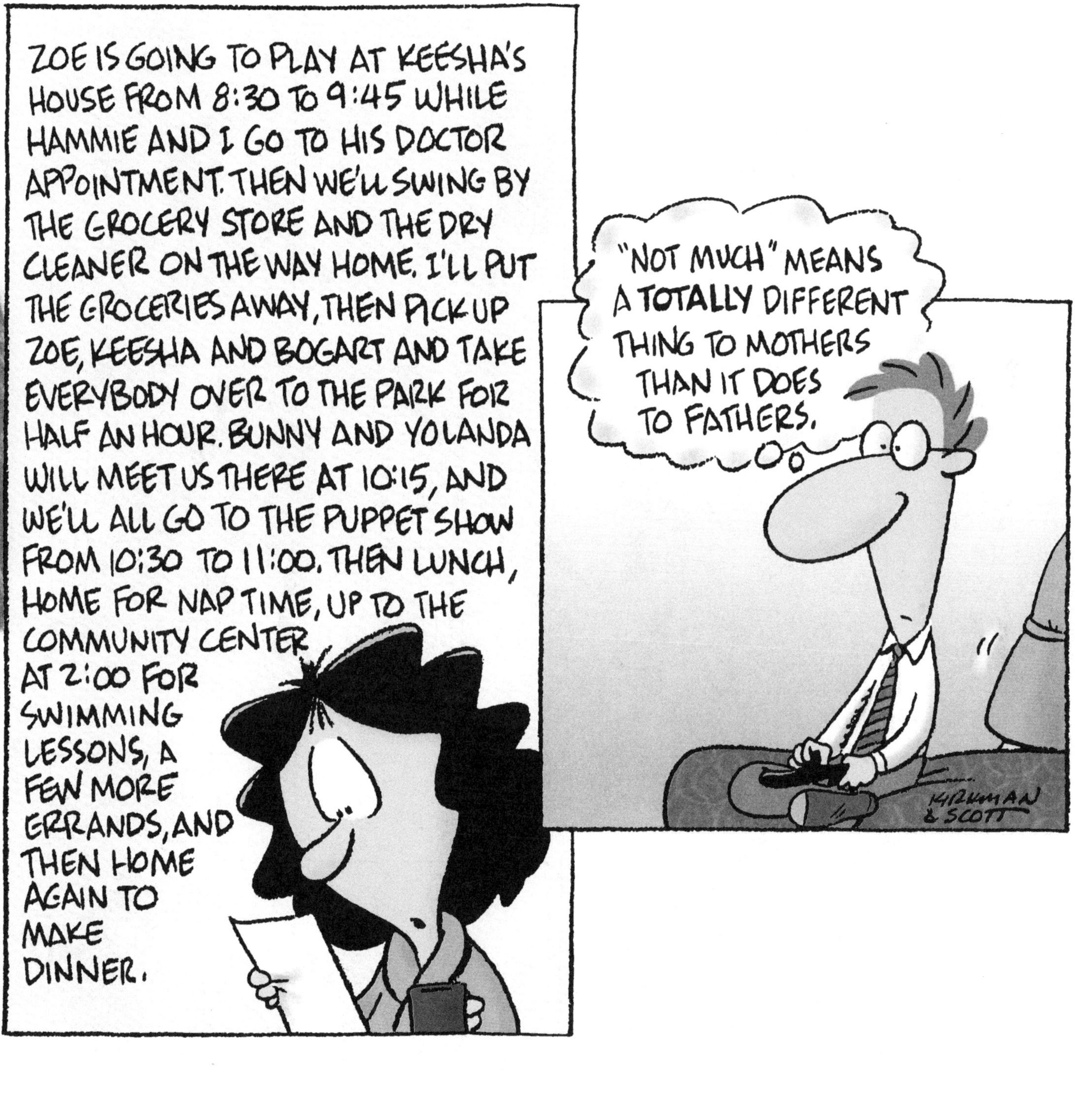
ZOE IS GOING TO PLAY AT KEESHA'S HOUSE FROM 8:30 TO 9:45 WHILE HAMMIE AND I GO TO HIS DOCTOR APPOINTMENT. THEN WE'LL SWING BY THE GROCERY STORE AND THE DRY CLEANER ON THE WAY HOME. I'LL PUT THE GROCERIES AWAY, THEN PICK UP ZOE, KEESHA AND BOGART AND TAKE EVERYBODY OVER TO THE PARK FOR HALF AN HOUR. BUNNY AND YOLANDA WILL MEET US THERE AT 10:15, AND WE'LL ALL GO TO THE PUPPET SHOW FROM 10:30 TO 11:00. THEN LUNCH, HOME FOR NAP TIME, UP TO THE COMMUNITY CENTER AT 2:00 FOR SWIMMING LESSONS, A FEW MORE ERRANDS, AND THEN HOME AGAIN TO MAKE DINNER.
"NOT MUCH" MEANS A **TOTALLY** DIFFERENT THING TO MOTHERS THAN IT DOES TO FATHERS.
KIRKMAN & SCOTT

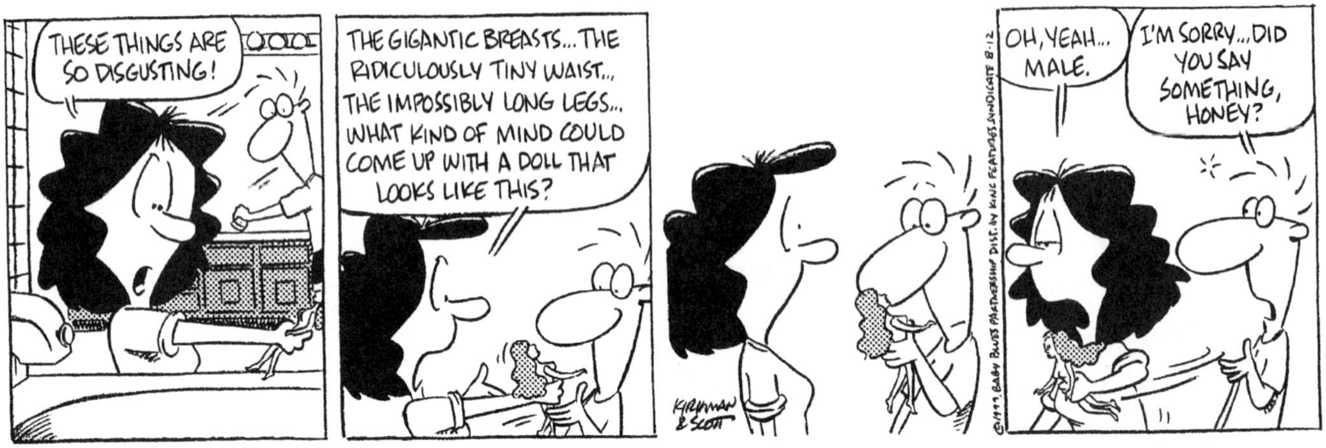
THESE THINGS ARE SO DISGUSTING!
THE GIGANTIC BREASTS... THE RIDICULOUSLY TINY WAIST... THE IMPOSSIBLY LONG LEGS... WHAT KIND OF MIND COULD COME UP WITH A DOLL THAT LOOKS LIKE THIS?
KIRKMAN & SCOTT
OH, YEAH... MALE.
I'M SORRY... DID YOU SAY SOMETHING, HONEY?

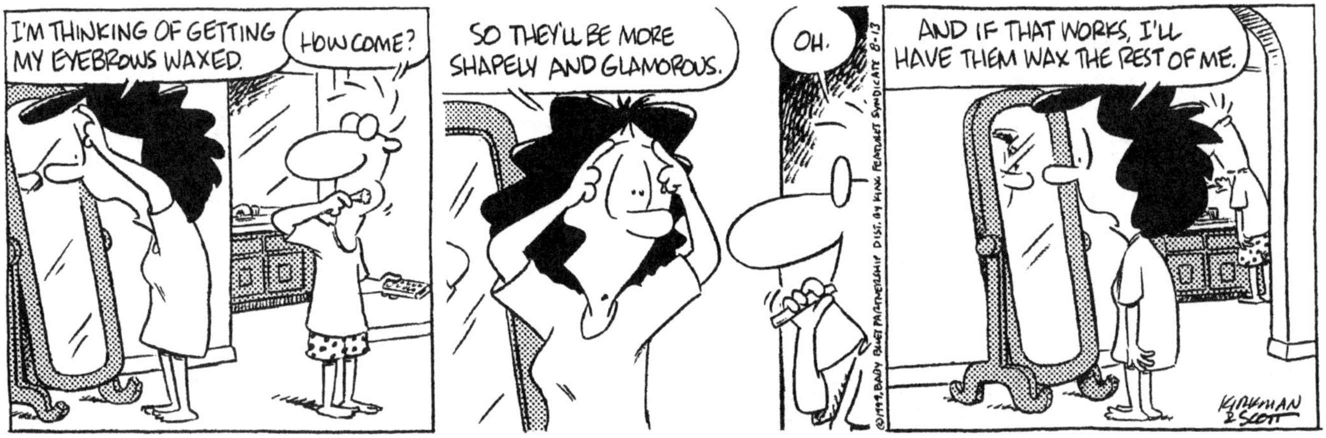
I'M THINKING OF GETTING MY EYEBROWS WAXED.
HOW COME?
SO THEY'LL BE MORE SHAPELY AND GLAMOROUS.
OH.
AND IF THAT WORKS, I'LL HAVE THEM WAX THE REST OF ME.
KIRKMAN & SCOTT

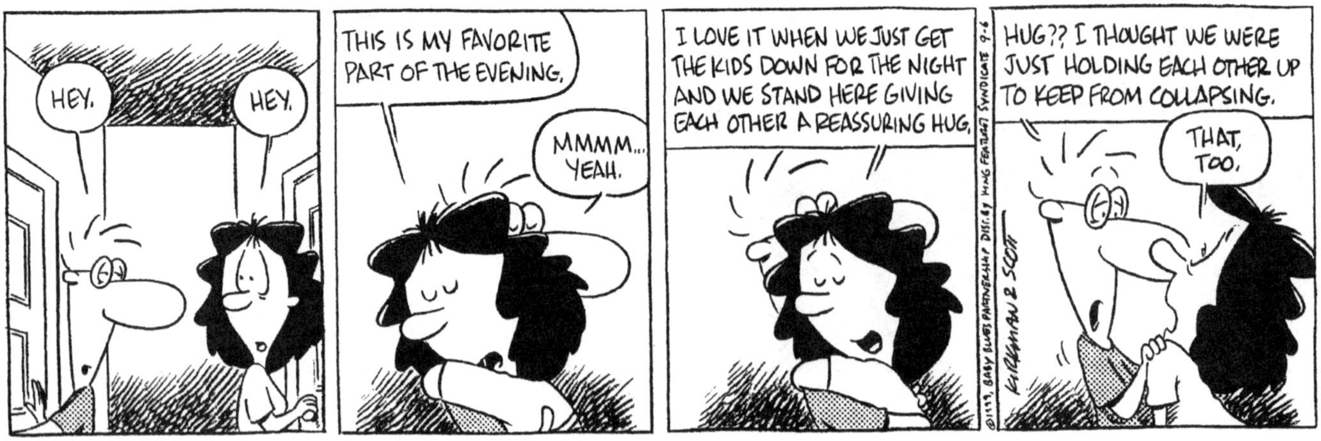
HEY.
HEY.
THIS IS MY FAVORITE PART OF THE EVENING.
MMMM... YEAH.
I LOVE IT WHEN WE JUST GET THE KIDS DOWN FOR THE NIGHT AND WE STAND HERE GIVING EACH OTHER A REASSURING HUG.
KIRKMAN & SCOTT
HUG?? I THOUGHT WE WERE JUST HOLDING EACH OTHER UP TO KEEP FROM COLLAPSING.
THAT, TOO.

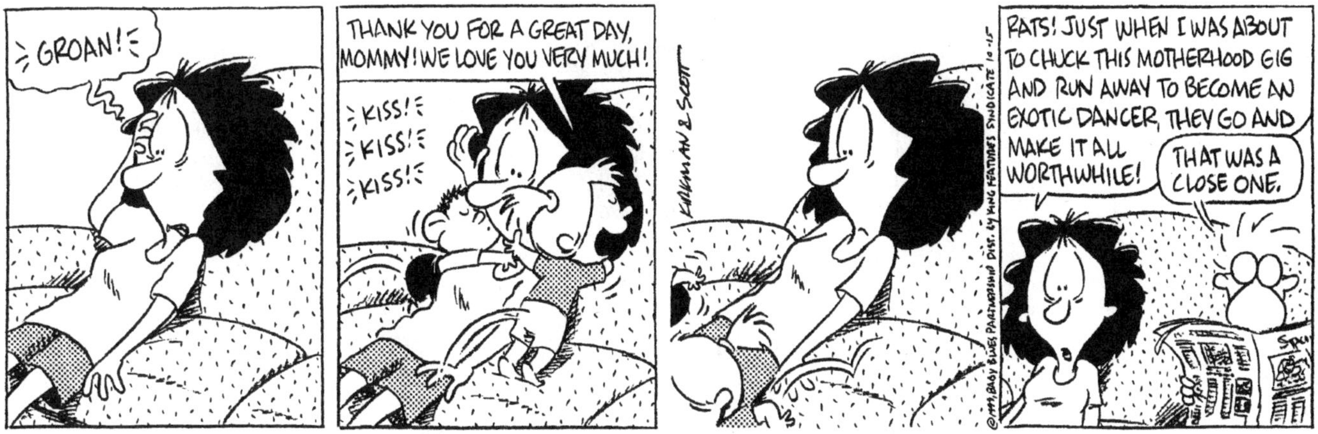
GROAN!
THANK YOU FOR A GREAT DAY, MOMMY! WE LOVE YOU VERY MUCH!
KISS! KISS! KISS!
KIRKMAN & SCOTT
RATS! JUST WHEN I WAS ABOUT TO CHUCK THIS MOTHERHOOD GIG AND RUN AWAY TO BECOME AN EXOTIC DANCER, THEY GO AND MAKE IT ALL WORTHWHILE!
THAT WAS A CLOSE ONE.

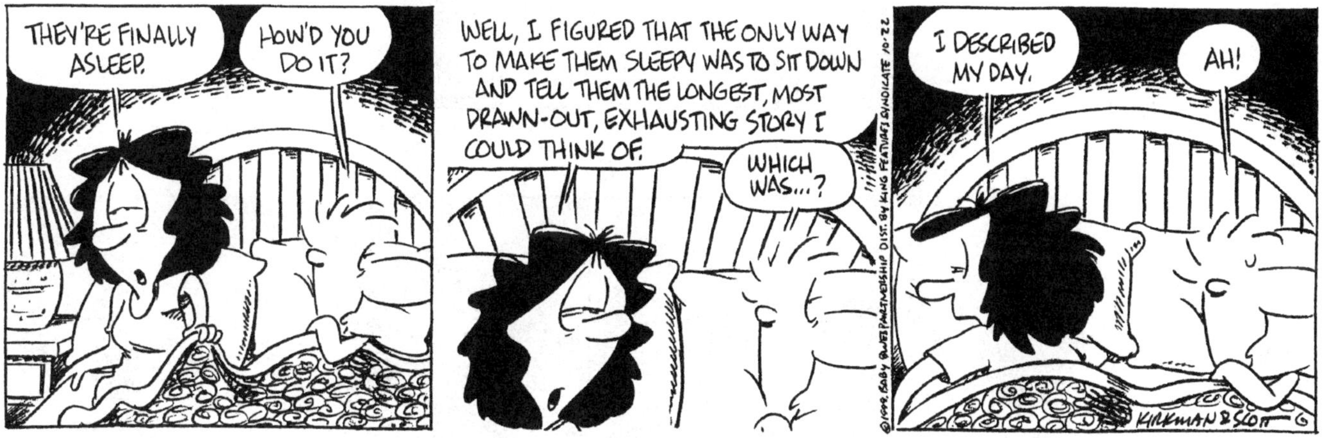
THEY'RE FINALLY ASLEEP.
HOW'D YOU DO IT?
WELL, I FIGURED THAT THE ONLY WAY TO MAKE THEM SLEEPY WAS TO SIT DOWN AND TELL THEM THE LONGEST, MOST DRAWN-OUT, EXHAUSTING STORY I COULD THINK OF.
WHICH WAS...?
I DESCRIBED MY DAY.
AH!
KIRKMAN & SCOTT

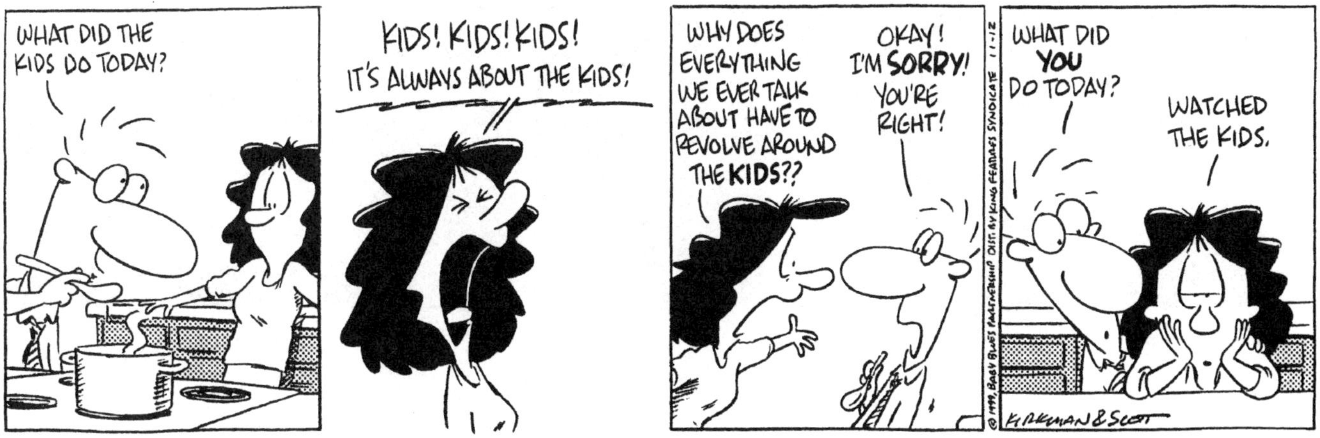
WHAT DID THE KIDS DO TODAY?
KIDS! KIDS! KIDS! IT'S ALWAYS ABOUT THE KIDS!
WHY DOES EVERYTHING WE EVER TALK ABOUT HAVE TO REVOLVE AROUND THE KIDS??
OKAY! I'M SORRY! YOU'RE RIGHT!
WHAT DID YOU DO TODAY?
WATCHED THE KIDS.
KIRKMAN & SCOTT

BABY BLUES®
BY RICK KIRKMAN / JERRY SCOTT
C A L

3-19
KIRKMAN & SCOTT
©2000, BABY BLUES PARTNERSHIP DIST. BY KING FEATURES SYNDICATE
HOW ABOUT A LITTLE BITE OF YOUR ICE CREAM?
N—
—OHH-KAYY...
SOMEBODY'S SHARING SKILLS NEED SOME WORK...
SOMEBODY'S LUCKY THE KIDS WERE WATCHING.

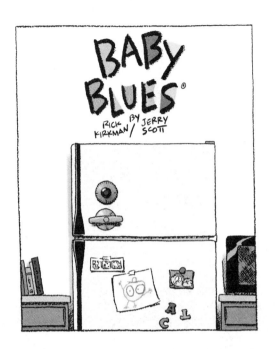

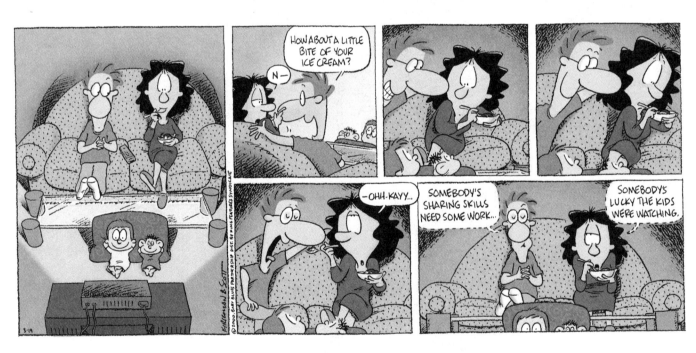

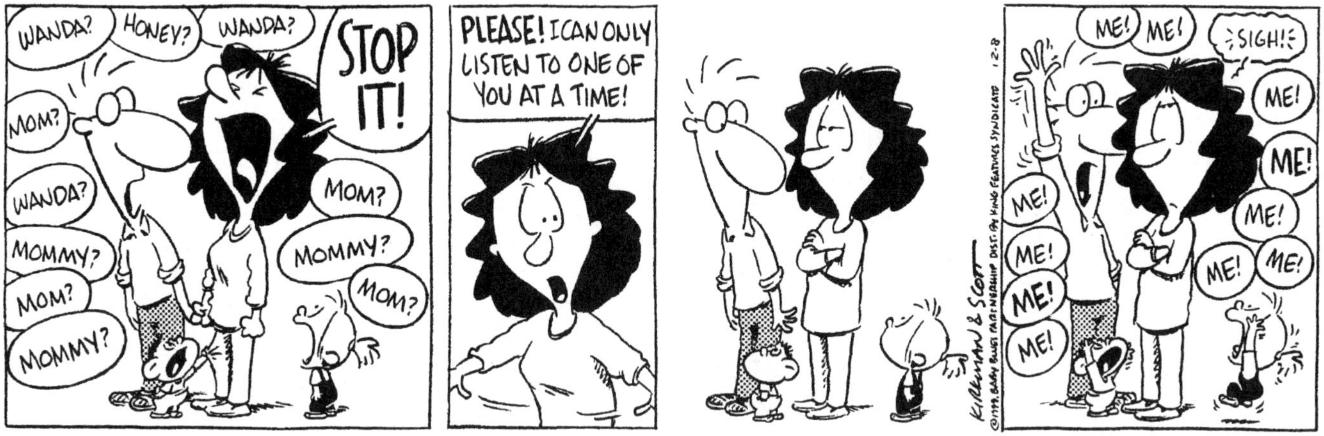
WANDA?
HONEY?
WANDA?
MOM?
WANDA?
MOMMY?
MOM?
MOMMY?
STOP IT!
MOM?
MOMMY?
MOM?
PLEASE! I CAN ONLY LISTEN TO ONE OF YOU AT A TIME!
KIRKMAN & SCOTT
ME!
ME!
SIGH!
ME!
ME!
ME!
ME!
ME!
ME!
ME!
ME!
ME!

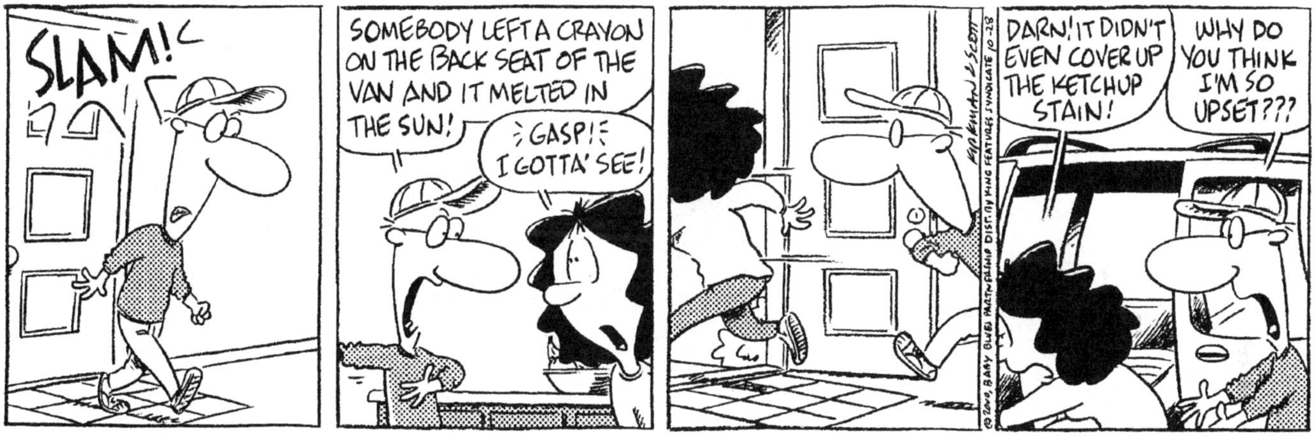
SLAM!
SOMEBODY LEFT A CRAYON ON THE BACK SEAT OF THE VAN AND IT MELTED IN THE SUN!
GASP! I GOTTA' SEE!
KIRKMAN & SCOTT
DARN! IT DIDN'T EVEN COVER UP THE KETCHUP STAIN!
WHY DO YOU THINK I'M SO UPSET???

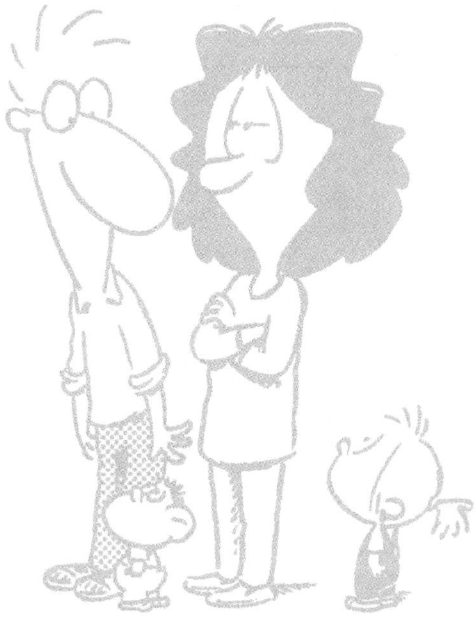

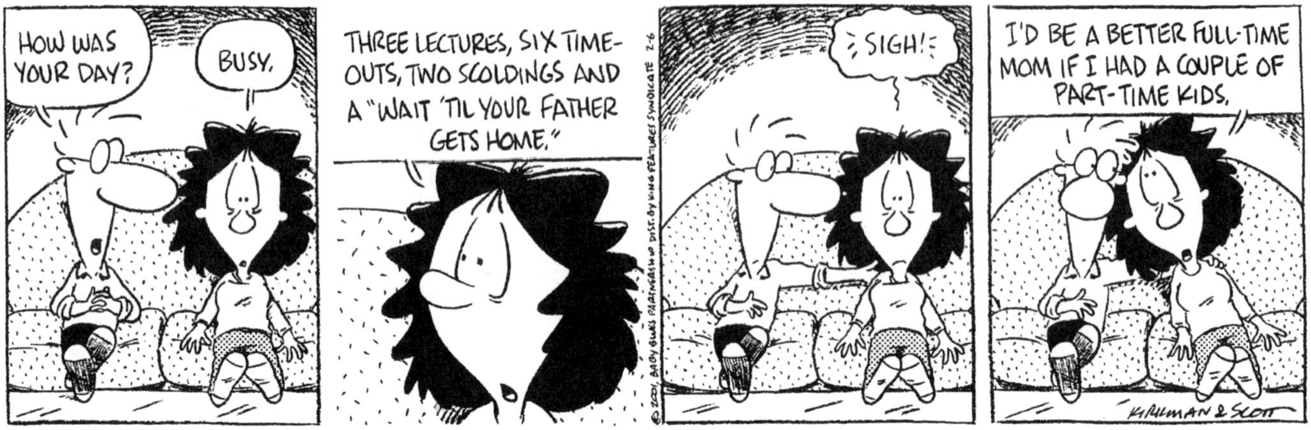
HOW WAS YOUR DAY?
BUSY.
THREE LECTURES, SIX TIME-OUTS, TWO SCOLDINGS AND A "WAIT 'TIL YOUR FATHER GETS HOME."
© 2001, BABY BLUES PARTNERSHIP DIST. BY KING FEATURES SYNDICATE 2-6
SIGH!
I'D BE A BETTER FULL-TIME MOM IF I HAD A COUPLE OF PART-TIME KIDS.
KIRKMAN & SCOTT

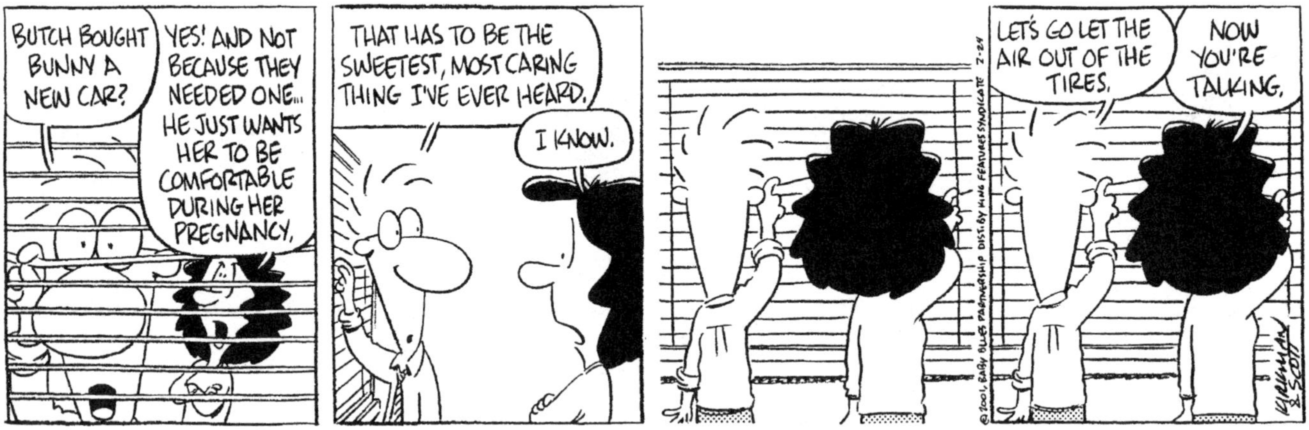
BUTCH BOUGHT BUNNY A NEW CAR?
YES! AND NOT BECAUSE THEY NEEDED ONE... HE JUST WANTS HER TO BE COMFORTABLE DURING HER PREGNANCY.
THAT HAS TO BE THE SWEETEST, MOST CARING THING I'VE EVER HEARD.
I KNOW.
© 2001, BABY BLUES PARTNERSHIP DIST. BY KING FEATURES SYNDICATE 2-24
LET'S GO LET THE AIR OUT OF THE TIRES.
NOW YOU'RE TALKING.
KIRKMAN & SCOTT

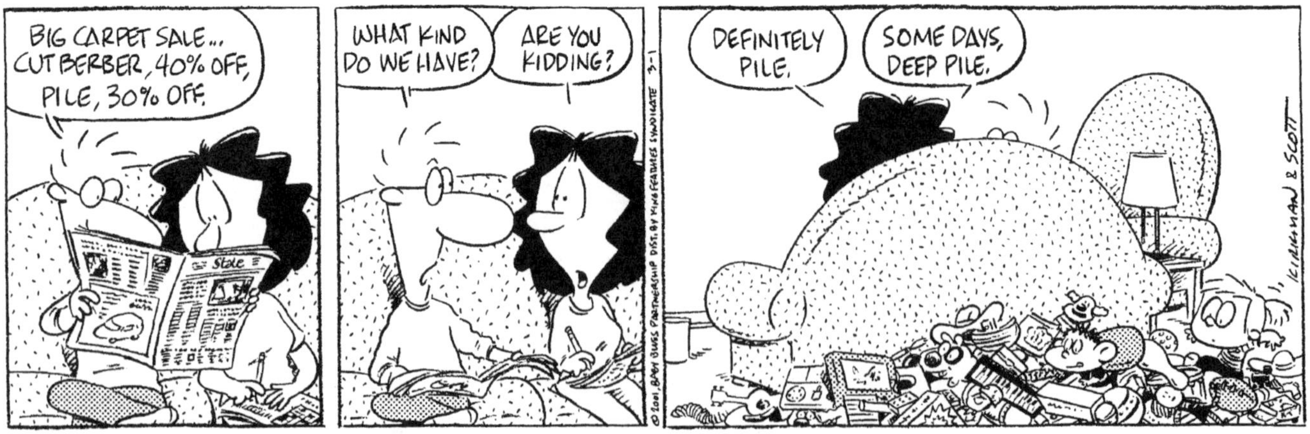
BIG CARPET SALE... CUT BERBER, 40% OFF, PILE, 30% OFF.
WHAT KIND DO WE HAVE?
ARE YOU KIDDING?
© 2001, BABY BLUES PARTNERSHIP DIST. BY KING FEATURES SYNDICATE 3-1
DEFINITELY PILE.
SOME DAYS, DEEP PILE.
KIRKMAN & SCOTT

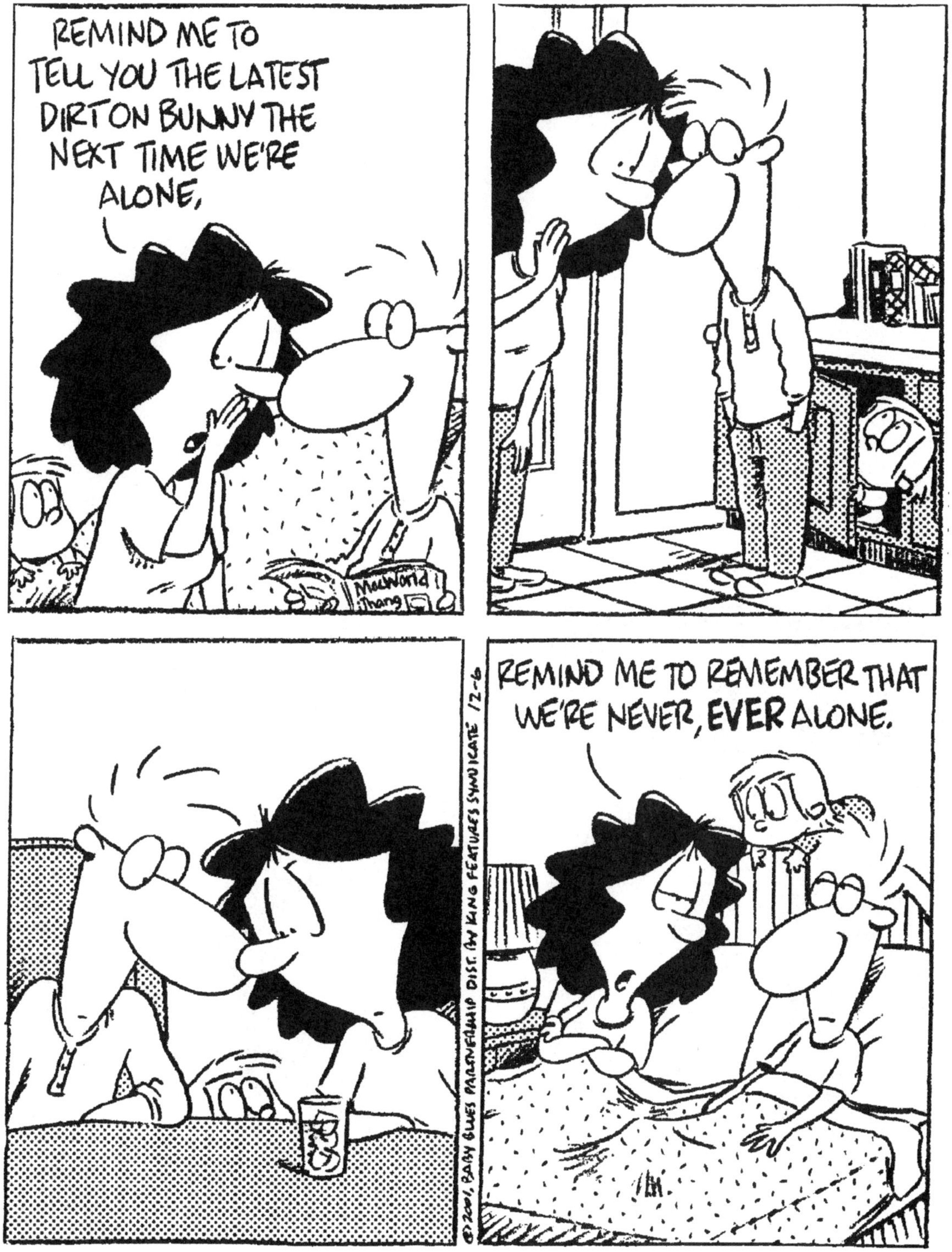
REMIND ME TO TELL YOU THE LATEST DIRT ON BUNNY THE NEXT TIME WE'RE ALONE,
MacWorld Thang
REMIND ME TO REMEMBER THAT WE'RE NEVER, EVER ALONE.
©2001, BABY BLUES PARTNERSHIP DIST. BY KING FEATURES SYNDICATE 12-6

BABY BLUES®
BY
RICK KIRKMAN / JERRY SCOTT

HAPPY FATHER'S DAY!
WOW! WHAT'S ALL THIS?
WELL, WE MADE YOU SOME COLD TOAST AND WEAK COFFEE.
OH. GOODIE.
AND AFTER YOU OPEN YOUR PRESENTS, WE'RE GOING TO DISAPPEAR FOR A WHILE, LEAVING YOU TO CLEAN UP THE INCREDIBLE MESS WE LEFT IN THE KITCHEN.
HUH?
6-18
THEN WE'RE GOING TO PIN A HUGE UGLY FLOWER ON YOUR SHIRT AND TAKE YOU OUT TO BRUNCH AT A BIG, IMPERSONAL HOTEL RESTAURANT WHERE THEY SERVE VATS OF RUNNY SCRAMBLED EGGS AND UNDERCOOKED BACON THAT TASTE LIKE THEY WERE PREPARED IN A PRISON KITCHEN. AND, OF COURSE, THEY'LL HAVE CHAMPAGNE BY THE PITCHER.
THIS IS BEGINNING TO SOUND A LOT LIKE WHAT WE DID FOR MOTHER'S DAY...
♪TURNABOUT IS FAIR PLAY!♪
GET DRESSED! LET'S GO!
YAY!
KIRKMAN & SCOTT

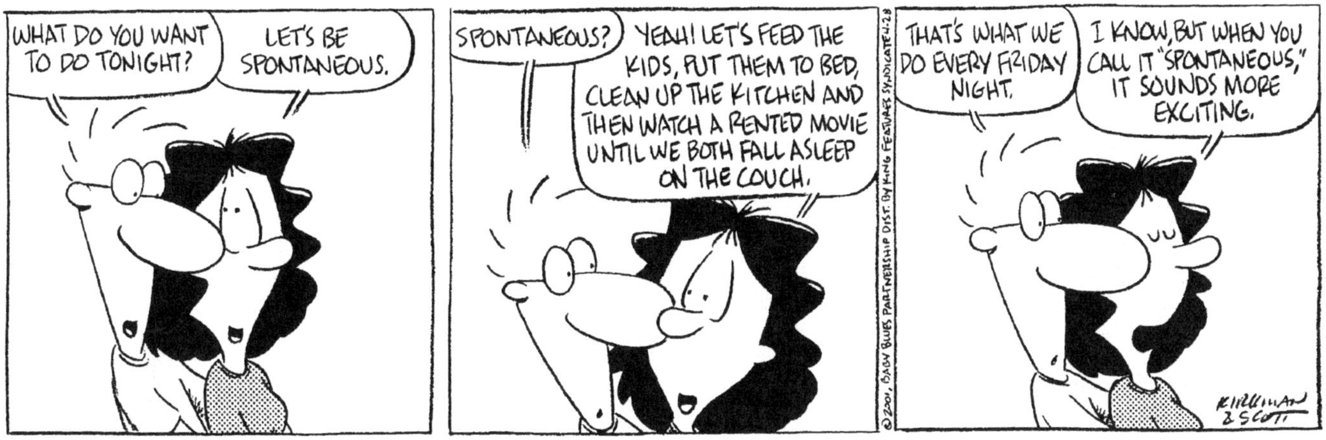
WHAT DO YOU WANT TO DO TONIGHT?
LET'S BE SPONTANEOUS.
SPONTANEOUS?
YEAH! LET'S FEED THE KIDS, PUT THEM TO BED, CLEAN UP THE KITCHEN AND THEN WATCH A RENTED MOVIE UNTIL WE BOTH FALL ASLEEP ON THE COUCH.
THAT'S WHAT WE DO EVERY FRIDAY NIGHT.
I KNOW, BUT WHEN YOU CALL IT "SPONTANEOUS," IT SOUNDS MORE EXCITING.
KIRKMAN & SCOTT

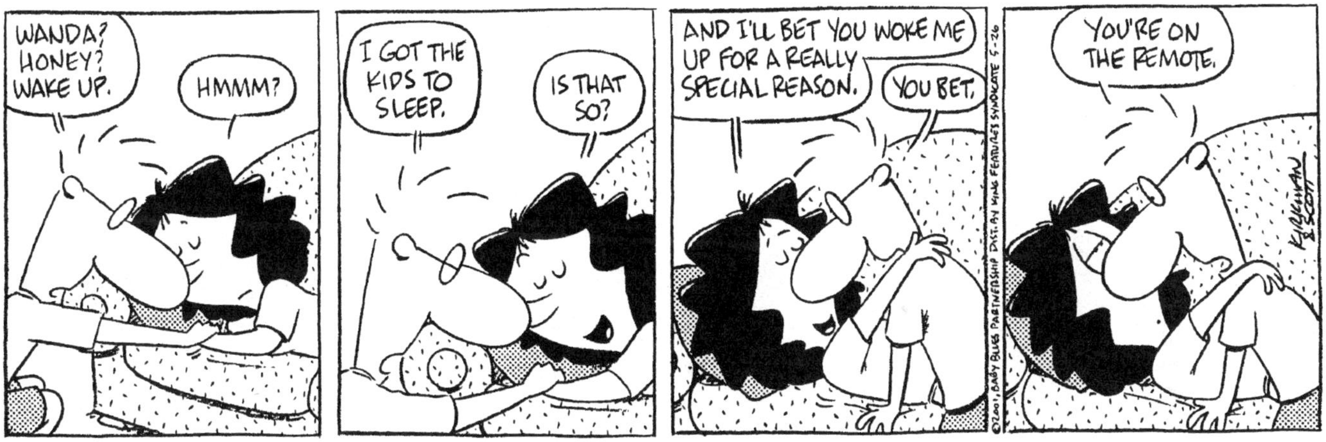
WANDA? HONEY? WAKE UP.
HMMM?
I GOT THE KIDS TO SLEEP.
IS THAT SO?
AND I'LL BET YOU WOKE ME UP FOR A REALLY SPECIAL REASON.
YOU BET.
YOU'RE ON THE REMOTE.
KIRKMAN & SCOTT

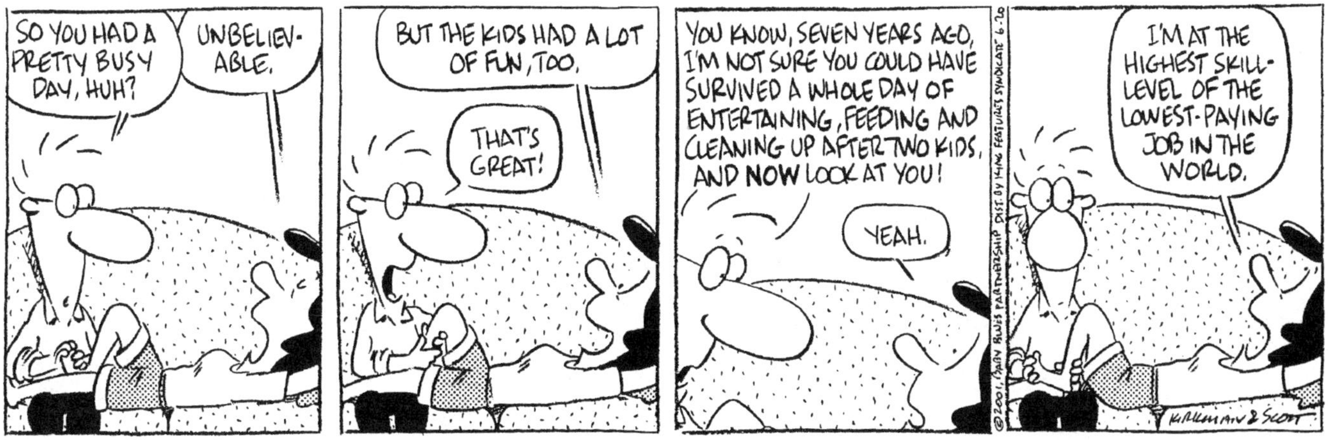
SO YOU HAD A PRETTY BUSY DAY, HUH?
UNBELIEV-ABLE.
BUT THE KIDS HAD A LOT OF FUN, TOO.
THAT'S GREAT!
YOU KNOW, SEVEN YEARS AGO, I'M NOT SURE YOU COULD HAVE SURVIVED A WHOLE DAY OF ENTERTAINING, FEEDING AND CLEANING UP AFTER TWO KIDS. AND NOW LOOK AT YOU!
YEAH.
I'M AT THE HIGHEST SKILL-LEVEL OF THE LOWEST-PAYING JOB IN THE WORLD.
KIRKMAN & SCOTT

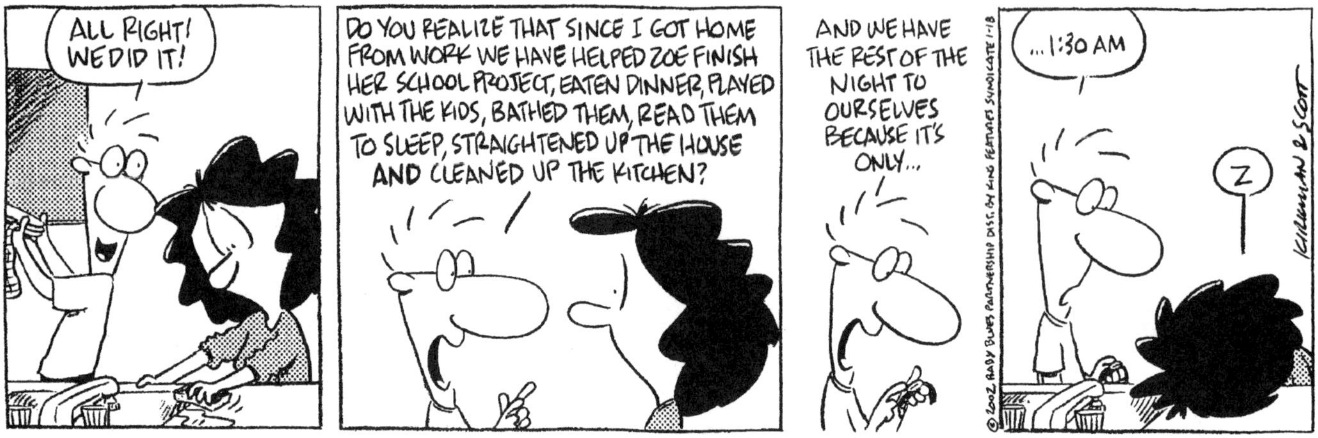
ALL RIGHT! WE DID IT!
DO YOU REALIZE THAT SINCE I GOT HOME FROM WORK WE HAVE HELPED ZOE FINISH HER SCHOOL PROJECT, EATEN DINNER, PLAYED WITH THE KIDS, BATHED THEM, READ THEM TO SLEEP, STRAIGHTENED UP THE HOUSE AND CLEANED UP THE KITCHEN?
AND WE HAVE THE REST OF THE NIGHT TO OURSELVES BECAUSE IT'S ONLY...
...1:30 AM
Z
KIRKMAN & SCOTT
© 2002, BABY BLUES PARTNERSHIP DIST. BY KING FEATURES SYNDICATE 1-18

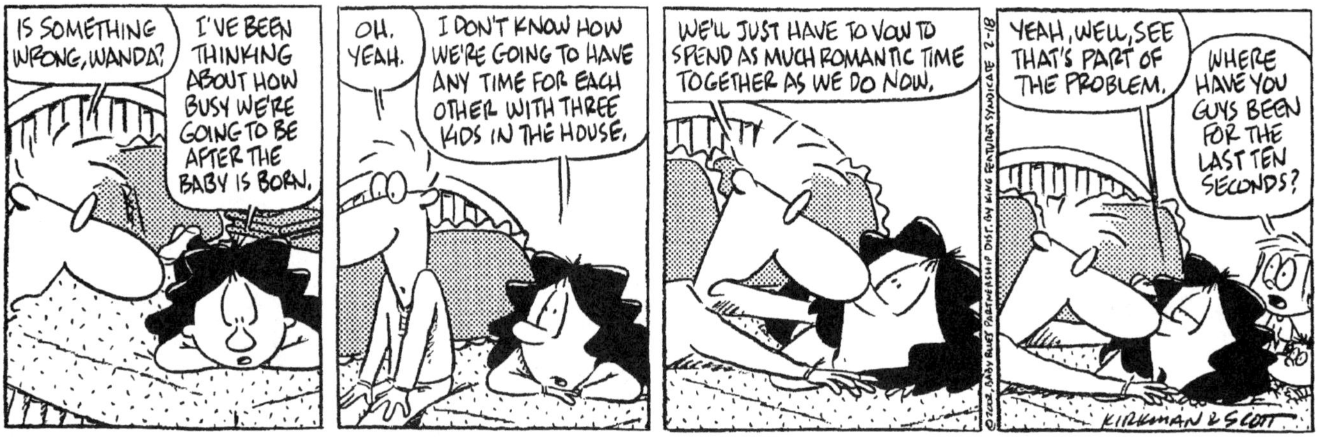
IS SOMETHING WRONG, WANDA?
I'VE BEEN THINKING ABOUT HOW BUSY WE'RE GOING TO BE AFTER THE BABY IS BORN.
OH. YEAH.
I DON'T KNOW HOW WE'RE GOING TO HAVE ANY TIME FOR EACH OTHER WITH THREE KIDS IN THE HOUSE.
WE'LL JUST HAVE TO VOW TO SPEND AS MUCH ROMANTIC TIME TOGETHER AS WE DO NOW.
YEAH, WELL, SEE THAT'S PART OF THE PROBLEM.
WHERE HAVE YOU GUYS BEEN FOR THE LAST TEN SECONDS?
KIRKMAN & SCOTT
© 2002, BABY BLUES PARTNERSHIP DIST. BY KING FEATURES SYNDICATE 2-18

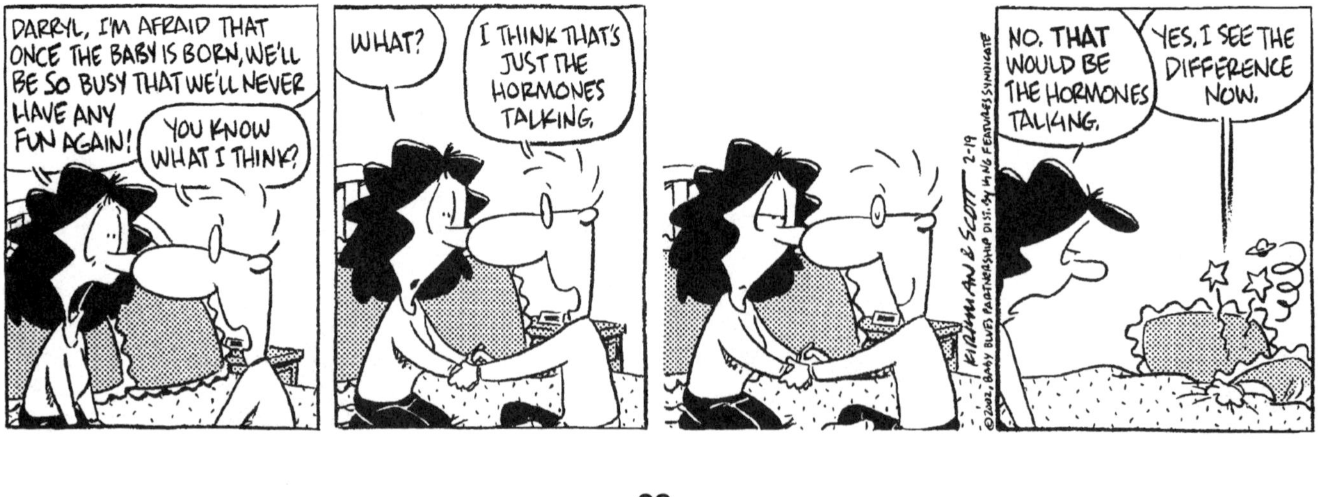
DARRYL, I'M AFRAID THAT ONCE THE BABY IS BORN, WE'LL BE SO BUSY THAT WE'LL NEVER HAVE ANY FUN AGAIN!
YOU KNOW WHAT I THINK?
WHAT?
I THINK THAT'S JUST THE HORMONES TALKING.
NO. THAT WOULD BE THE HORMONES TALKING.
YES. I SEE THE DIFFERENCE NOW.
KIRKMAN & SCOTT
© 2002, BABY BLUES PARTNERSHIP DIST. BY KING FEATURES SYNDICATE 2-19

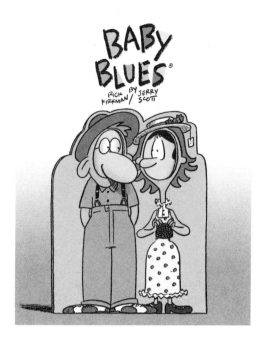

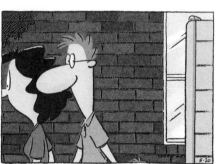

BABY BLUES®

BY RICK KIRKMAN / JERRY SCOTT

8-20
DON'T LOOK NOW, BUT YOU'VE **GOT** TO SEE THAT FAMILY OVER THERE!
WHERE?
I JUST GOT A GLIMPSE OF THEM, BUT TALK ABOUT YOUR SMALL-TOWN GOOBERS!
SHHHH! THEY'LL HEAR YOU!
TO 6 PM
THE GUY IS PROBABLY ABOUT MY AGE, BUT HE LOOKS LIKE HE HASN'T EXERCISED IN ABOUT FIVE YEARS...
YEAH?
AND THE WIFE ISN'T MUCH BETTER! SHE HAS BAGS UNDER HER EYES THAT WOULDN'T QUALIFY AS CARRY-ON LUGGAGE, AND A HAIRSTYLE THAT WENT OUT IN THE EIGHTIES!
REALLY?
OH! AND TO COMPLETE THE EN-SEMBLE, THEY'RE DRAGGING A COUPLE OF MESSY, SNOT-NOSED KIDS ALONG IN A WAGON!
A **WAGON??**
BANK
KIRKMAN & SCOTT
I THINK I'M GOING TO CRY.

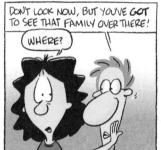

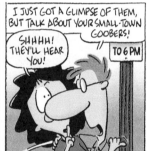

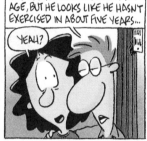

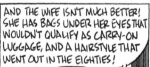

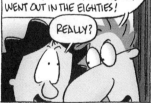

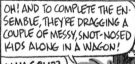

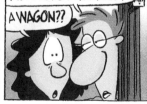

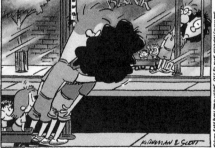

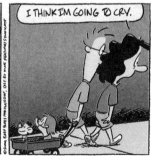

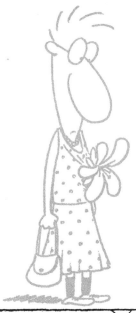

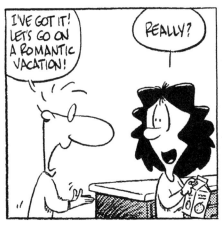

I'VE GOT IT! LET'S GO ON A ROMANTIC VACATION!
REALLY?
YES! JUST THE TWO OF US ALONE IN A HOTEL!
ONE LAST FLING BEFORE THE BABY IS BORN!
ONE LAST FLING BEFORE YOU BLOW UP LIKE A PUFFER FISH!
© 2002, BABY BLUES PARTNERSHIP DIST. BY KING FEATURES SYNDICATE 2-20
A REALLY **SEXY** PUFFER FISH, I MEAN.
THAT JUST COST YOU AN UPGRADE TO A SUITE.
KIRKMAN & SCOTT

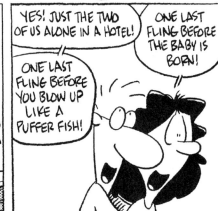

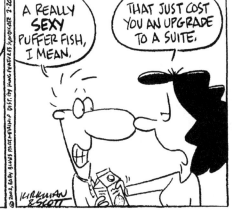

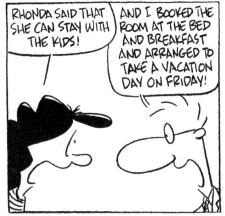

RHONDA SAID THAT SHE CAN STAY WITH THE KIDS!
AND I BOOKED THE ROOM AT THE BED AND BREAKFAST AND ARRANGED TO TAKE A VACATION DAY ON FRIDAY!
JUST THINK... LONG WALKS ON THE BEACH... ROMANTIC DINNERS BY CANDLELIGHT...
OUR OWN IN-ROOM SPA... COZY EVENINGS BY THE FIRE...
KIRKMAN & SCOTT
© 2002, BABY BLUES PARTNERSHIP DIST. BY KING FEATURES SYNDICATE 2-23
I JUST HOPE THE KIDS DON'T MISS US TOO MUCH.
ALL THE TV WE WANT TO WATCH... NOTHING BUT PIZZA AND MACARONI FOR THREE DAYS...
HOW SOON DO THEY LEAVE?

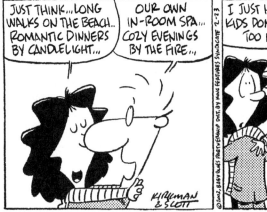

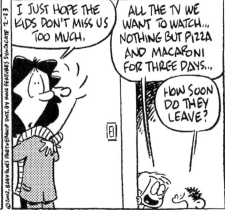

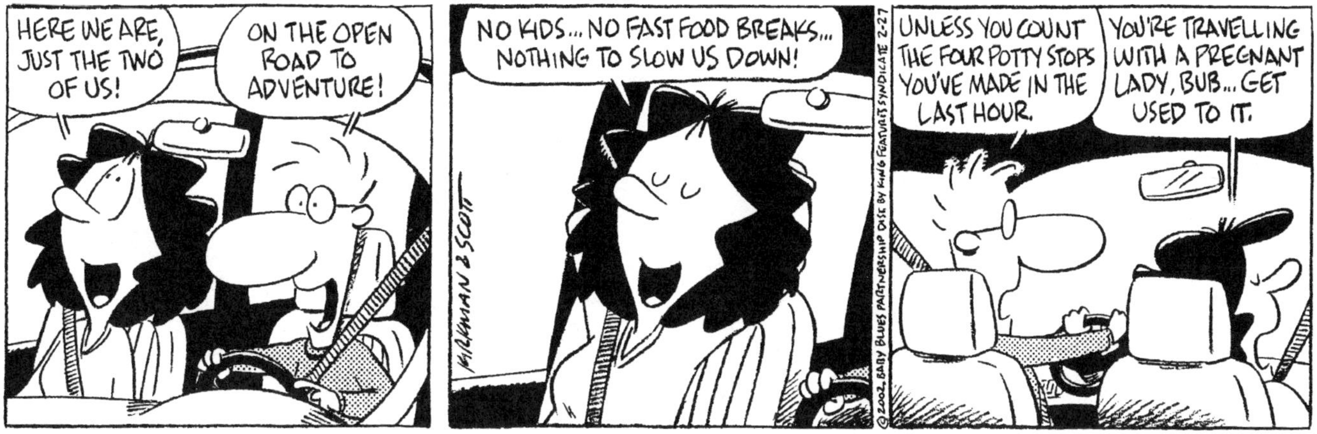
HERE WE ARE, JUST THE TWO OF US!
ON THE OPEN ROAD TO ADVENTURE!
NO KIDS... NO FAST FOOD BREAKS... NOTHING TO SLOW US DOWN!
UNLESS YOU COUNT THE FOUR POTTY STOPS YOU'VE MADE IN THE LAST HOUR.
YOU'RE TRAVELLING WITH A PREGNANT LADY, BUB... GET USED TO IT.
KIRKMAN & SCOTT
© 2002, BABY BLUES PARTNERSHIP DIST. BY KING FEATURES SYNDICATE 2-27

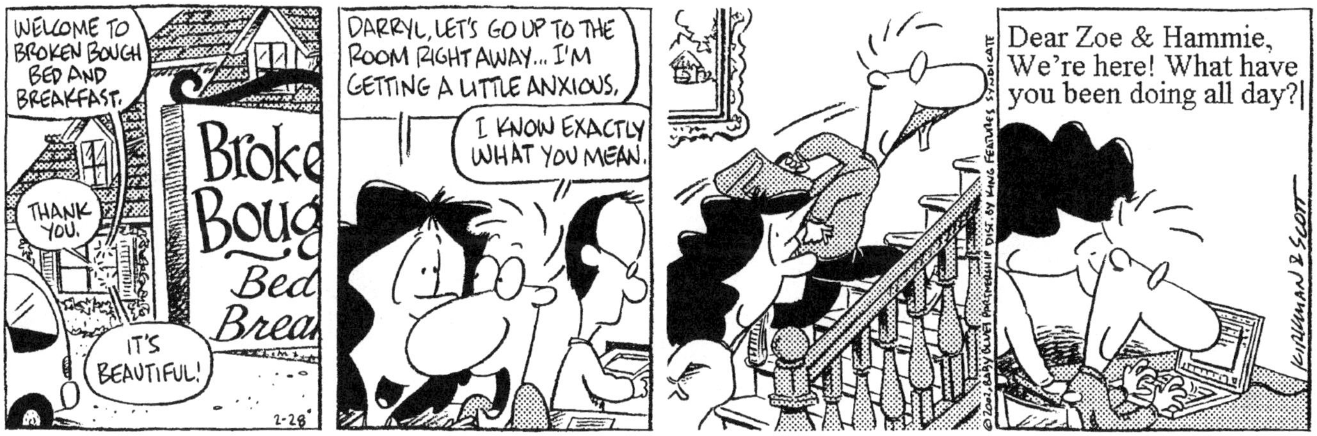
WELCOME TO BROKEN BOUGH BED AND BREAKFAST.
THANK YOU.
IT'S BEAUTIFUL!
2-28
DARRYL, LET'S GO UP TO THE ROOM RIGHT AWAY... I'M GETTING A LITTLE ANXIOUS.
I KNOW EXACTLY WHAT YOU MEAN.
© 2002, BABY BLUES PARTNERSHIP DIST. BY KING FEATURES SYNDICATE
Dear Zoe & Hammie,
We're here! What have you been doing all day?
KIRKMAN & SCOTT

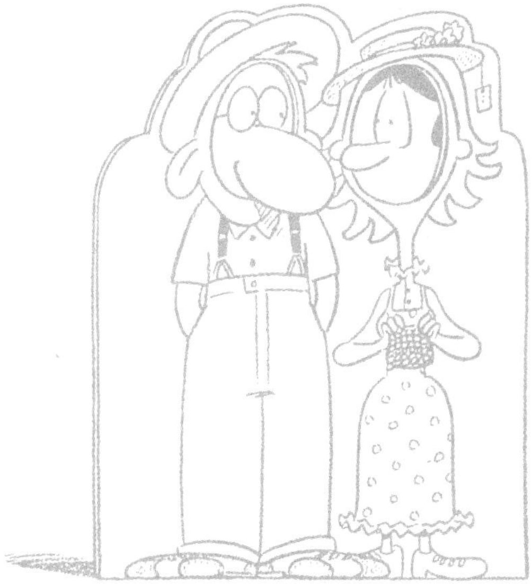

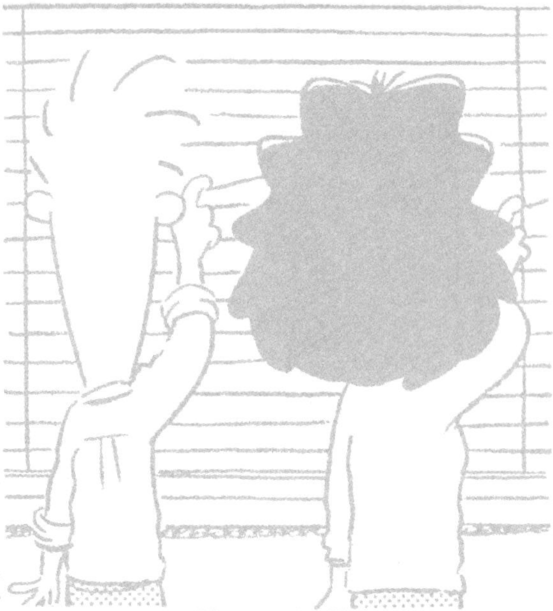

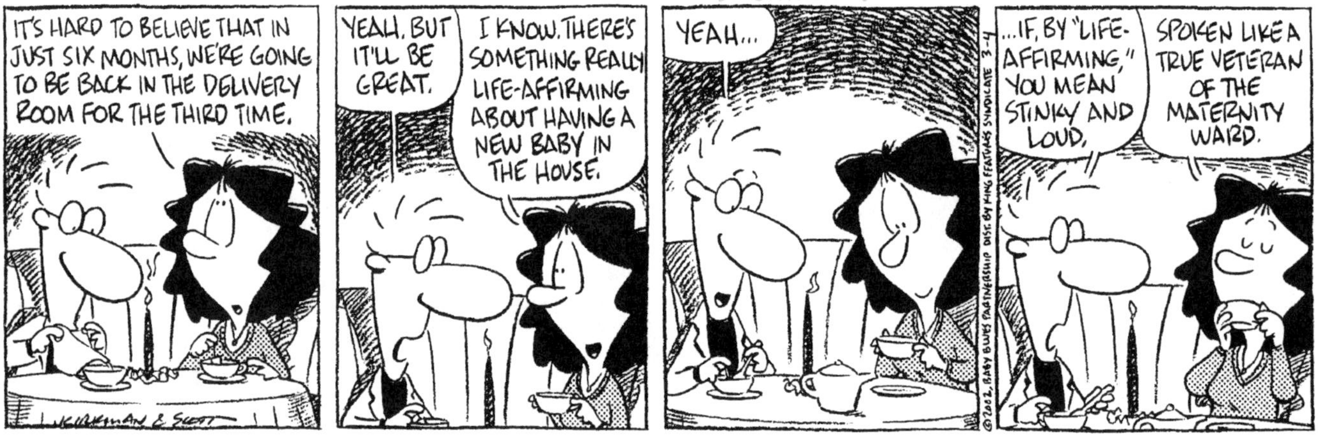
IT'S HARD TO BELIEVE THAT IN JUST SIX MONTHS, WE'RE GOING TO BE BACK IN THE DELIVERY ROOM FOR THE THIRD TIME.
KIRKMAN & SCOTT
YEAH. BUT IT'LL BE GREAT.
I KNOW. THERE'S SOMETHING REALLY LIFE-AFFIRMING ABOUT HAVING A NEW BABY IN THE HOUSE.
YEAH...
©2002, BABY BLUES PARTNERSHIP DIST. BY KING FEATURES SYNDICATE 3-4
...IF, BY "LIFE-AFFIRMING," YOU MEAN STINKY AND LOUD.
SPOKEN LIKE A TRUE VETERAN OF THE MATERNITY WARD.

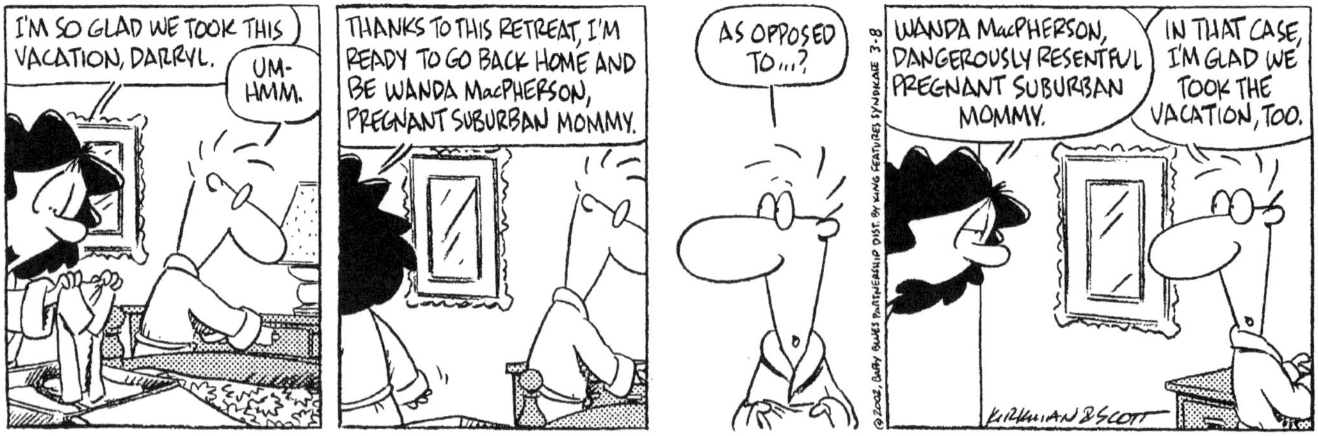
I'M SO GLAD WE TOOK THIS VACATION, DARRYL.
UM-HMM.
THANKS TO THIS RETREAT, I'M READY TO GO BACK HOME AND BE WANDA MacPHERSON, PREGNANT SUBURBAN MOMMY.
AS OPPOSED TO...?
©2002, BABY BLUES PARTNERSHIP DIST. BY KING FEATURES SYNDICATE 3-8
WANDA MacPHERSON, DANGEROUSLY RESENTFUL PREGNANT SUBURBAN MOMMY.
IN THAT CASE, I'M GLAD WE TOOK THE VACATION, TOO.
KIRKMAN & SCOTT

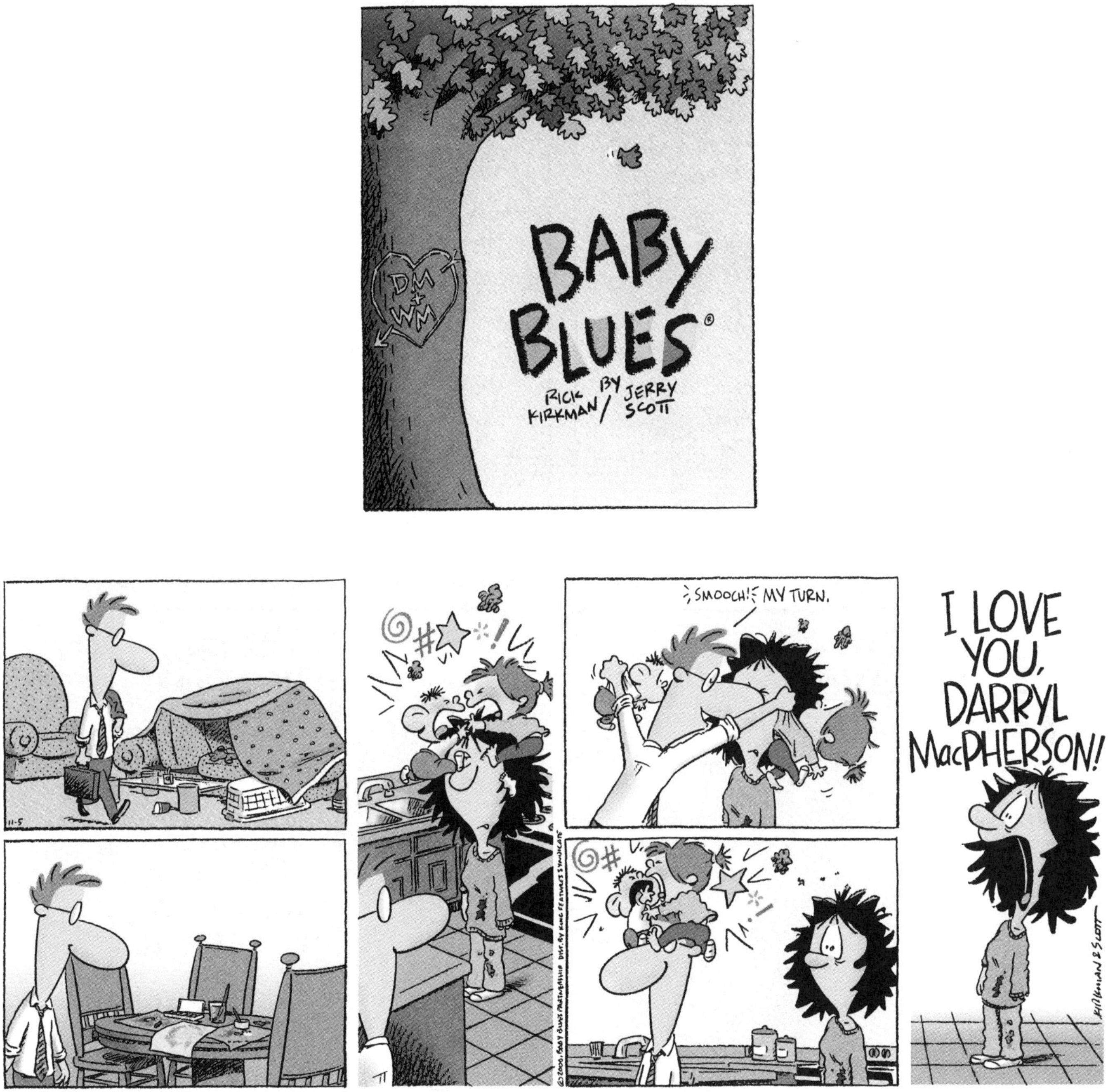

DM + WM
BABY BLUES®
BY RICK KIRKMAN / JERRY SCOTT
11-5
©2000, BABY BLUES PARTNERSHIP DIST. BY KING FEATURES SYNDICATE
SMOOCH!
MY TURN.
I LOVE YOU, DARRYL MacPHERSON!
KIRKMAN & SCOTT

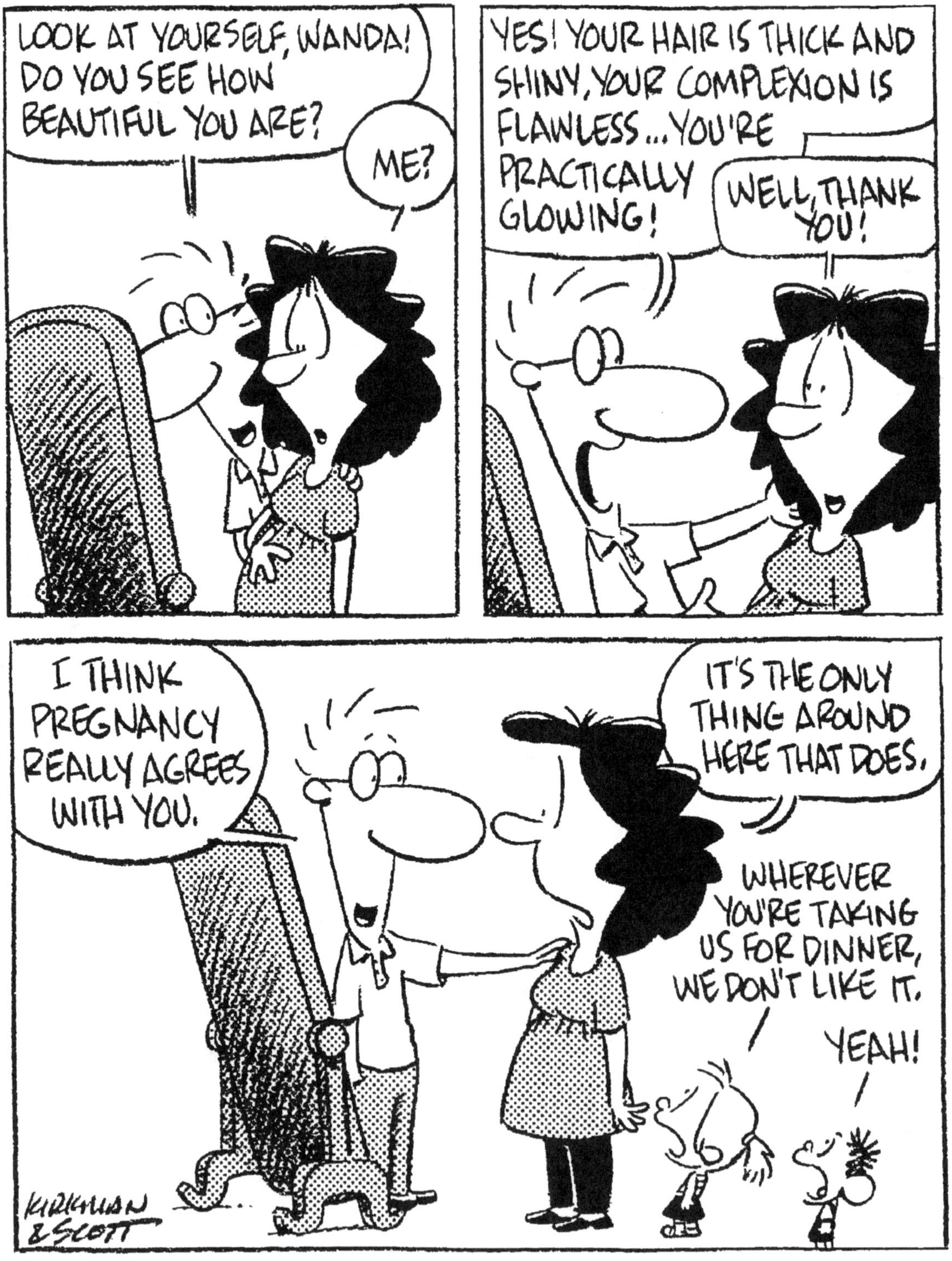

LOOK AT YOURSELF, WANDA! DO YOU SEE HOW BEAUTIFUL YOU ARE?
ME?
YES! YOUR HAIR IS THICK AND SHINY, YOUR COMPLEXION IS FLAWLESS... YOU'RE PRACTICALLY GLOWING!
WELL, THANK YOU!
I THINK PREGNANCY REALLY AGREES WITH YOU.
IT'S THE ONLY THING AROUND HERE THAT DOES.
WHEREVER YOU'RE TAKING US FOR DINNER, WE DON'T LIKE IT.
YEAH!
KIRKMAN & SCOTT

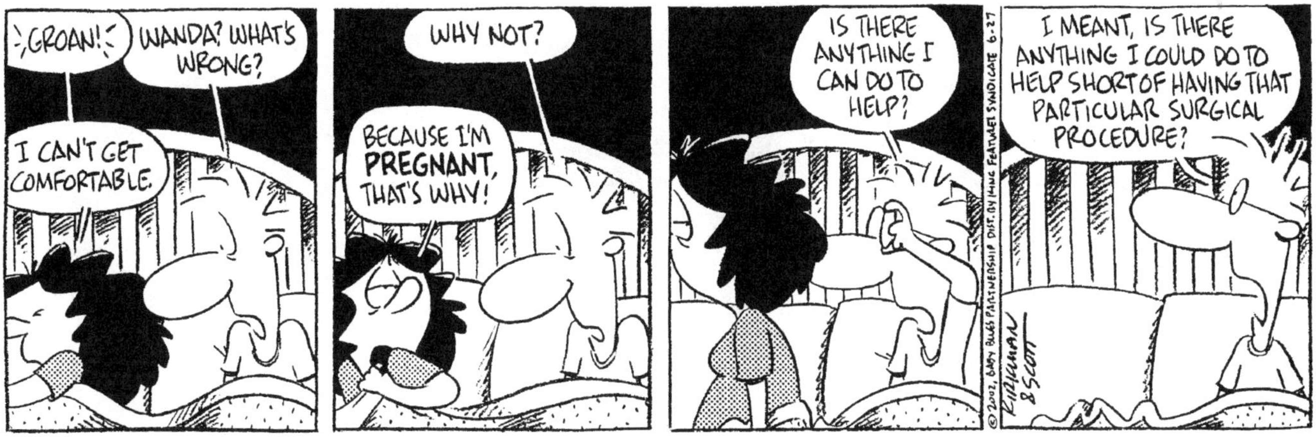
GROAN!
WANDA? WHAT'S WRONG?
I CAN'T GET COMFORTABLE.
WHY NOT?
BECAUSE I'M **PREGNANT**, THAT'S WHY!
IS THERE ANYTHING I CAN DO TO HELP?
I MEANT, IS THERE ANYTHING I COULD DO TO HELP SHORT OF HAVING THAT PARTICULAR SURGICAL PROCEDURE?
KIRKMAN & SCOTT
© 2002, BABY BLUES PARTNERSHIP DIST. BY KING FEATURES SYNDICATE 6-27

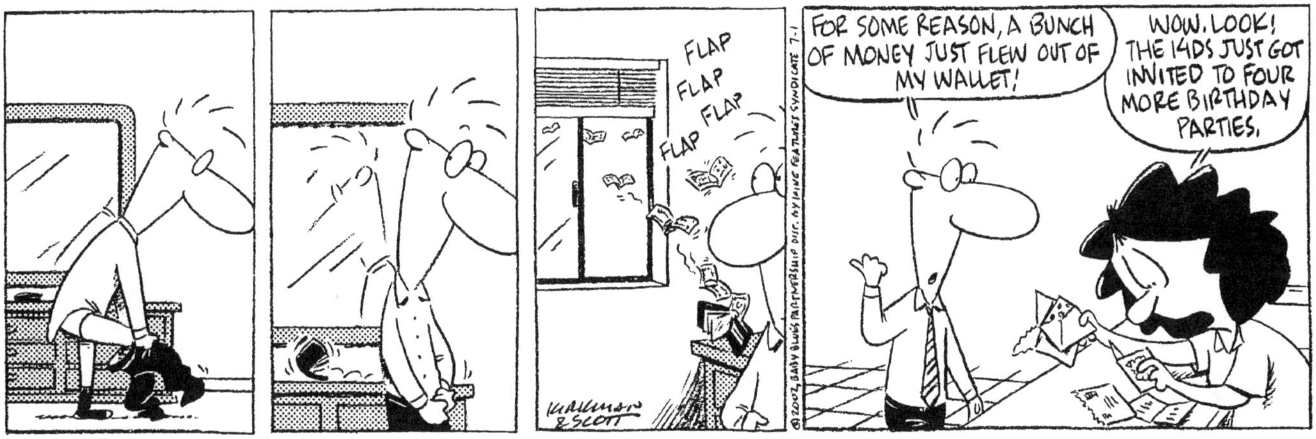
FLAP
FLAP
FLAP FLAP
FLAP
KIRKMAN & SCOTT
© 2002, BABY BLUES PARTNERSHIP DIST. BY KING FEATURES SYNDICATE 7-1
FOR SOME REASON, A BUNCH OF MONEY JUST FLEW OUT OF MY WALLET!
WOW. LOOK! THE KIDS JUST GOT INVITED TO FOUR MORE BIRTHDAY PARTIES.

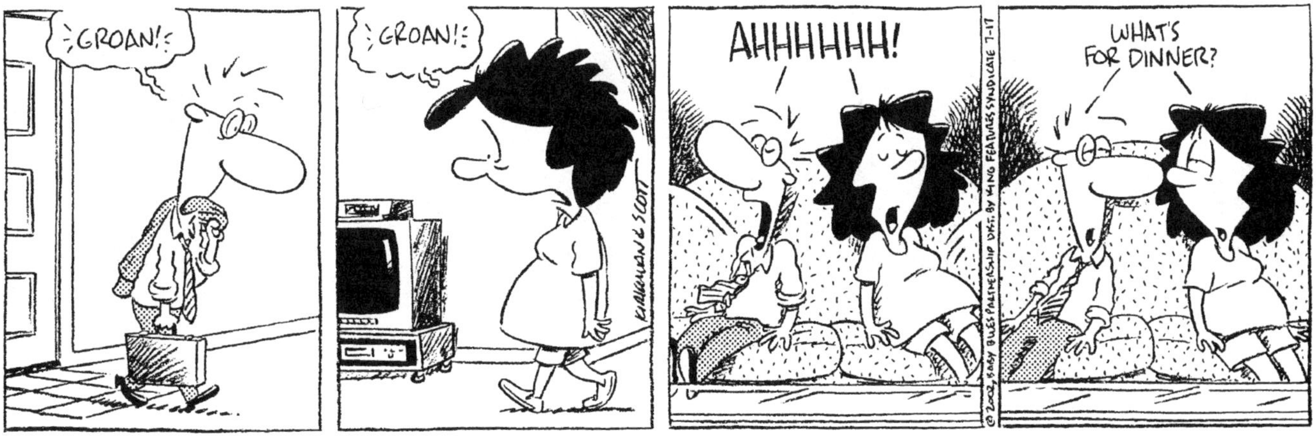
GROAN!
GROAN!
KIRKMAN & SCOTT
AHHHHHH!
© 2002, BABY BLUES PARTNERSHIP DIST. BY KING FEATURES SYNDICATE 7-17
WHAT'S FOR DINNER?

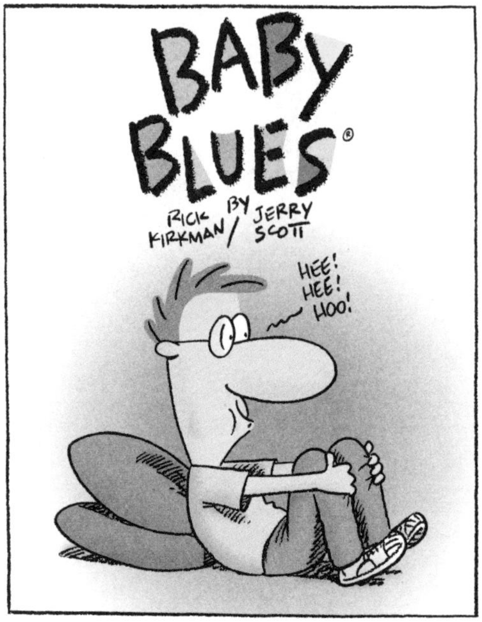
BABY BLUES®
BY RICK KIRKMAN / JERRY SCOTT
HEE! HEE! HOO!

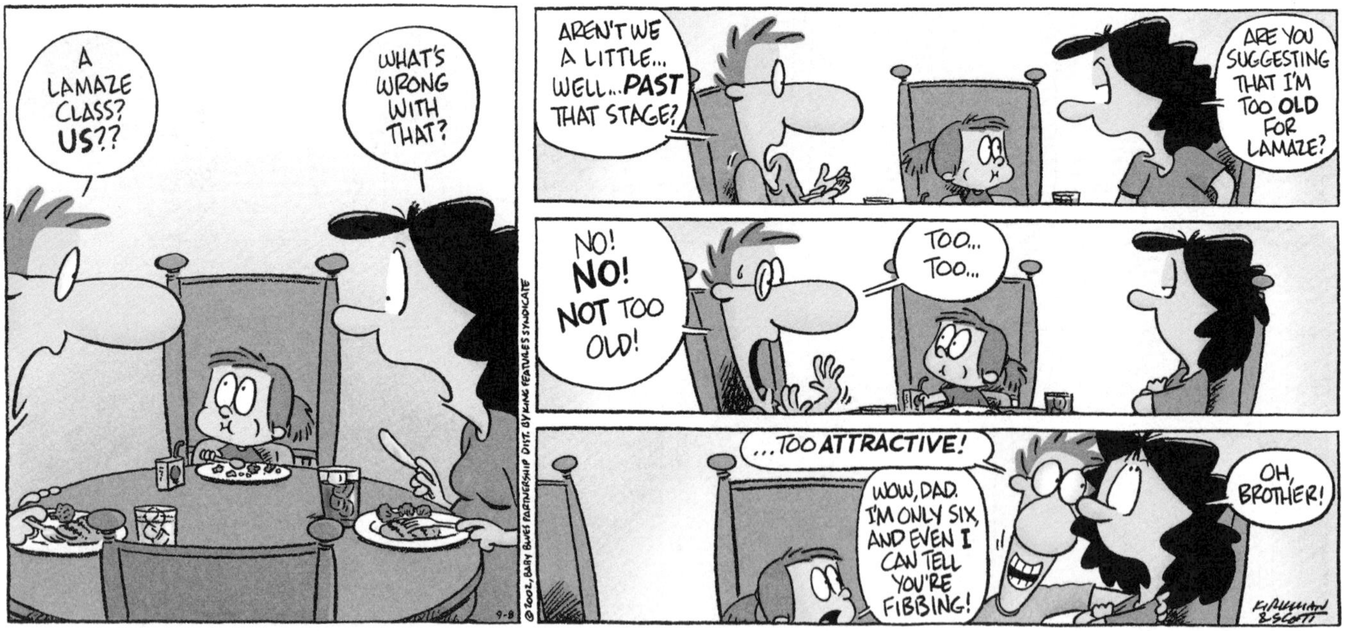
A LAMAZE CLASS? US??
WHAT'S WRONG WITH THAT?
AREN'T WE A LITTLE... WELL...PAST THAT STAGE?
ARE YOU SUGGESTING THAT I'M TOO OLD FOR LAMAZE?
NO! NO! NOT TOO OLD!
TOO... TOO...
...TOO ATTRACTIVE!
WOW, DAD. I'M ONLY SIX, AND EVEN I CAN TELL YOU'RE FIBBING!
OH, BROTHER!
©2002, BABY BLUES PARTNERSHIP DIST. BY KING FEATURES SYNDICATE
9-8
KIRKMAN & SCOTT

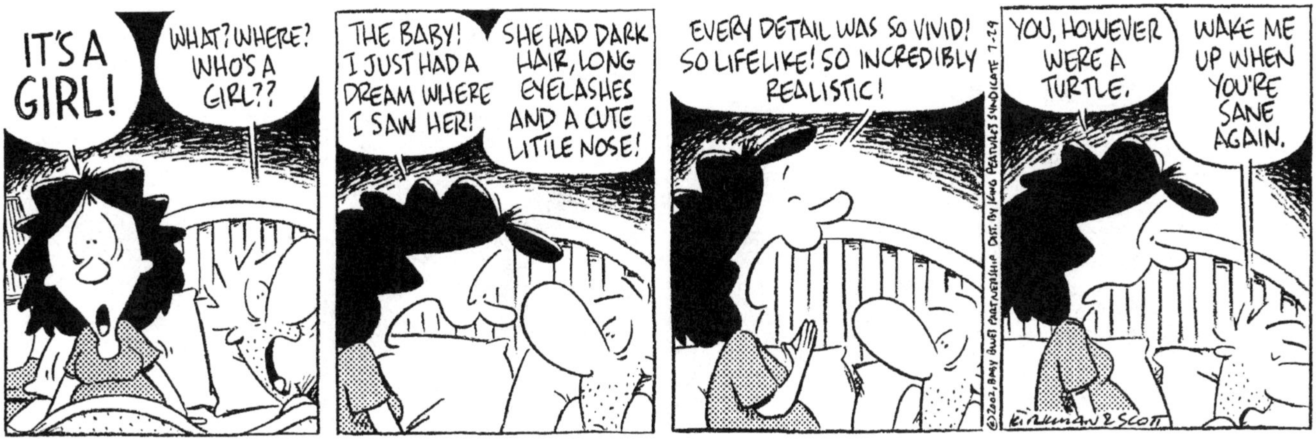
IT'S A GIRL!
WHAT? WHERE? WHO'S A GIRL??
THE BABY! I JUST HAD A DREAM WHERE I SAW HER!
SHE HAD DARK HAIR, LONG EYELASHES AND A CUTE LITTLE NOSE!
EVERY DETAIL WAS SO VIVID! SO LIFELIKE! SO INCREDIBLY REALISTIC!
YOU, HOWEVER WERE A TURTLE.
WAKE ME UP WHEN YOU'RE SANE AGAIN.
© 2002, BABY BLUES PARTNERSHIP DIST. BY KING FEATURES SYNDICATE 7-29
KIRKMAN & SCOTT

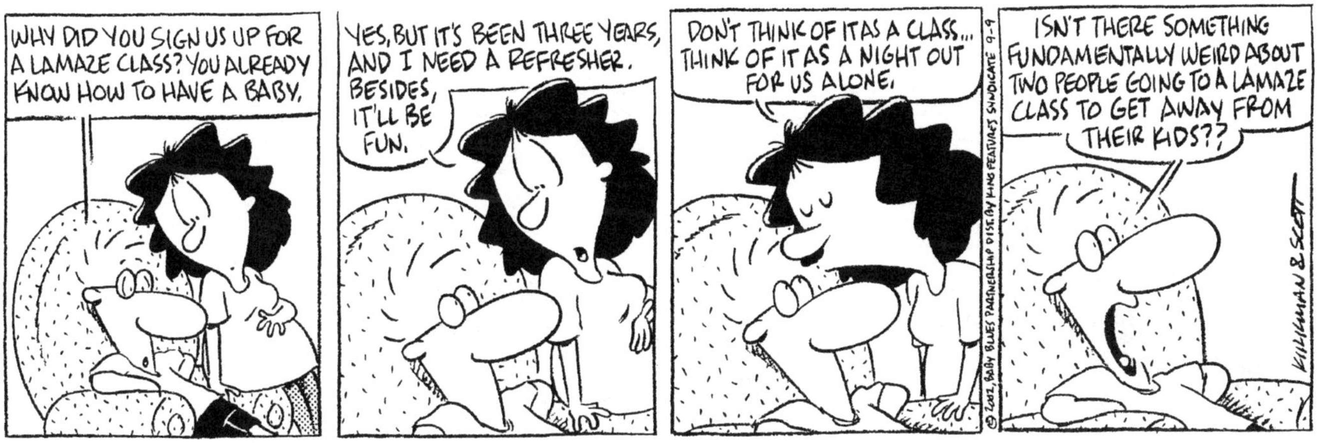
WHY DID YOU SIGN US UP FOR A LAMAZE CLASS? YOU ALREADY KNOW HOW TO HAVE A BABY.
YES, BUT IT'S BEEN THREE YEARS, AND I NEED A REFRESHER.
BESIDES, IT'LL BE FUN.
DON'T THINK OF IT AS A CLASS... THINK OF IT AS A NIGHT OUT FOR US ALONE.
ISN'T THERE SOMETHING FUNDAMENTALLY WEIRD ABOUT TWO PEOPLE GOING TO A LAMAZE CLASS TO GET AWAY FROM THEIR KIDS??
© 2002, BABY BLUES PARTNERSHIP DIST. BY KING FEATURES SYNDICATE 9-9
KIRKMAN & SCOTT

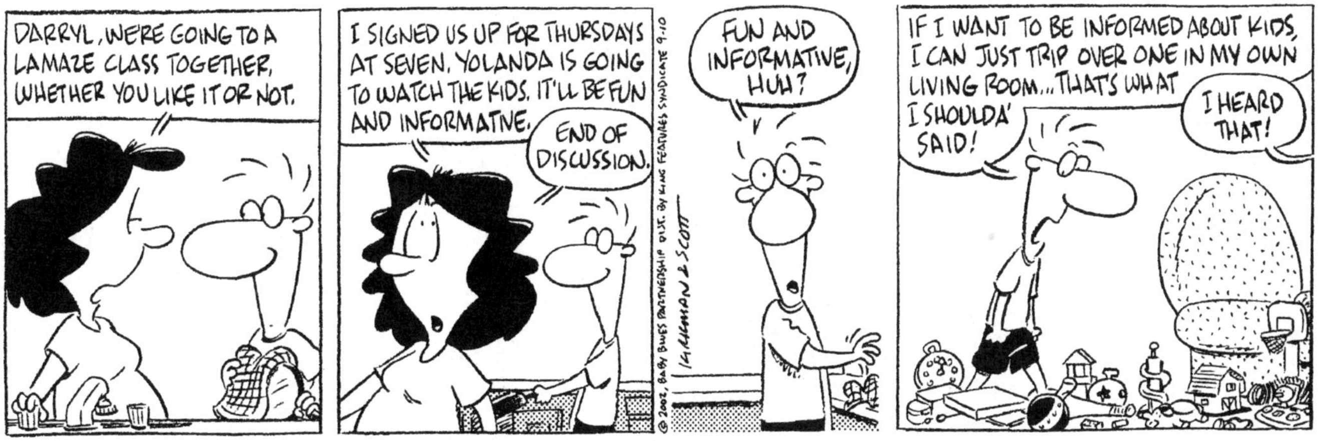
DARRYL, WE'RE GOING TO A LAMAZE CLASS TOGETHER, WHETHER YOU LIKE IT OR NOT.
I SIGNED US UP FOR THURSDAYS AT SEVEN. YOLANDA IS GOING TO WATCH THE KIDS. IT'LL BE FUN AND INFORMATIVE.
END OF DISCUSSION.
FUN AND INFORMATIVE, HUH?
IF I WANT TO BE INFORMED ABOUT KIDS, I CAN JUST TRIP OVER ONE IN MY OWN LIVING ROOM... THAT'S WHAT I SHOULDA' SAID!
I HEARD THAT!
© 2002, BABY BLUES PARTNERSHIP DIST. BY KING FEATURES SYNDICATE 9-10
KIRKMAN & SCOTT

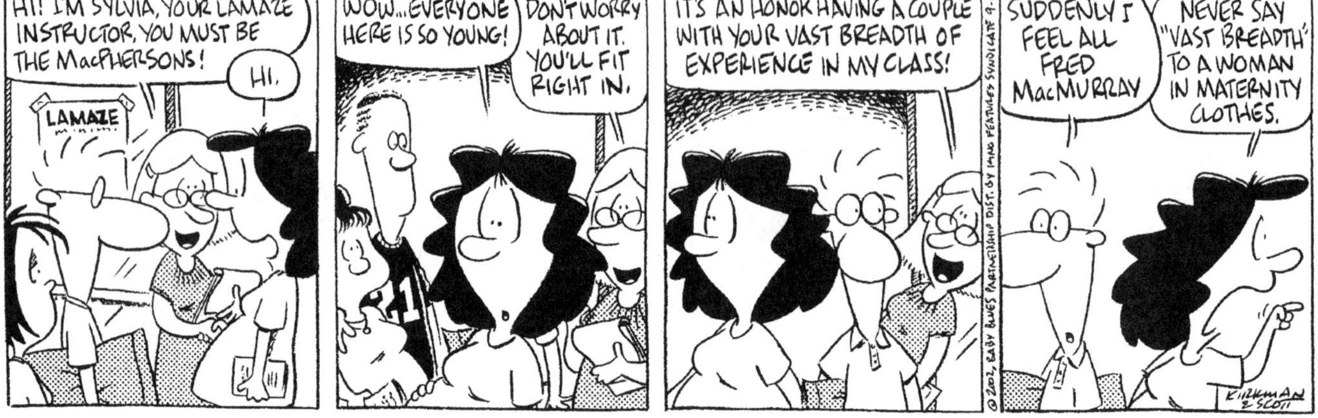
HI! I'M SYLVIA, YOUR LAMAZE INSTRUCTOR. YOU MUST BE THE MacPHERSONS!
HI.
LAMAZE
WOW...EVERYONE HERE IS SO YOUNG!
DON'T WORRY ABOUT IT. YOU'LL FIT RIGHT IN.
IT'S AN HONOR HAVING A COUPLE WITH YOUR VAST BREADTH OF EXPERIENCE IN MY CLASS!
SUDDENLY I FEEL ALL FRED MacMURRAY
NEVER SAY "VAST BREADTH" TO A WOMAN IN MATERNITY CLOTHES.
© 2002, BABY BLUES PARTNERSHIP DIST. BY KING FEATURES SYNDICATE 9-11
KIRKMAN & SCOTT

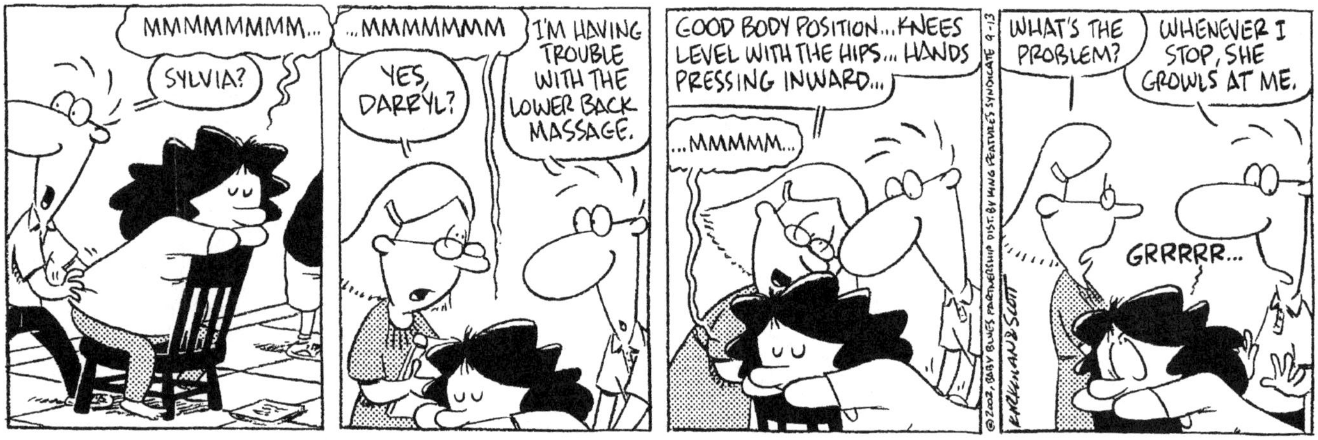
MMMMMMMM...
SYLVIA?
...MMMMMMM
YES, DARRYL?
I'M HAVING TROUBLE WITH THE LOWER BACK MASSAGE.
GOOD BODY POSITION... KNEES LEVEL WITH THE HIPS... HANDS PRESSING INWARD...
...MMMMM...
WHAT'S THE PROBLEM?
WHENEVER I STOP, SHE GROWLS AT ME.
GRRRRR...
© 2002, BABY BLUES PARTNERSHIP DIST. BY KING FEATURES SYNDICATE 9-13
KIRKMAN & SCOTT

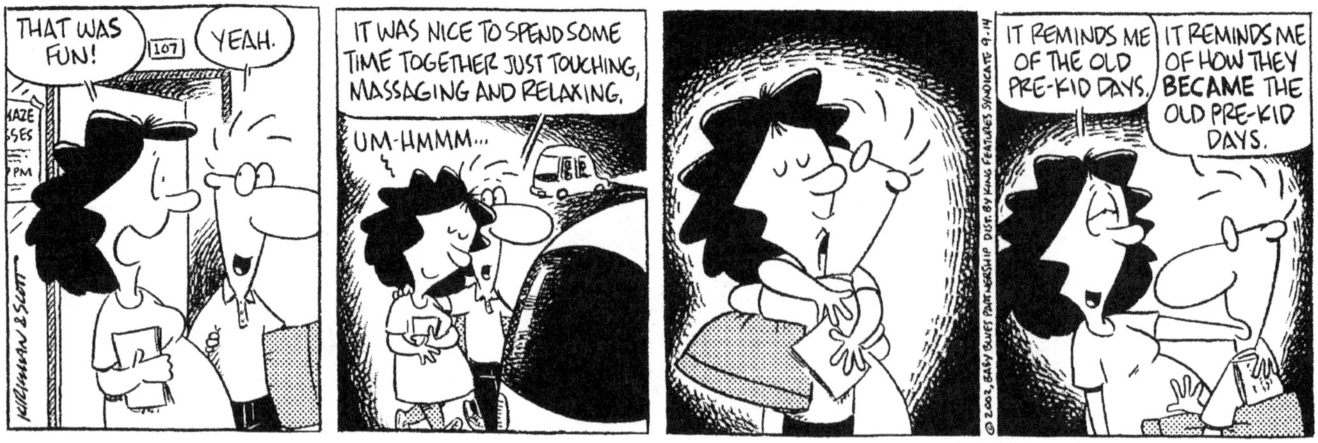
THAT WAS FUN!
107
YEAH.
IT WAS NICE TO SPEND SOME TIME TOGETHER JUST TOUCHING, MASSAGING AND RELAXING.
UM-HMMM...
IT REMINDS ME OF THE OLD PRE-KID DAYS.
IT REMINDS ME OF HOW THEY BECAME THE OLD PRE-KID DAYS.
© 2002, BABY BLUES PARTNERSHIP DIST. BY KING FEATURES SYNDICATE 9-14
KIRKMAN & SCOTT

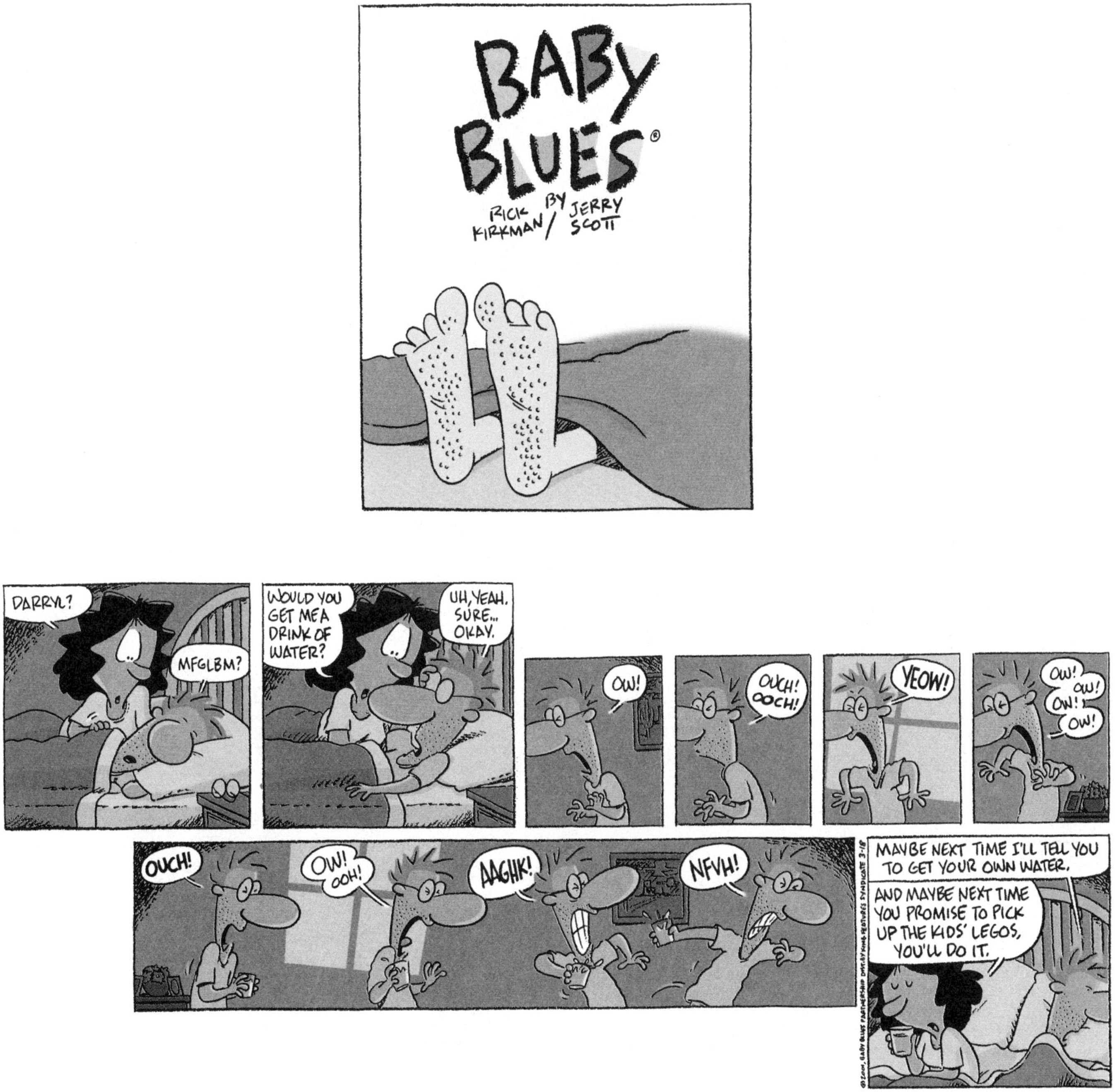
BABY BLUES®
BY RICK KIRKMAN / JERRY SCOTT
DARRYL?
MFGLBM?
WOULD YOU GET ME A DRINK OF WATER?
UH, YEAH. SURE... OKAY.
OW!
OUCH! OOCH!
YEOW!
OW! OW! OW! OW!
OUCH!
OW! OOH!
AAGHK!
NFVH!
MAYBE NEXT TIME I'LL TELL YOU TO GET YOUR OWN WATER.
AND MAYBE NEXT TIME YOU PROMISE TO PICK UP THE KIDS' LEGOS, YOU'LL DO IT.

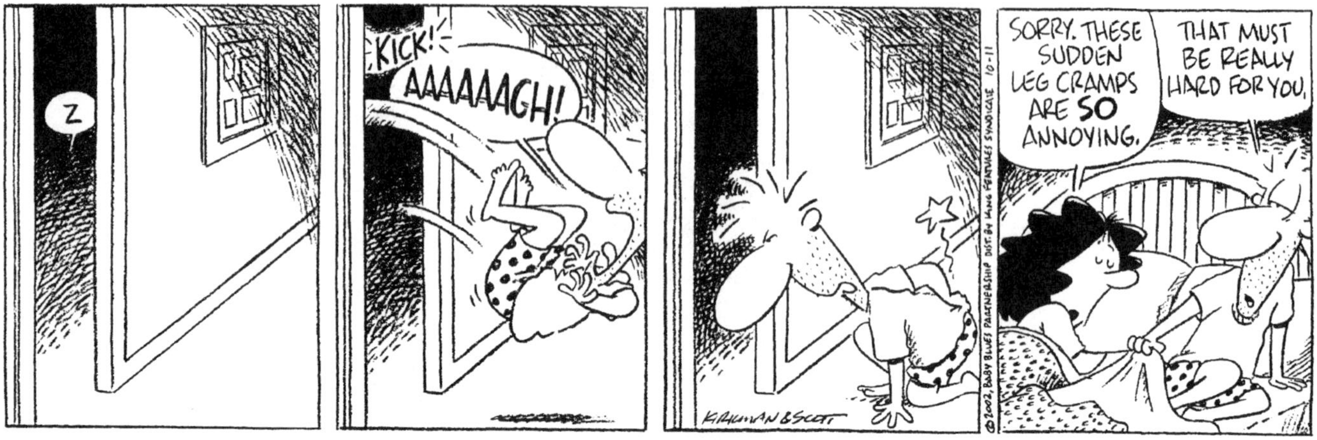
Z
KICK!
AAAAAAGH!
SORRY. THESE SUDDEN LEG CRAMPS ARE **SO** ANNOYING.
THAT MUST BE REALLY HARD FOR YOU.

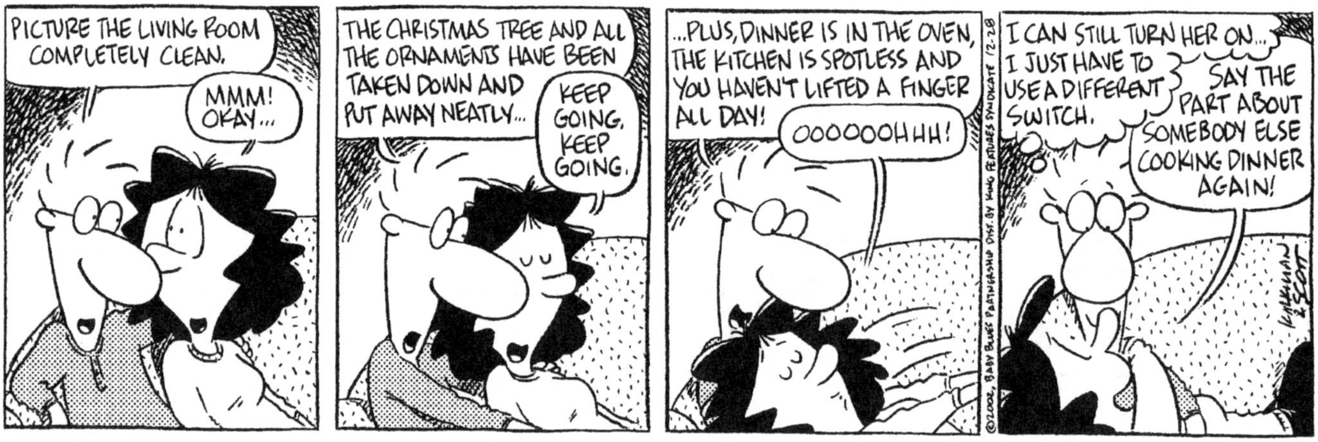
PICTURE THE LIVING ROOM COMPLETELY CLEAN.
MMM! OKAY...
THE CHRISTMAS TREE AND ALL THE ORNAMENTS HAVE BEEN TAKEN DOWN AND PUT AWAY NEATLY...
KEEP GOING. KEEP GOING.
...PLUS, DINNER IS IN THE OVEN, THE KITCHEN IS SPOTLESS AND YOU HAVEN'T LIFTED A FINGER ALL DAY!
OOOOOOHHH!
I CAN STILL TURN HER ON... I JUST HAVE TO USE A DIFFERENT SWITCH.
SAY THE PART ABOUT SOMEBODY ELSE COOKING DINNER AGAIN!

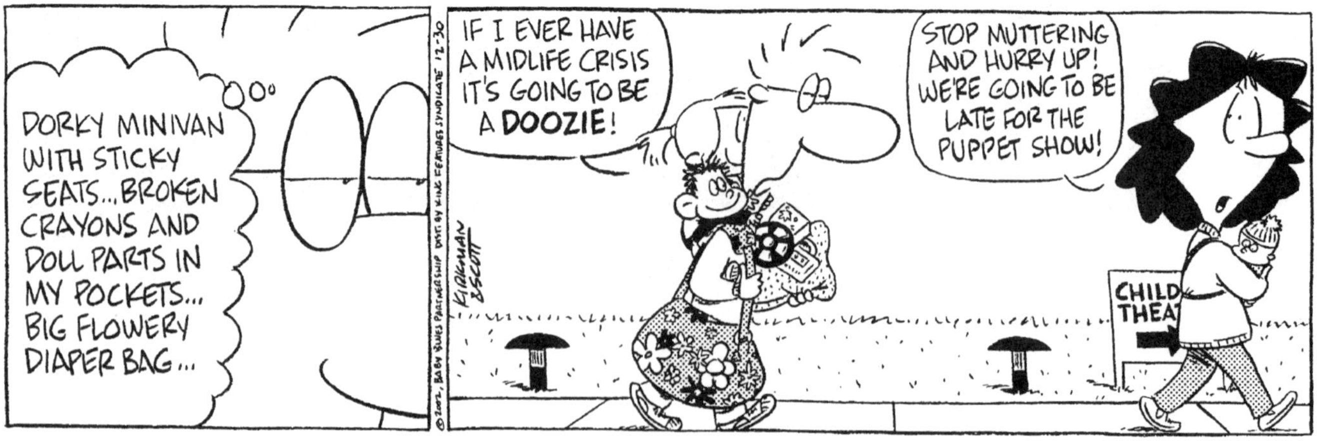
DORKY MINIVAN WITH STICKY SEATS... BROKEN CRAYONS AND DOLL PARTS IN MY POCKETS... BIG FLOWERY DIAPER BAG...
IF I EVER HAVE A MIDLIFE CRISIS IT'S GOING TO BE A **DOOZIE**!
STOP MUTTERING AND HURRY UP! WE'RE GOING TO BE LATE FOR THE PUPPET SHOW!
CHILD THEA

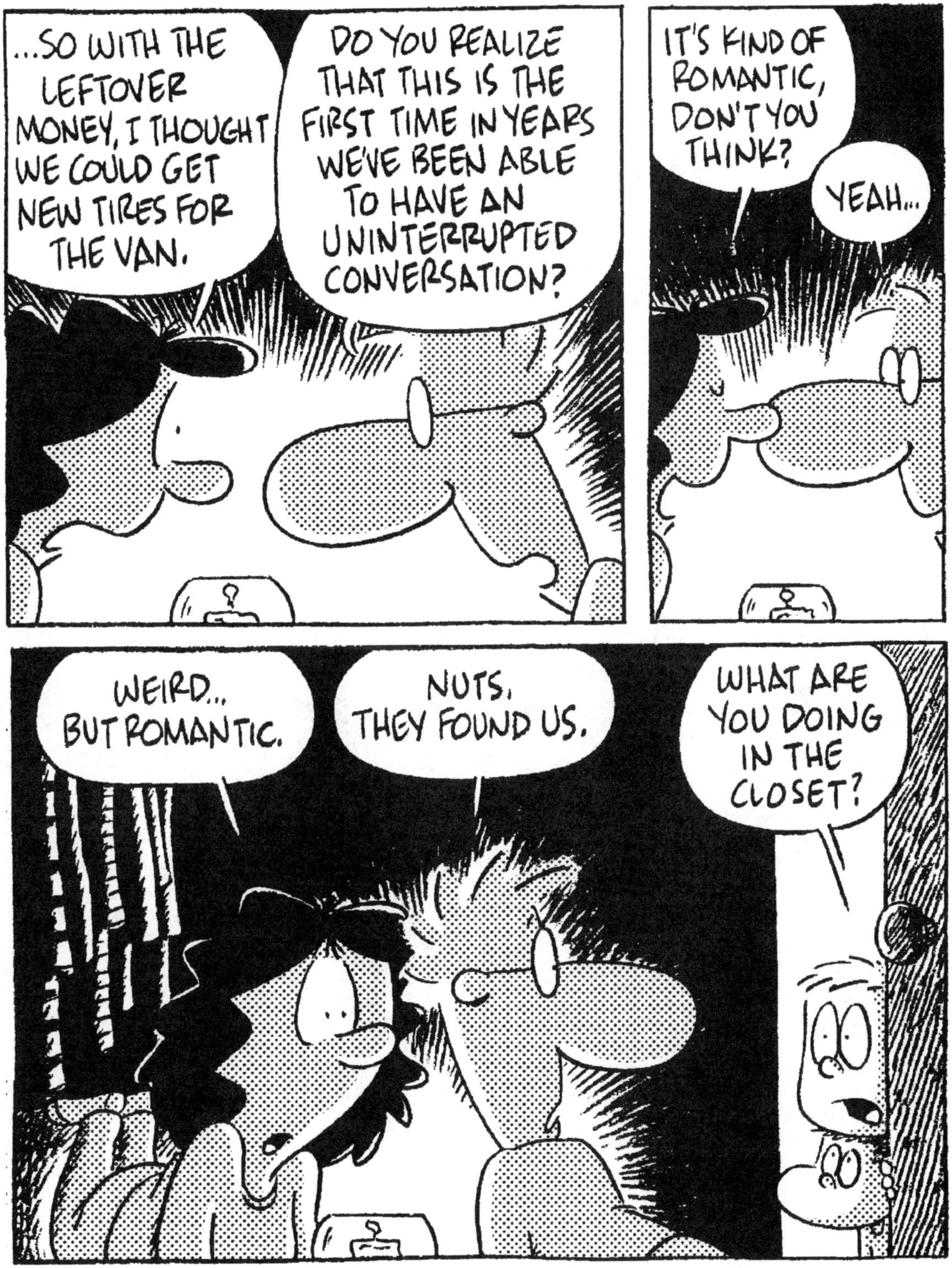
...SO WITH THE LEFTOVER MONEY, I THOUGHT WE COULD GET NEW TIRES FOR THE VAN.
DO YOU REALIZE THAT THIS IS THE FIRST TIME IN YEARS WE'VE BEEN ABLE TO HAVE AN UNINTERRUPTED CONVERSATION?
IT'S KIND OF ROMANTIC, DON'T YOU THINK?
YEAH...
WEIRD... BUT ROMANTIC.
NUTS. THEY FOUND US.
WHAT ARE YOU DOING IN THE CLOSET?

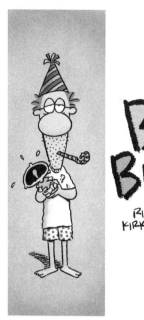

BABY BLUES®
BY RICK KIRKMAN / JERRY SCOTT

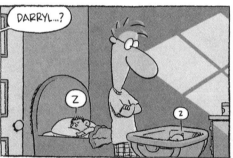

DARRYL...?
Z
Z
WHAT ARE YOU DOING UP?
I WAS JUST THINKING...
FOR AS LONG AS I CAN REMEMBER, I'VE PICTURED MYSELF AS A GUY WITH A BIG FAMILY, AND NOW LOOK AT ME.
©2002, BABY BLUES PARTNERSHIP DIST. BY KING FEATURES SYNDICATE
I DID IT, WANDA! I'VE ACHEIVED MY DREAM.
THANKS TO YOU, I HAVE THE UNBELIEVABLE PRIVILEGE OF SHARING THE LIFE OF YET ANOTHER BEAUTIFUL CHILD!
BBBBBWWWAAAAAAAAAAAAAAAAAAAAAAAAA!
KIRKMAN & SCOTT 11-17
I THINK I'LL GO CELEBRATE.
GET BACK HERE!!

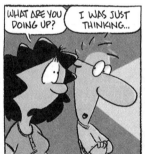

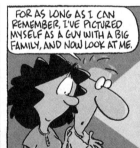

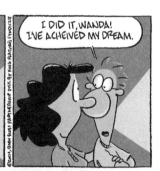

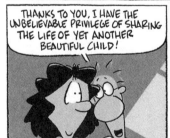

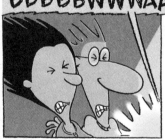

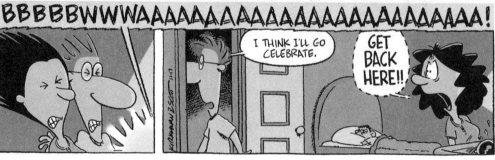

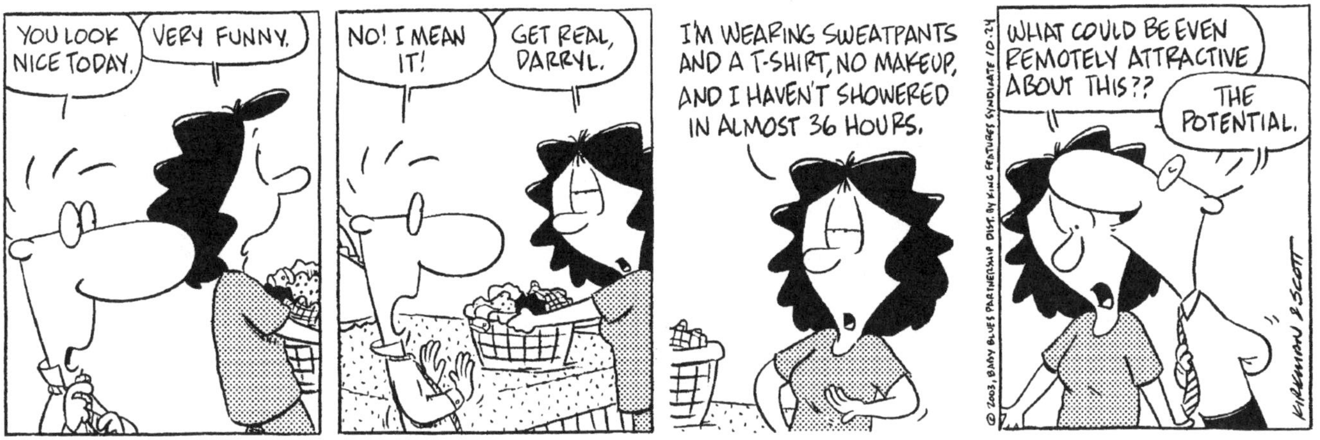
YOU LOOK NICE TODAY.
VERY FUNNY.
NO! I MEAN IT!
GET REAL, DARRYL.
I'M WEARING SWEATPANTS AND A T-SHIRT, NO MAKEUP, AND I HAVEN'T SHOWERED IN ALMOST 36 HOURS.
WHAT COULD BE EVEN REMOTELY ATTRACTIVE ABOUT THIS??
THE POTENTIAL.
© 2003, BABY BLUES PARTNERSHIP DIST. BY KING FEATURES SYNDICATE 10-24
KIRKMAN & SCOTT

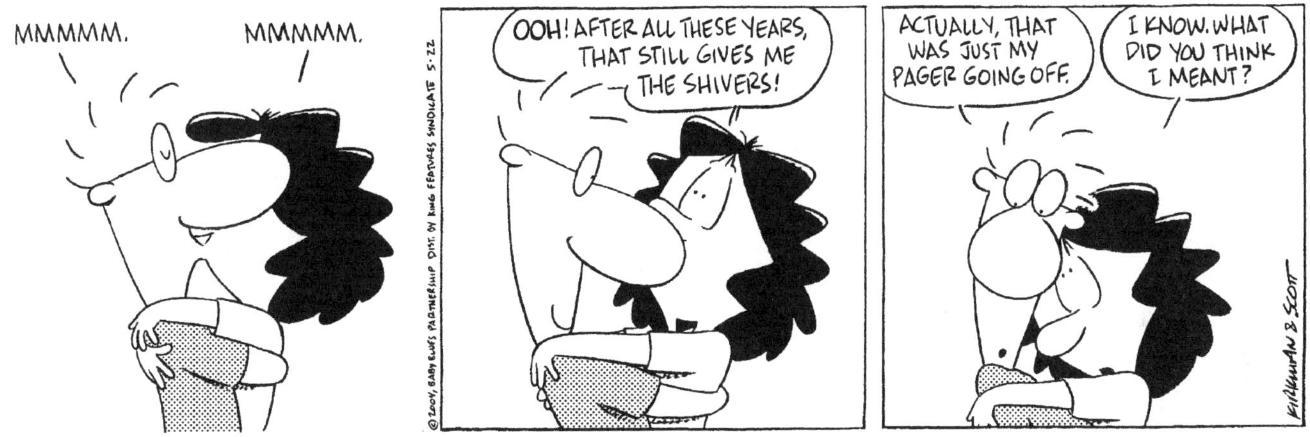
MMMMM.
MMMMM.
OOH! AFTER ALL THESE YEARS, THAT STILL GIVES ME THE SHIVERS!
ACTUALLY, THAT WAS JUST MY PAGER GOING OFF.
I KNOW. WHAT DID YOU THINK I MEANT?
© 2004, BABY BLUES PARTNERSHIP DIST. BY KING FEATURES SYNDICATE 5-22
KIRKMAN & SCOTT

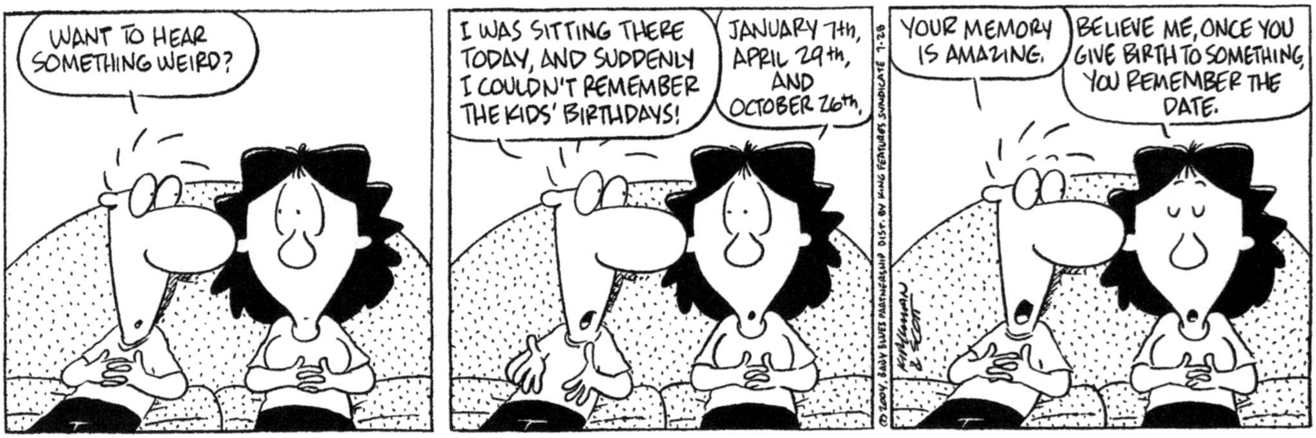
WANT TO HEAR SOMETHING WEIRD?
I WAS SITTING THERE TODAY, AND SUDDENLY I COULDN'T REMEMBER THE KIDS' BIRTHDAYS!
JANUARY 7th, APRIL 29th, AND OCTOBER 26th.
YOUR MEMORY IS AMAZING.
BELIEVE ME, ONCE YOU GIVE BIRTH TO SOMETHING, YOU REMEMBER THE DATE.
© 2004, BABY BLUES PARTNERSHIP DIST. BY KING FEATURES SYNDICATE 7-28
KIRKMAN & SCOTT

PASSION

DURING THE KIDYEARS

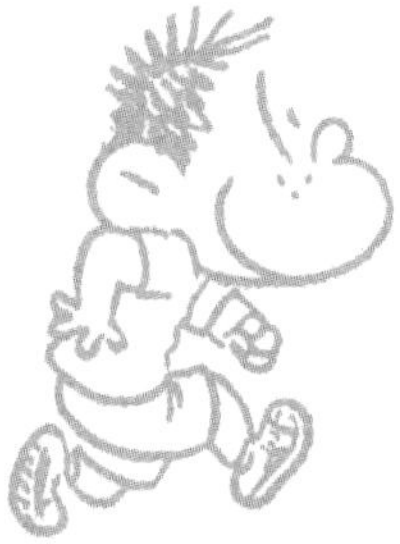

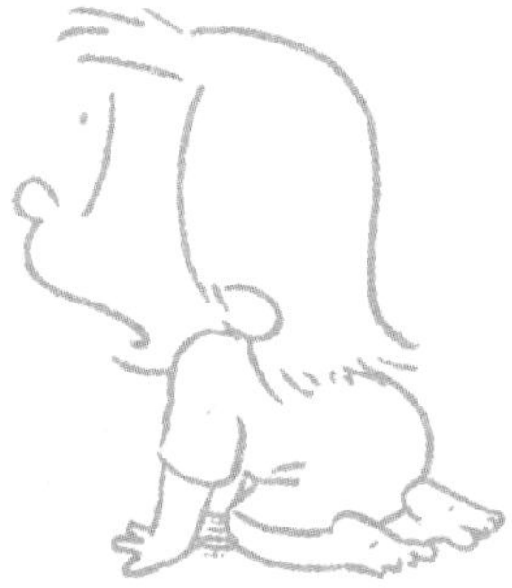

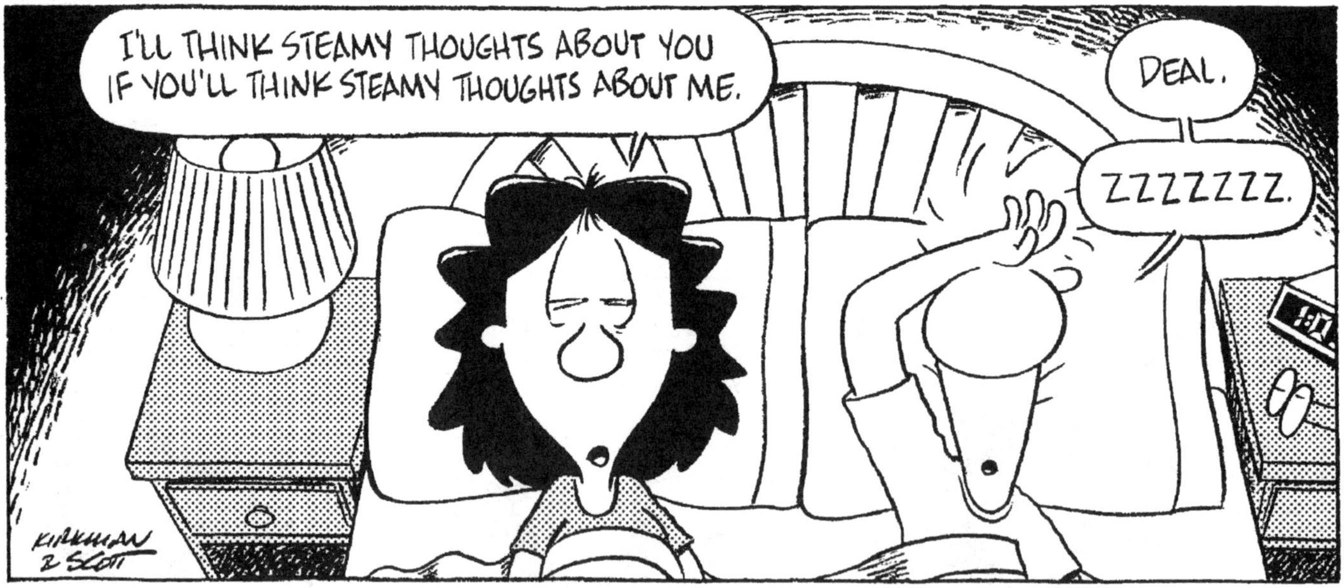
I'LL THINK STEAMY THOUGHTS ABOUT YOU IF YOU'LL THINK STEAMY THOUGHTS ABOUT ME.
DEAL.
ZZZZZZZ.
KIRKMAN & SCOTT

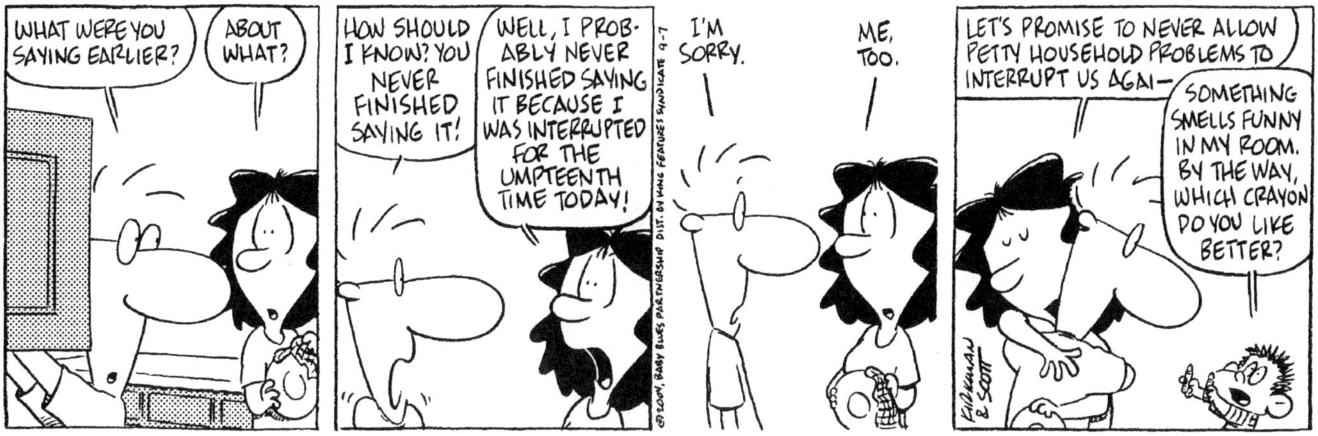
WHAT WERE YOU SAYING EARLIER?
ABOUT WHAT?
HOW SHOULD I KNOW? YOU NEVER FINISHED SAYING IT!
WELL, I PROBABLY NEVER FINISHED SAYING IT BECAUSE I WAS INTERRUPTED FOR THE UMPTEENTH TIME TODAY!
© 2001, BABY BLUES PARTNERSHIP DIST. BY KING FEATURES SYNDICATE 9-7
I'M SORRY.
ME, TOO.
LET'S PROMISE TO NEVER ALLOW PETTY HOUSEHOLD PROBLEMS TO INTERRUPT US AGAI—
SOMETHING SMELLS FUNNY IN MY ROOM. BY THE WAY, WHICH CRAYON DO YOU LIKE BETTER?
KIRKMAN & SCOTT

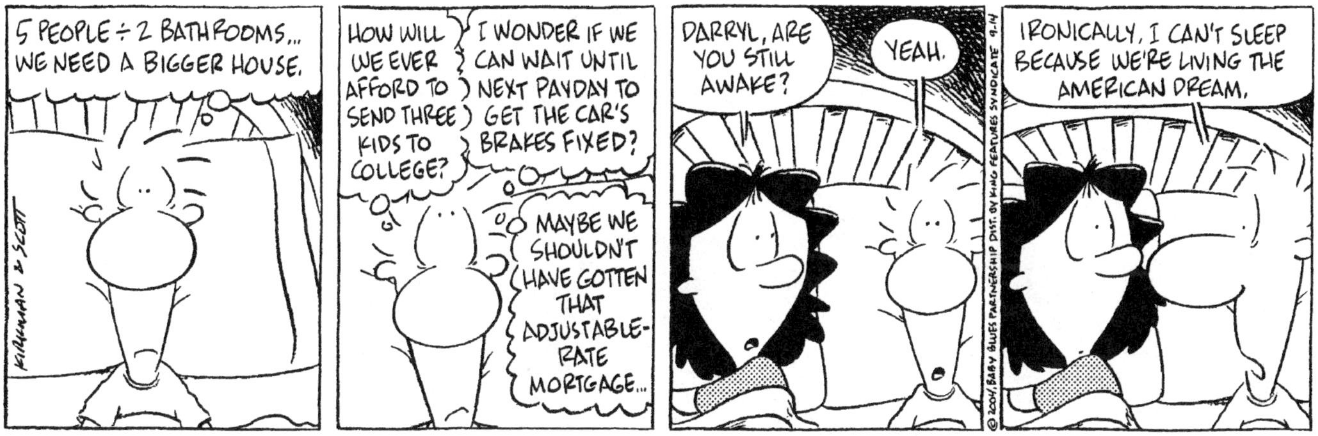
5 PEOPLE ÷ 2 BATHROOMS... WE NEED A BIGGER HOUSE.
KIRKMAN & SCOTT
HOW WILL WE EVER AFFORD TO SEND THREE KIDS TO COLLEGE?
I WONDER IF WE CAN WAIT UNTIL NEXT PAYDAY TO GET THE CAR'S BRAKES FIXED?
MAYBE WE SHOULDN'T HAVE GOTTEN THAT ADJUSTABLE-RATE MORTGAGE...
DARRYL, ARE YOU STILL AWAKE?
YEAH.
© 2001, BABY BLUES PARTNERSHIP DIST. BY KING FEATURES SYNDICATE 9-14
IRONICALLY, I CAN'T SLEEP BECAUSE WE'RE LIVING THE AMERICAN DREAM.

A Really, Really, Really Bad Answer:

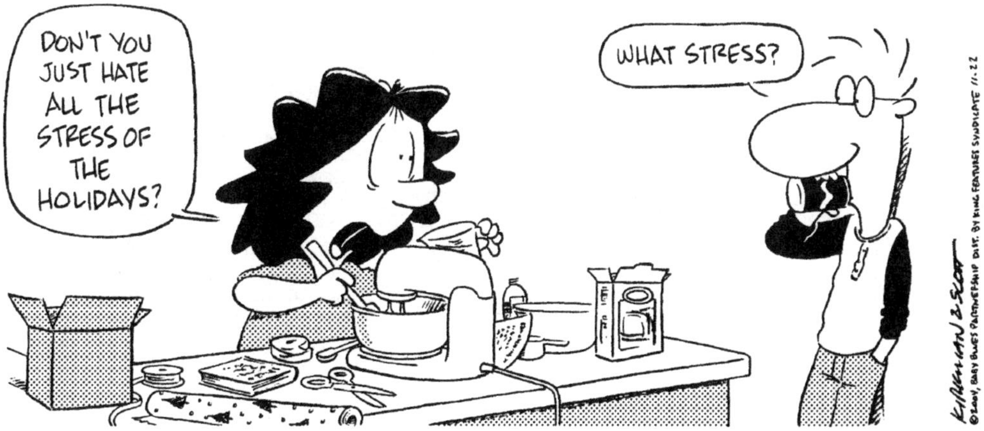
DON'T YOU JUST HATE ALL THE STRESS OF THE HOLIDAYS?
WHAT STRESS?
KIRKMAN & SCOTT
© 2001, BABY BLUES PARTNERSHIP DIST. BY KING FEATURES SYNDICATE 11-22

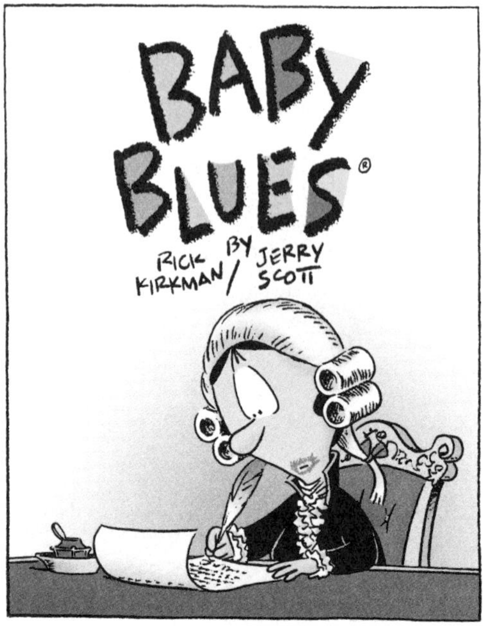
BABY BLUES®
BY RICK KIRKMAN / JERRY SCOTT

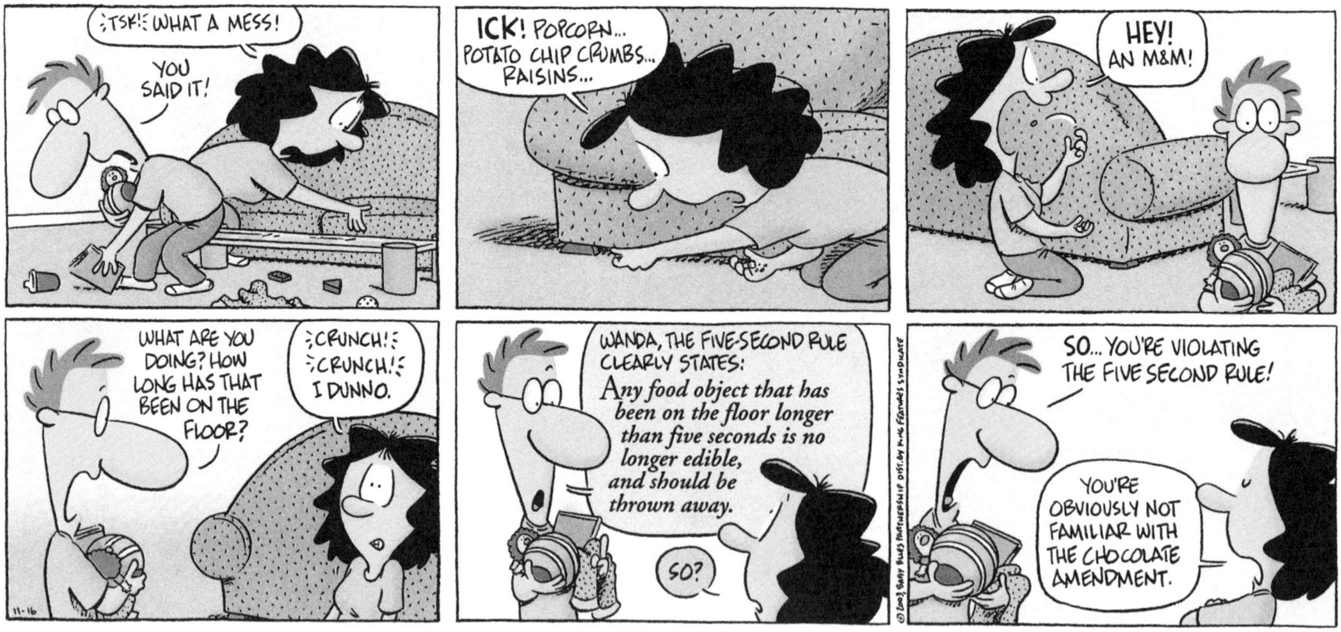
TSK! WHAT A MESS!
YOU SAID IT!
ICK! POPCORN... POTATO CHIP CRUMBS... RAISINS...
HEY! AN M&M!
WHAT ARE YOU DOING? HOW LONG HAS THAT BEEN ON THE FLOOR?
CRUNCH! CRUNCH! I DUNNO.
WANDA, THE FIVE-SECOND RULE CLEARLY STATES: Any food object that has been on the floor longer than five seconds is no longer edible, and should be thrown away.
SO?
SO... YOU'RE VIOLATING THE FIVE SECOND RULE!
YOU'RE OBVIOUSLY NOT FAMILIAR WITH THE CHOCOLATE AMENDMENT.
11-16
©2003 BABY BLUES PARTNERSHIP DIST. BY KING FEATURES SYNDICATE

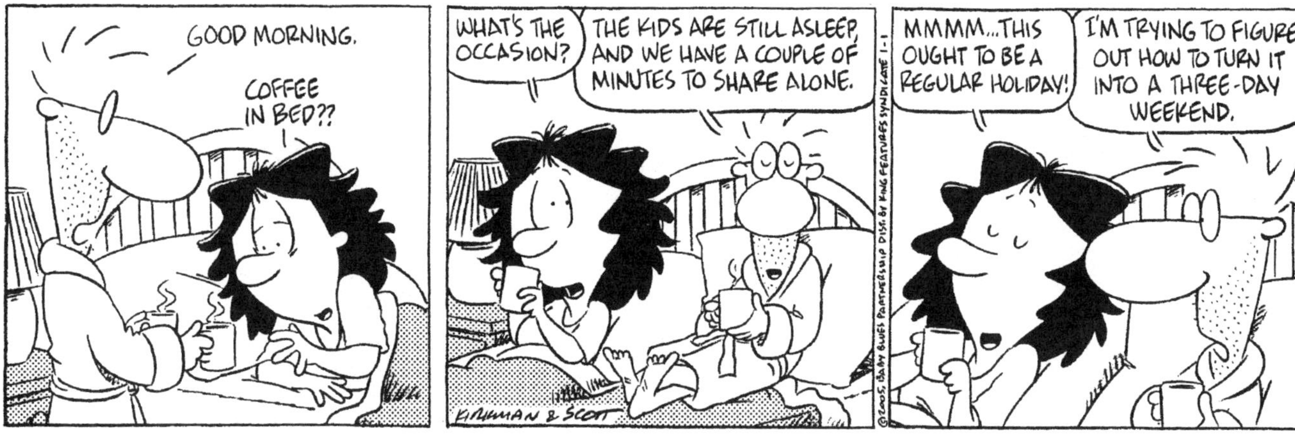
GOOD MORNING.
COFFEE IN BED??
WHAT'S THE OCCASION?
THE KIDS ARE STILL ASLEEP, AND WE HAVE A COUPLE OF MINUTES TO SHARE ALONE.
MMMM...THIS OUGHT TO BE A REGULAR HOLIDAY!
I'M TRYING TO FIGURE OUT HOW TO TURN IT INTO A THREE-DAY WEEKEND.

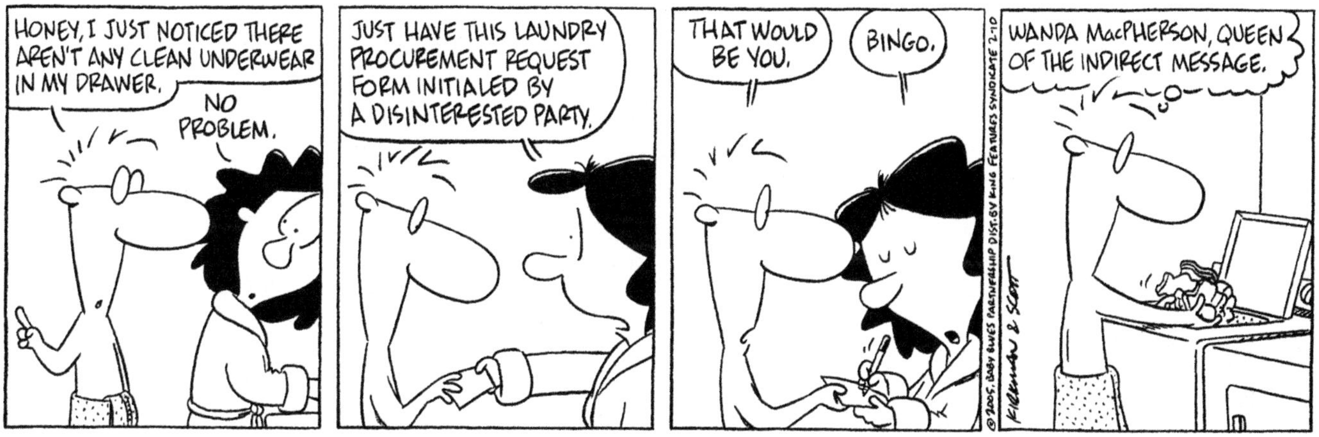
HONEY, I JUST NOTICED THERE AREN'T ANY CLEAN UNDERWEAR IN MY DRAWER.
NO PROBLEM.
JUST HAVE THIS LAUNDRY PROCUREMENT REQUEST FORM INITIALED BY A DISINTERESTED PARTY.
THAT WOULD BE YOU.
BINGO.
WANDA MacPHERSON, QUEEN OF THE INDIRECT MESSAGE.

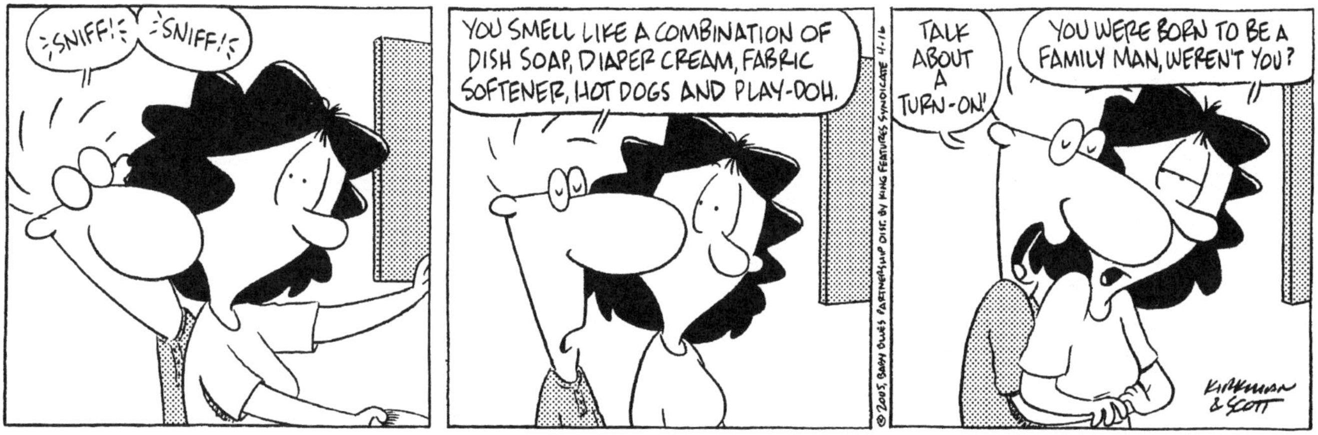
SNIFF!
SNIFF!
YOU SMELL LIKE A COMBINATION OF DISH SOAP, DIAPER CREAM, FABRIC SOFTENER, HOT DOGS AND PLAY-DOH.
TALK ABOUT A TURN-ON!
YOU WERE BORN TO BE A FAMILY MAN, WEREN'T YOU?

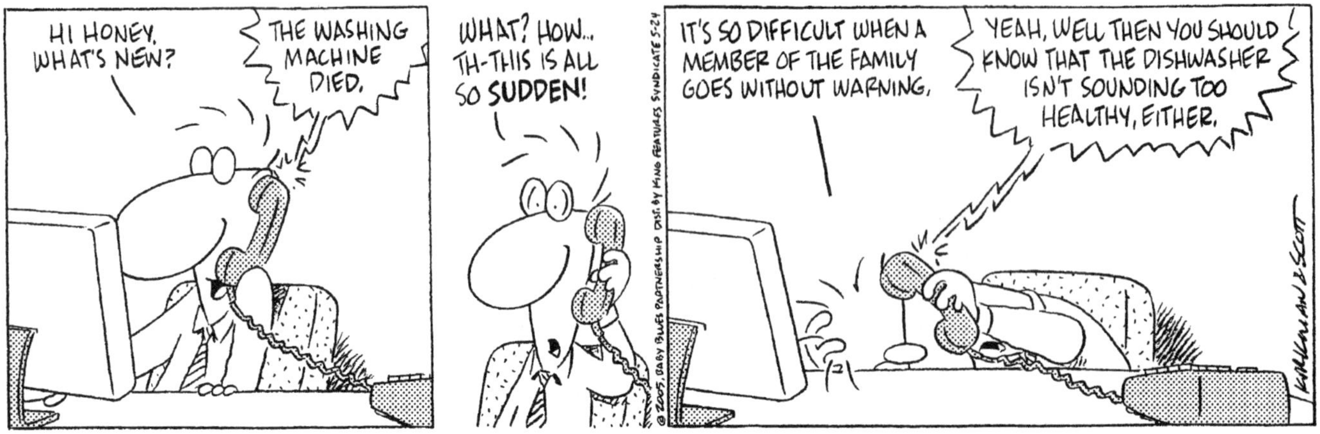
HI HONEY. WHAT'S NEW?
THE WASHING MACHINE DIED.
WHAT? HOW... TH-THIS IS ALL SO SUDDEN!
© 2005, BABY BLUES PARTNERSHIP DIST. BY KING FEATURES SYNDICATE 5-24
IT'S SO DIFFICULT WHEN A MEMBER OF THE FAMILY GOES WITHOUT WARNING.
YEAH, WELL THEN YOU SHOULD KNOW THAT THE DISHWASHER ISN'T SOUNDING TOO HEALTHY, EITHER.
KIRKMAN & SCOTT

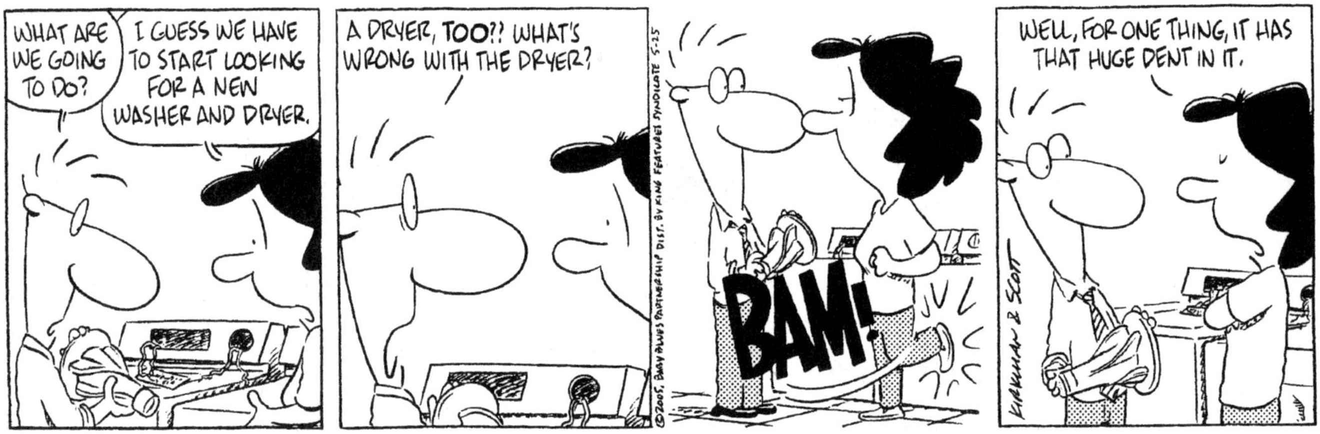
WHAT ARE WE GOING TO DO?
I GUESS WE HAVE TO START LOOKING FOR A NEW WASHER AND DRYER.
A DRYER, TOO?? WHAT'S WRONG WITH THE DRYER?
© 2005, BABY BLUES PARTNERSHIP DIST. BY KING FEATURES SYNDICATE 5-25
BAM!
KIRKMAN & SCOTT
WELL, FOR ONE THING, IT HAS THAT HUGE DENT IN IT.

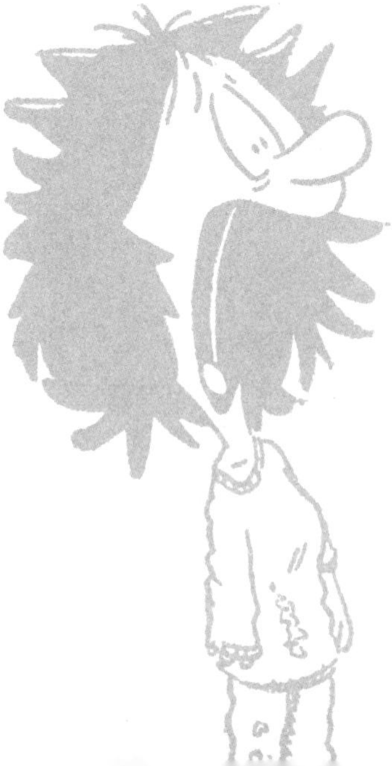

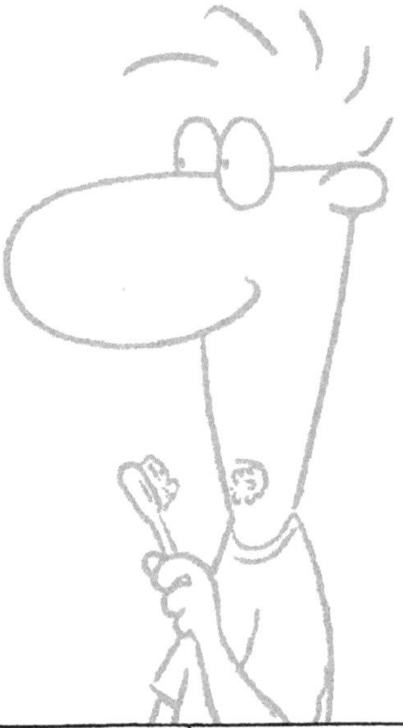

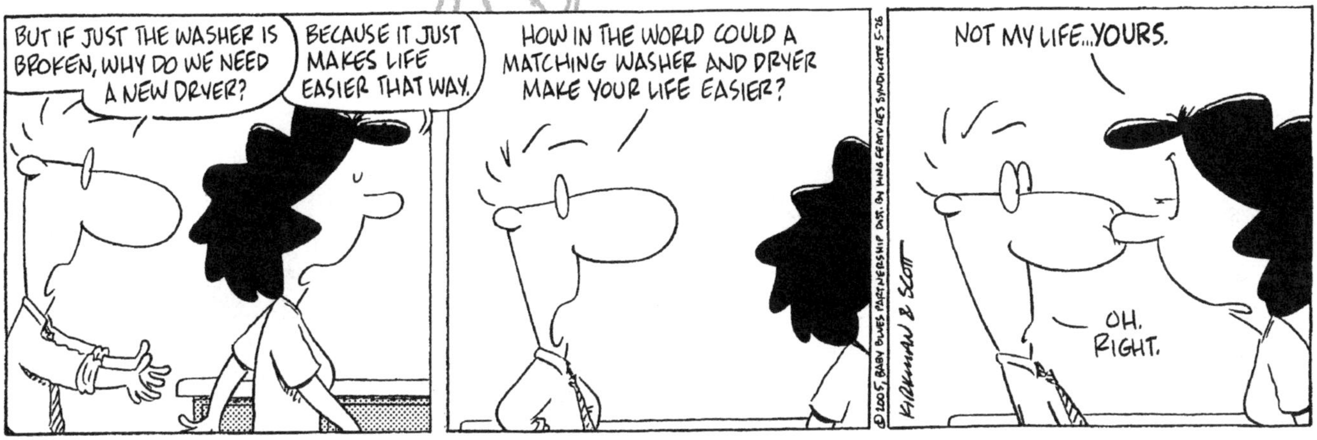

BUT IF JUST THE WASHER IS BROKEN, WHY DO WE NEED A NEW DRYER?
BECAUSE IT JUST MAKES LIFE EASIER THAT WAY.
HOW IN THE WORLD COULD A MATCHING WASHER AND DRYER MAKE YOUR LIFE EASIER?
© 2005, BABY BLUES PARTNERSHIP DIST. BY KING FEATURES SYNDICATE 5-26
KIRKMAN & SCOTT
NOT MY LIFE...YOURS.
OH. RIGHT.

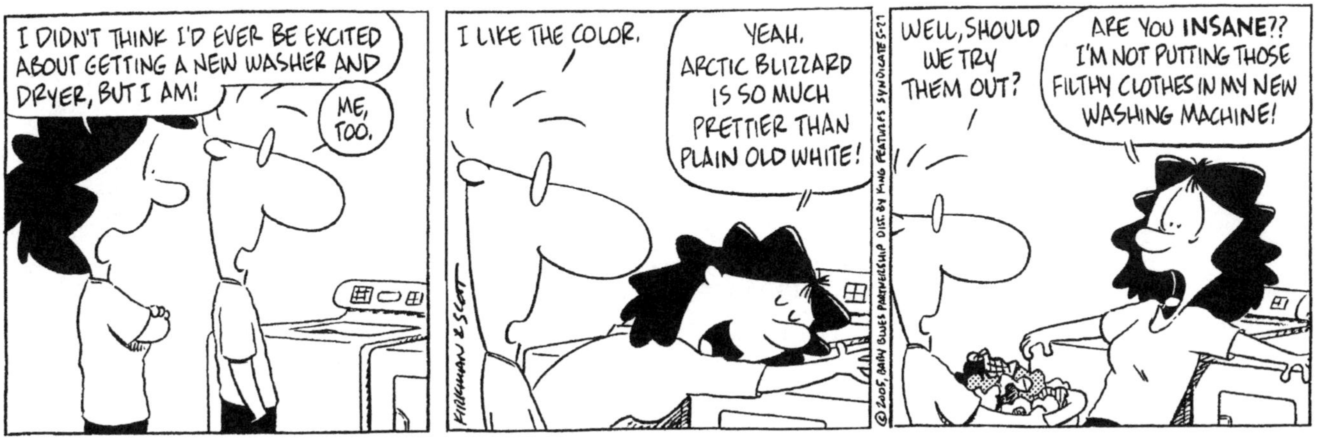

I DIDN'T THINK I'D EVER BE EXCITED ABOUT GETTING A NEW WASHER AND DRYER, BUT I AM!
ME, TOO.
KIRKMAN & SCOTT
I LIKE THE COLOR.
YEAH. ARCTIC BLIZZARD IS SO MUCH PRETTIER THAN PLAIN OLD WHITE!
© 2005, BABY BLUES PARTNERSHIP DIST. BY KING FEATURES SYNDICATE 5-27
WELL, SHOULD WE TRY THEM OUT?
ARE YOU INSANE?? I'M NOT PUTTING THOSE FILTHY CLOTHES IN MY NEW WASHING MACHINE!

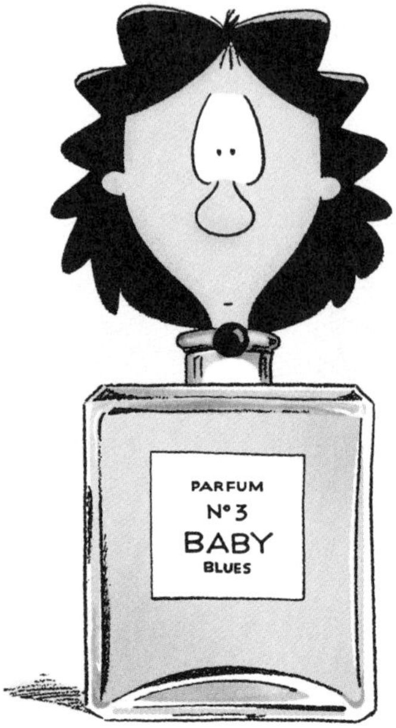
PARFUM
Nº 3
BABY
BLUES

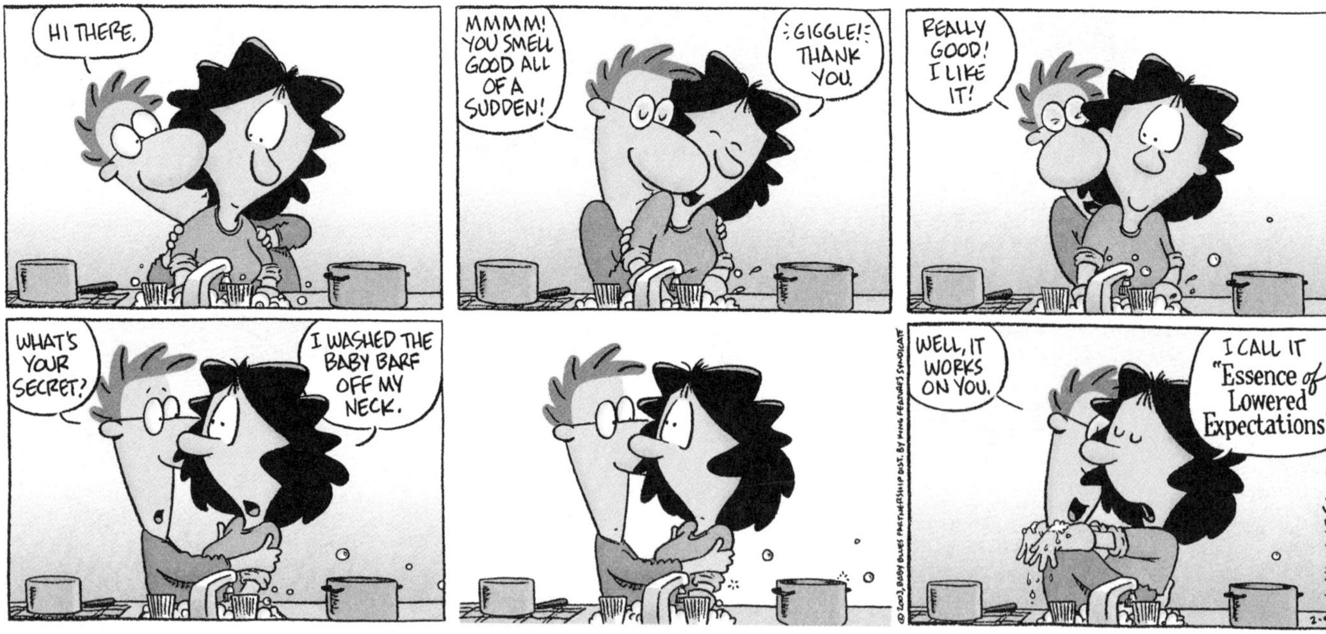
HI THERE.
MMMMM! YOU SMELL GOOD ALL OF A SUDDEN!
GIGGLE! THANK YOU.
REALLY GOOD! I LIKE IT!
WHAT'S YOUR SECRET?
I WASHED THE BABY BARF OFF MY NECK.
WELL, IT WORKS ON YOU.
I CALL IT "Essence of Lowered Expectations"
© 2003, BABY BLUES PARTNERSHIP DIST. BY KING FEATURES SYNDICATE
KIRKMAN & SCOTT
2-9

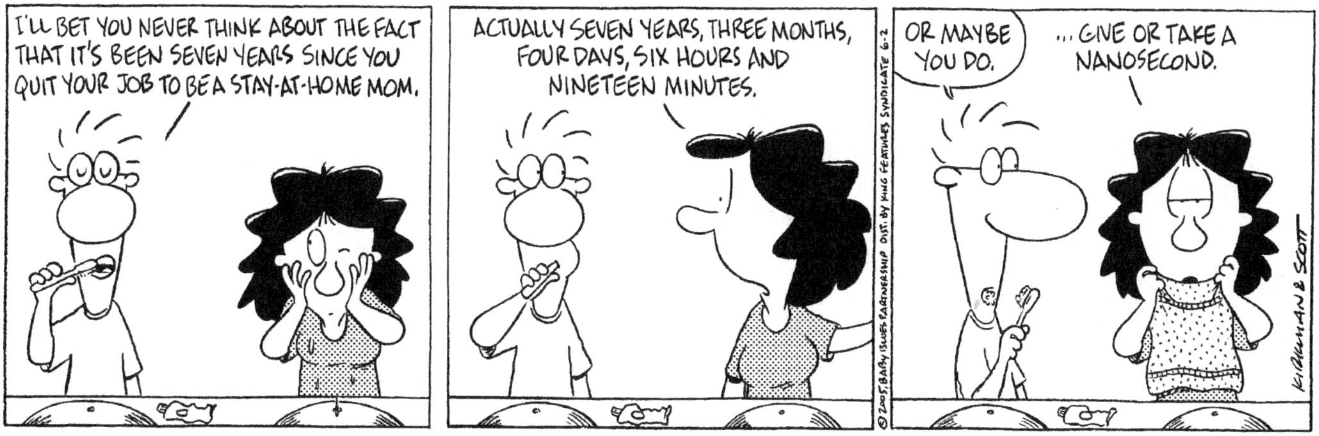
I'LL BET YOU NEVER THINK ABOUT THE FACT THAT IT'S BEEN SEVEN YEARS SINCE YOU QUIT YOUR JOB TO BE A STAY-AT-HOME MOM.
ACTUALLY SEVEN YEARS, THREE MONTHS, FOUR DAYS, SIX HOURS AND NINETEEN MINUTES.
© 2005, BABY BLUES PARTNERSHIP DIST. BY KING FEATURES SYNDICATE 6-2
OR MAYBE YOU DO.
...GIVE OR TAKE A NANOSECOND.
KIRKMAN & SCOTT

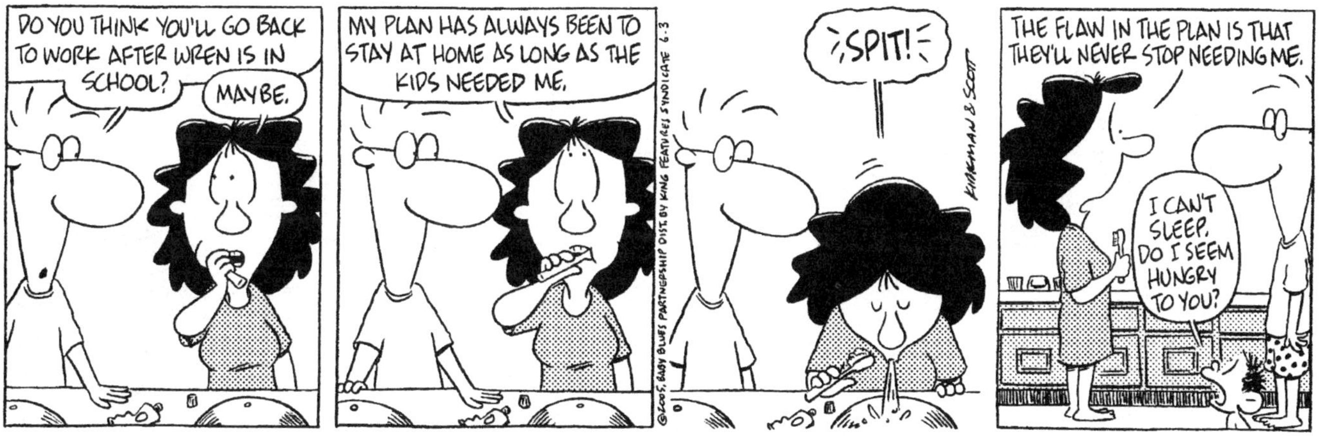
DO YOU THINK YOU'LL GO BACK TO WORK AFTER WREN IS IN SCHOOL?
MAYBE.
MY PLAN HAS ALWAYS BEEN TO STAY AT HOME AS LONG AS THE KIDS NEEDED ME.
© 2005, BABY BLUES PARTNERSHIP DIST. BY KING FEATURES SYNDICATE 6-3
SPIT!
KIRKMAN & SCOTT
THE FLAW IN THE PLAN IS THAT THEY'LL NEVER STOP NEEDING ME.
I CAN'T SLEEP. DO I SEEM HUNGRY TO YOU?

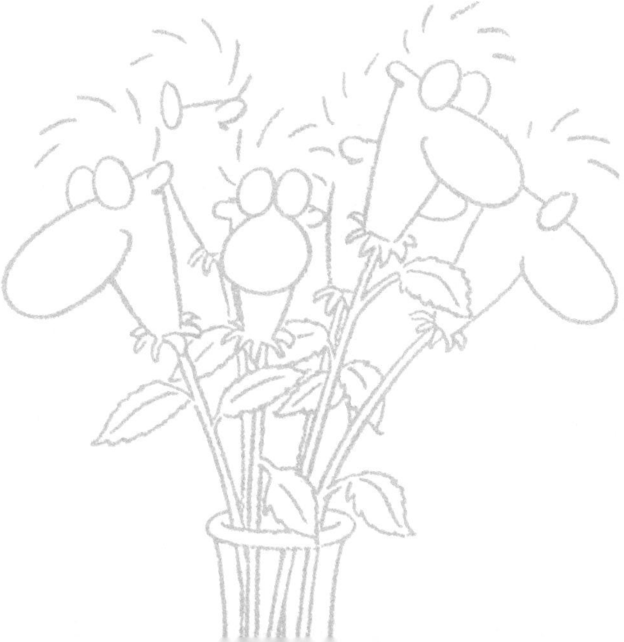

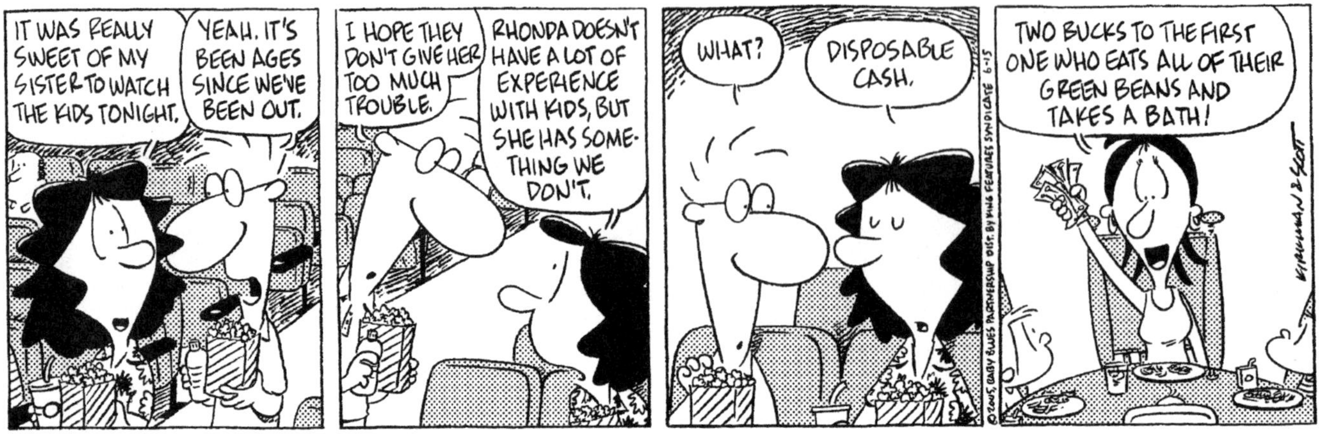
IT WAS REALLY SWEET OF MY SISTER TO WATCH THE KIDS TONIGHT.
YEAH. IT'S BEEN AGES SINCE WE'VE BEEN OUT.
I HOPE THEY DON'T GIVE HER TOO MUCH TROUBLE.
RHONDA DOESN'T HAVE A LOT OF EXPERIENCE WITH KIDS, BUT SHE HAS SOMETHING WE DON'T.
WHAT?
DISPOSABLE CASH.
©2005 BABY BLUES PARTNERSHIP DIST. BY KING FEATURES SYNDICATE 6-15
TWO BUCKS TO THE FIRST ONE WHO EATS ALL OF THEIR GREEN BEANS AND TAKES A BATH!
KIRKMAN & SCOTT

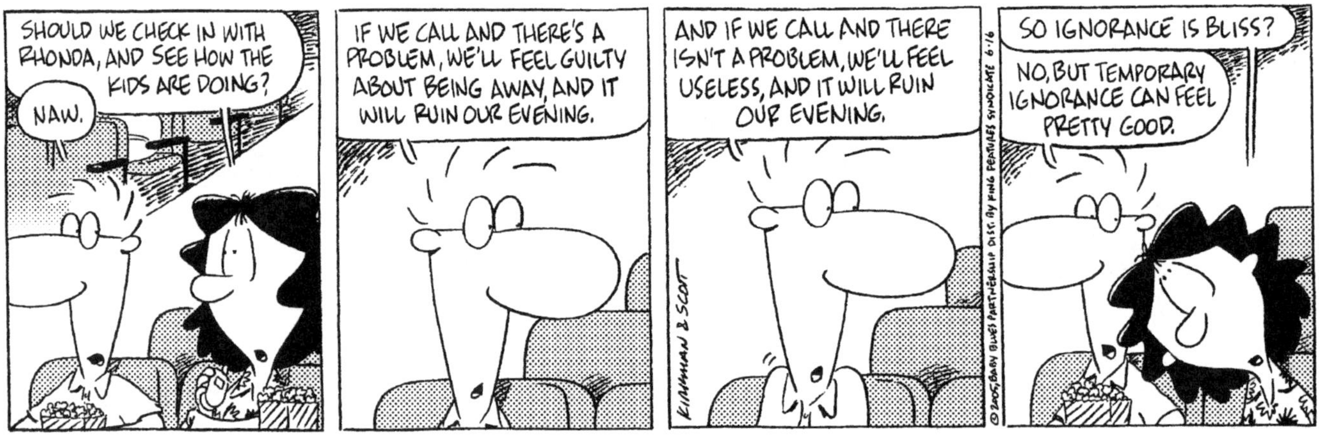
SHOULD WE CHECK IN WITH RHONDA, AND SEE HOW THE KIDS ARE DOING?
NAW.
IF WE CALL AND THERE'S A PROBLEM, WE'LL FEEL GUILTY ABOUT BEING AWAY, AND IT WILL RUIN OUR EVENING.
KIRKMAN & SCOTT
AND IF WE CALL AND THERE ISN'T A PROBLEM, WE'LL FEEL USELESS, AND IT WILL RUIN OUR EVENING.
©2005 BABY BLUES PARTNERSHIP DIST. BY KING FEATURES SYNDICATE 6-16
SO IGNORANCE IS BLISS?
NO, BUT TEMPORARY IGNORANCE CAN FEEL PRETTY GOOD.

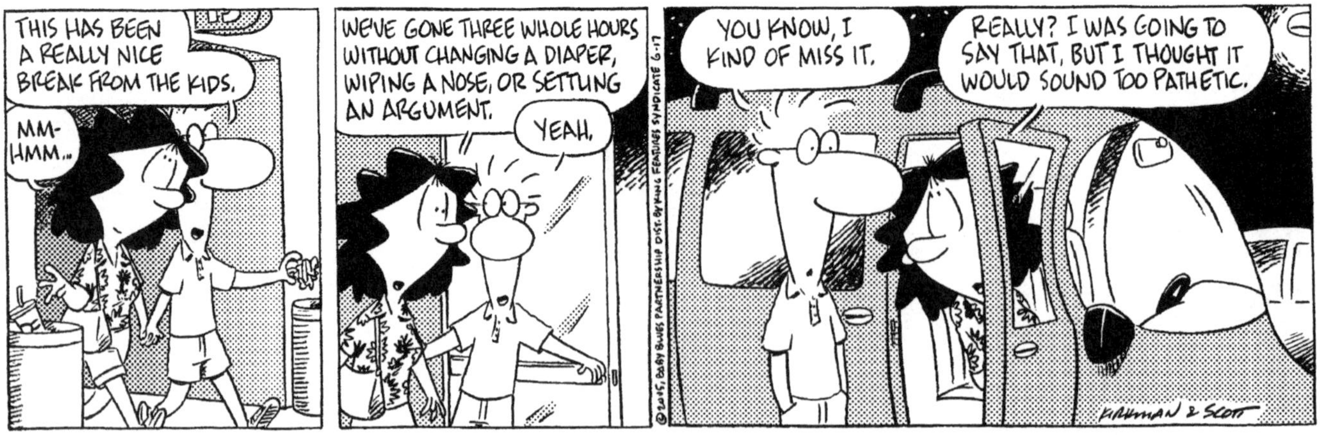
THIS HAS BEEN A REALLY NICE BREAK FROM THE KIDS.
MM-HMM..
WE'VE GONE THREE WHOLE HOURS WITHOUT CHANGING A DIAPER, WIPING A NOSE, OR SETTLING AN ARGUMENT.
YEAH.
©2005 BABY BLUES PARTNERSHIP DIST. BY KING FEATURES SYNDICATE 6-17
YOU KNOW, I KIND OF MISS IT.
REALLY? I WAS GOING TO SAY THAT, BUT I THOUGHT IT WOULD SOUND TOO PATHETIC.
KIRKMAN & SCOTT

BABY BLUES®
RICK KIRKMAN / BY JERRY SCOTT

HEY! LOOK AT THIS!
WHAT?
I THINK I MAY HAVE LOST A COUPLE OF POUNDS!
HOW??
I DON'T KNOW...
...BUT LOOK HOW LOOSE THIS WAIST-BAND IS!
THIS IS INCREDIBLE! I MEAN, I HAVEN'T EVEN BEEN TRYING!!
BUT HEY, DON'T BE TOO JEALOUS, SWEETIE. I PROBABLY JUST HAVE A HIGHER METABOLISM RATE THAN YOU DO.
WELL, I THINK I'LL GO HAVE A BIG BOWL OF ICE CREAM BEFORE I WASTE AWAY COMPLETELY!
ARE YOU GOING TO TELL DADDY THAT HE'S WEARING YOUR MATERNITY JEANS, OR SHOULD I?
OH, I WILL...
...EVENTUALLY.

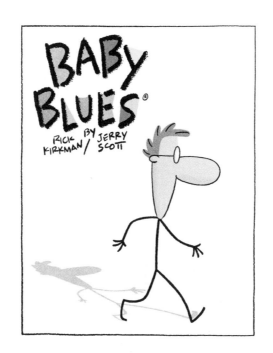

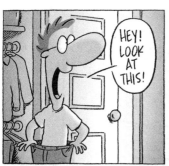

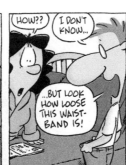

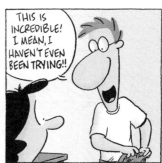

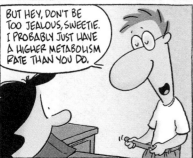

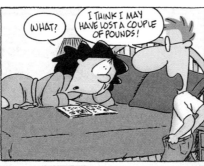

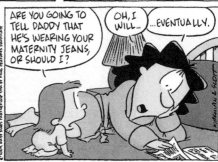

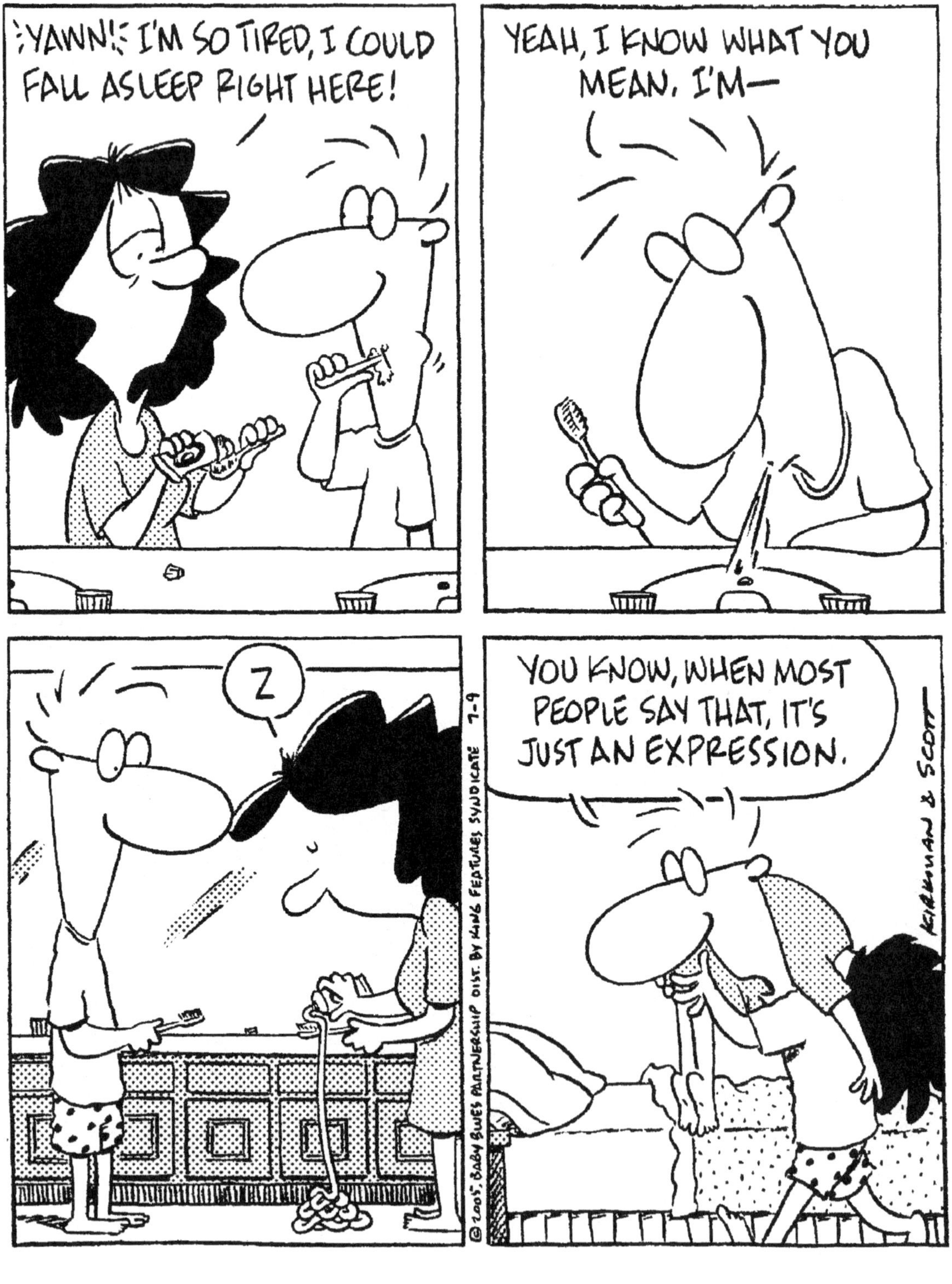

YAWN! I'M SO TIRED, I COULD FALL ASLEEP RIGHT HERE!
YEAH, I KNOW WHAT YOU MEAN. I'M—
Z
YOU KNOW, WHEN MOST PEOPLE SAY THAT, IT'S JUST AN EXPRESSION.
7-9
©2005, BABY BLUES PARTNERSHIP DIST. BY KING FEATURES SYNDICATE
KIRKMAN & SCOTT

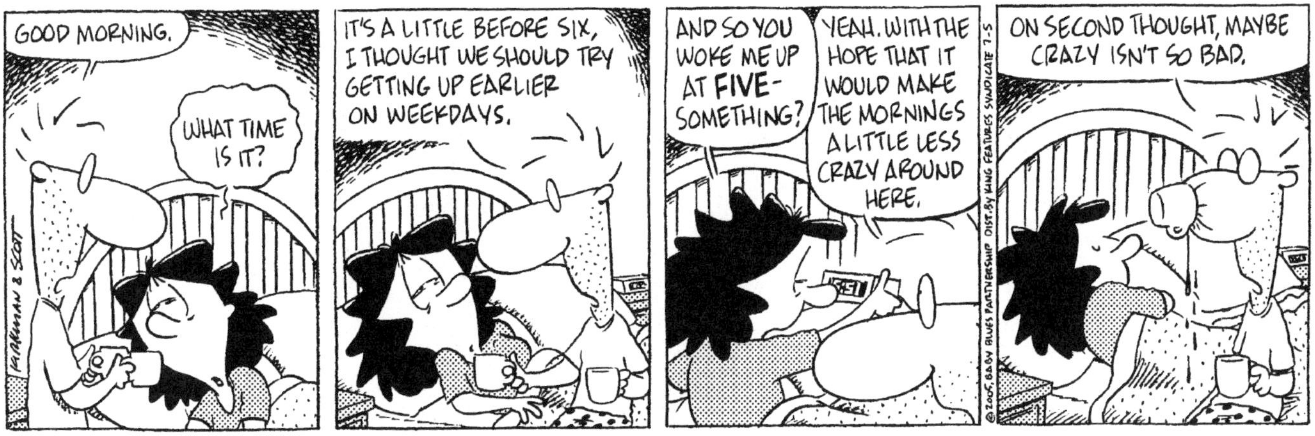
GOOD MORNING.
WHAT TIME IS IT?
IT'S A LITTLE BEFORE SIX, I THOUGHT WE SHOULD TRY GETTING UP EARLIER ON WEEKDAYS.
AND SO YOU WOKE ME UP AT FIVE-SOMETHING?
YEAH. WITH THE HOPE THAT IT WOULD MAKE THE MORNINGS A LITTLE LESS CRAZY AROUND HERE.
ON SECOND THOUGHT, MAYBE CRAZY ISN'T SO BAD.
KIRKMAN & SCOTT

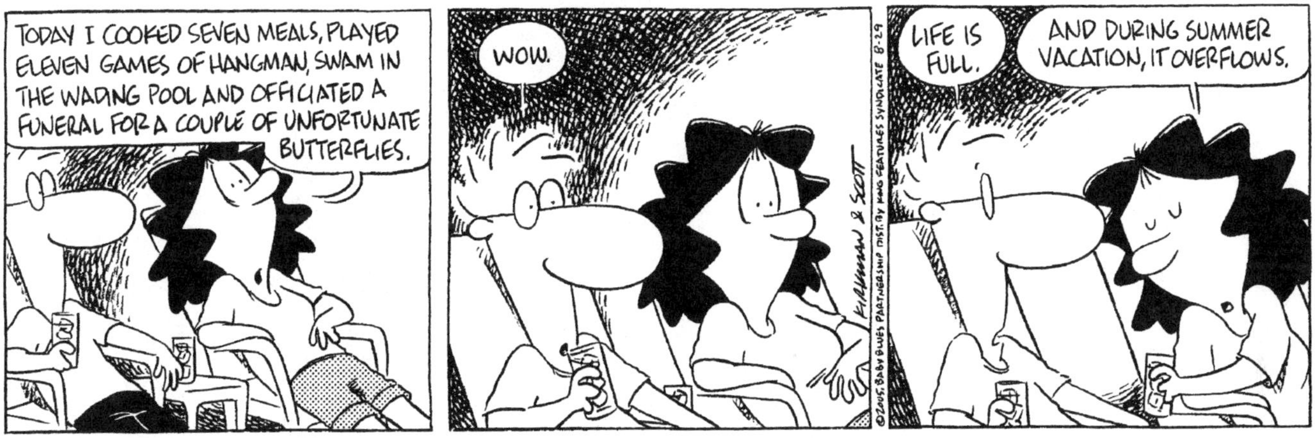
TODAY I COOKED SEVEN MEALS, PLAYED ELEVEN GAMES OF HANGMAN, SWAM IN THE WADING POOL AND OFFICIATED A FUNERAL FOR A COUPLE OF UNFORTUNATE BUTTERFLIES.
WOW.
LIFE IS FULL.
AND DURING SUMMER VACATION, IT OVERFLOWS.
KIRKMAN & SCOTT

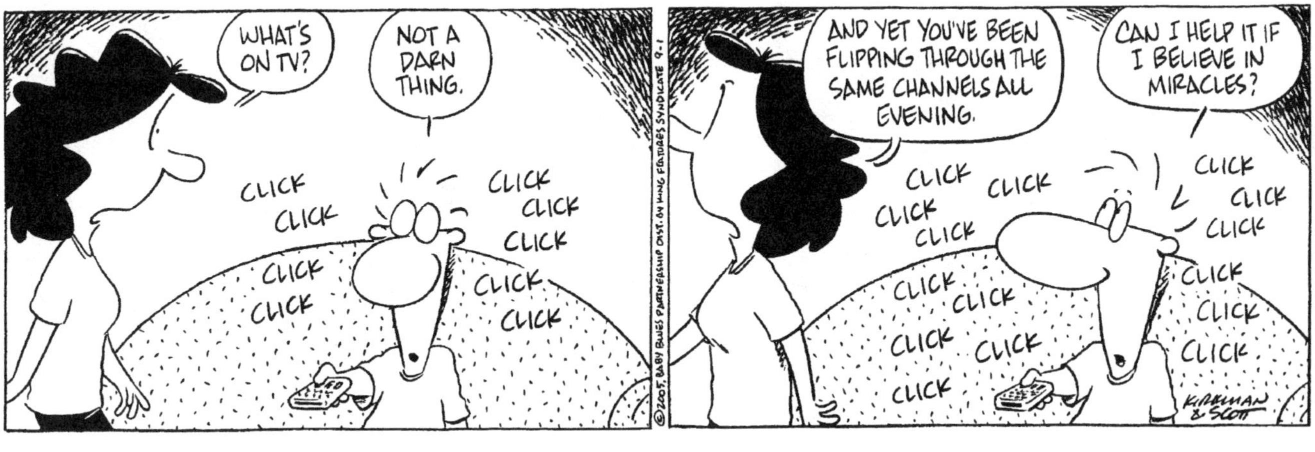
WHAT'S ON TV?
NOT A DARN THING.
CLICK CLICK CLICK CLICK CLICK CLICK CLICK CLICK CLICK
AND YET YOU'VE BEEN FLIPPING THROUGH THE SAME CHANNELS ALL EVENING.
CAN I HELP IT IF I BELIEVE IN MIRACLES?
CLICK CLICK CLICK CLICK CLICK CLICK CLICK CLICK CLICK CLICK CLICK CLICK CLICK
KIRKMAN & SCOTT

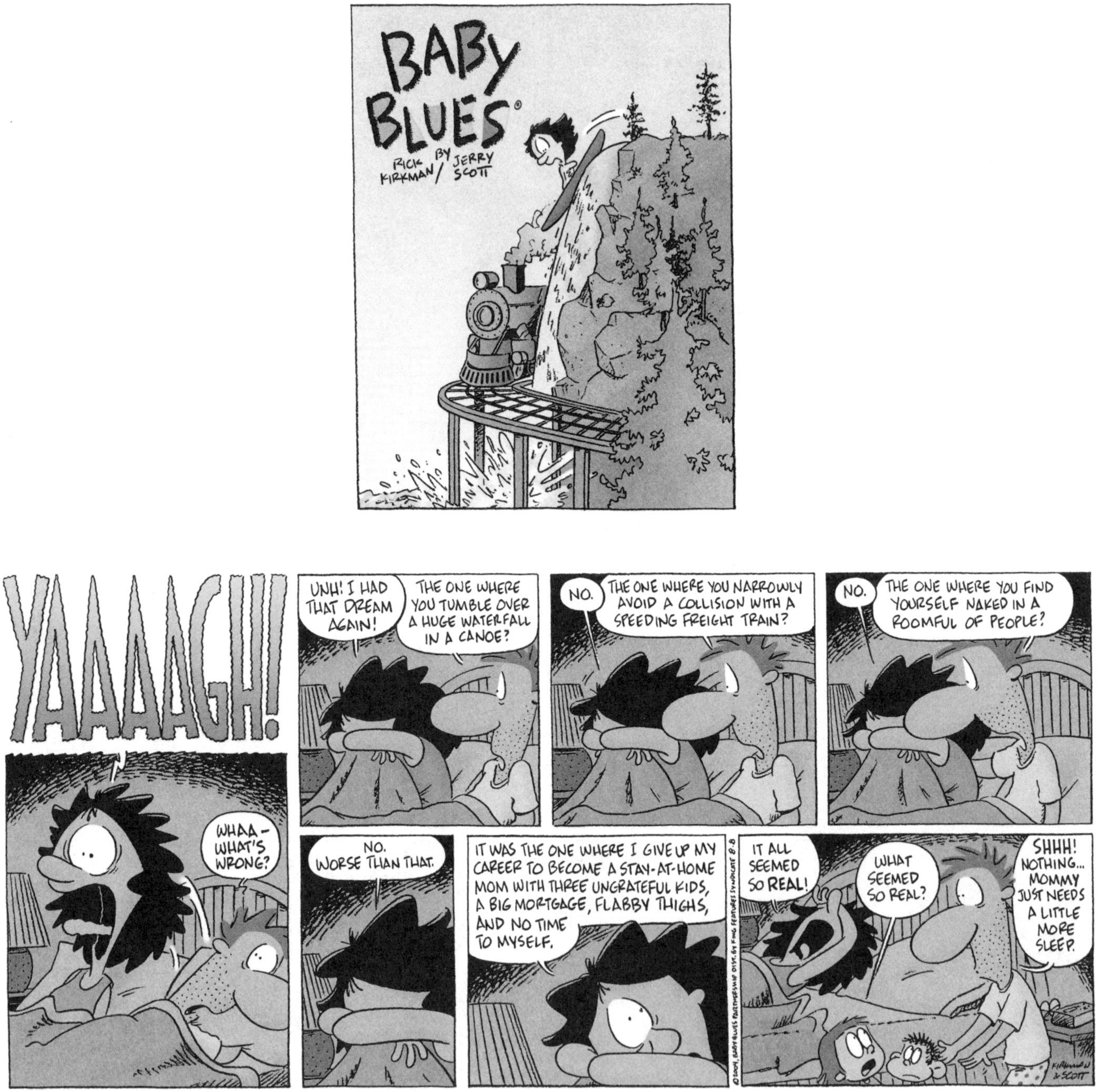

BABY BLUES®
BY RICK KIRKMAN / JERRY SCOTT
YAAAAGH!
WHAA-WHAT'S WRONG?
UNH! I HAD THAT DREAM AGAIN!
THE ONE WHERE YOU TUMBLE OVER A HUGE WATERFALL IN A CANOE?
NO.
THE ONE WHERE YOU NARROWLY AVOID A COLLISION WITH A SPEEDING FREIGHT TRAIN?
NO.
THE ONE WHERE YOU FIND YOURSELF NAKED IN A ROOMFUL OF PEOPLE?
NO. WORSE THAN THAT.
IT WAS THE ONE WHERE I GIVE UP MY CAREER TO BECOME A STAY-AT-HOME MOM WITH THREE UNGRATEFUL KIDS, A BIG MORTGAGE, FLABBY THIGHS, AND NO TIME TO MYSELF.
©2004, BABY BLUES PARTNERSHIP DIST. BY KING FEATURES SYNDICATE 8-8
IT ALL SEEMED SO REAL!
WHAT SEEMED SO REAL?
SHHH! NOTHING... MOMMY JUST NEEDS A LITTLE MORE SLEEP.
KIRKMAN & SCOTT

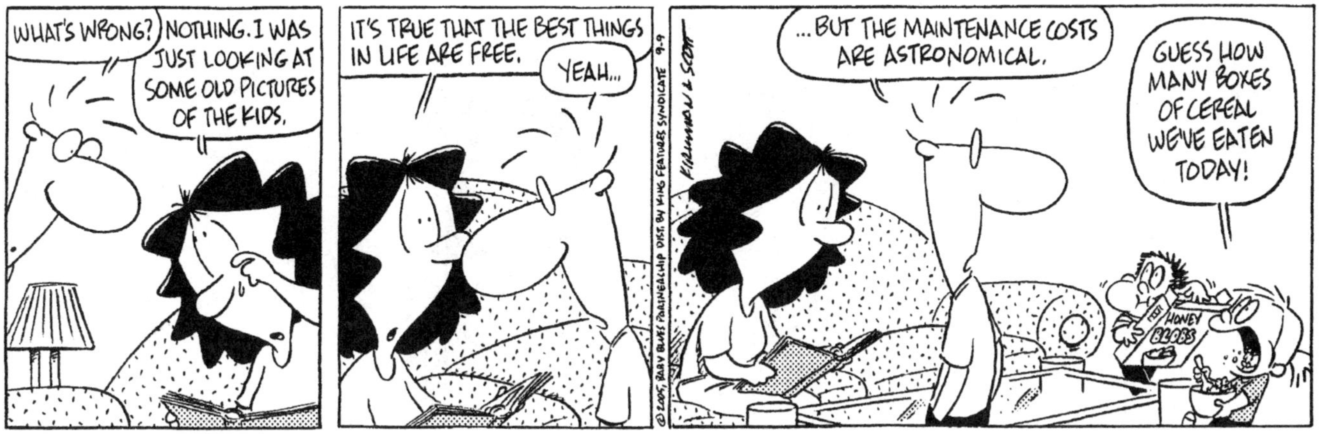
WHAT'S WRONG?
NOTHING. I WAS JUST LOOKING AT SOME OLD PICTURES OF THE KIDS.
IT'S TRUE THAT THE BEST THINGS IN LIFE ARE FREE.
YEAH...
KIRKMAN & SCOTT
© 2005, BABY BLUES PARTNERSHIP DIST. BY KING FEATURES SYNDICATE 9-9
...BUT THE MAINTENANCE COSTS ARE ASTRONOMICAL.
GUESS HOW MANY BOXES OF CEREAL WE'VE EATEN TODAY!
HONEY BLOBS

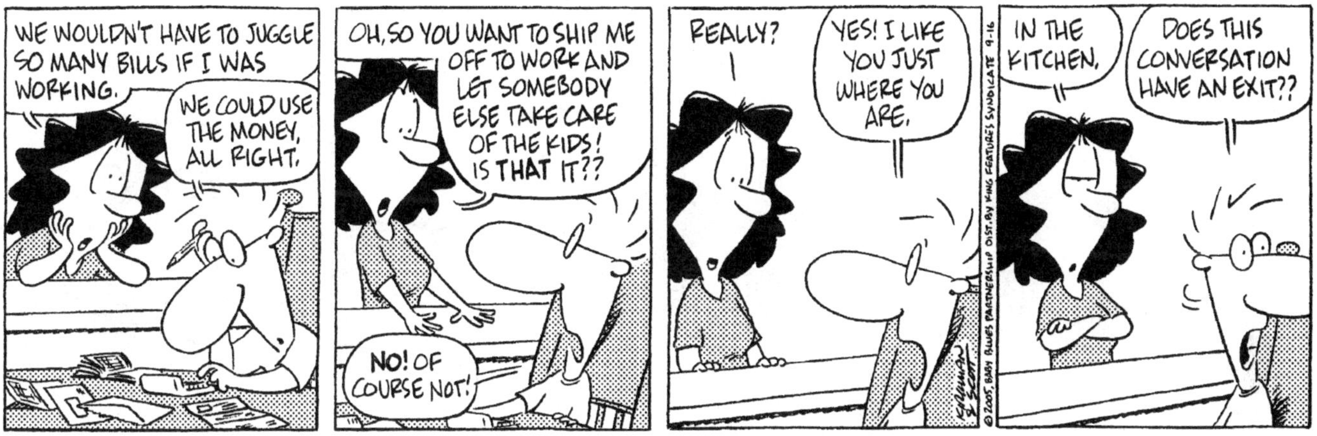
WE WOULDN'T HAVE TO JUGGLE SO MANY BILLS IF I WAS WORKING.
WE COULD USE THE MONEY, ALL RIGHT.
OH, SO YOU WANT TO SHIP ME OFF TO WORK AND LET SOMEBODY ELSE TAKE CARE OF THE KIDS! IS **THAT** IT??
NO! OF COURSE NOT!
REALLY?
YES! I LIKE YOU JUST WHERE YOU ARE.
KIRKMAN & SCOTT
© 2005, BABY BLUES PARTNERSHIP DIST. BY KING FEATURES SYNDICATE 9-16
IN THE KITCHEN.
DOES THIS CONVERSATION HAVE AN EXIT??

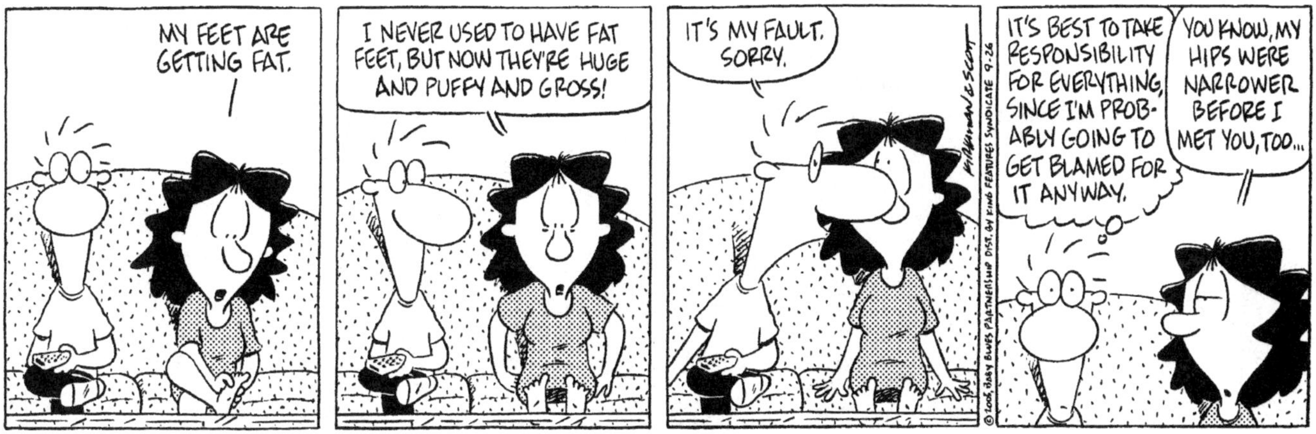
MY FEET ARE GETTING FAT.
I NEVER USED TO HAVE FAT FEET, BUT NOW THEY'RE HUGE AND PUFFY AND GROSS!
IT'S MY FAULT. SORRY.
KIRKMAN & SCOTT
© 2005 BABY BLUES PARTNERSHIP DIST. BY KING FEATURES SYNDICATE 9-26
IT'S BEST TO TAKE RESPONSIBILITY FOR EVERYTHING, SINCE I'M PROBABLY GOING TO GET BLAMED FOR IT ANYWAY.
YOU KNOW, MY HIPS WERE NARROWER BEFORE I MET YOU, TOO...

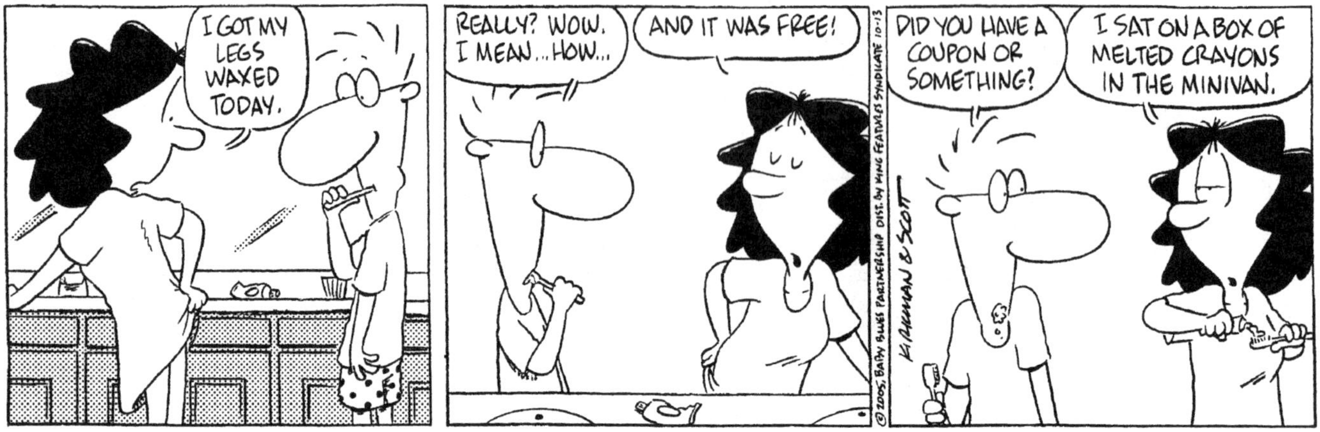
I GOT MY LEGS WAXED TODAY.
REALLY? WOW. I MEAN...HOW...
AND IT WAS FREE!
©2005, BABY BLUES PARTNERSHIP DIST. BY KING FEATURES SYNDICATE 10-13
KIRKMAN & SCOTT
DID YOU HAVE A COUPON OR SOMETHING?
I SAT ON A BOX OF MELTED CRAYONS IN THE MINIVAN.

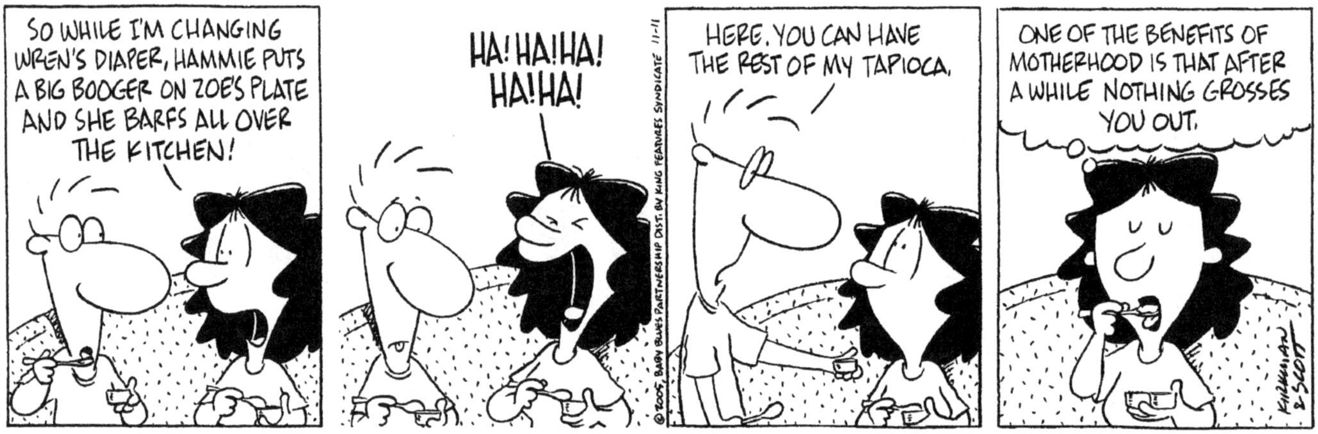
SO WHILE I'M CHANGING WREN'S DIAPER, HAMMIE PUTS A BIG BOOGER ON ZOE'S PLATE AND SHE BARFS ALL OVER THE KITCHEN!
HA! HA! HA! HA! HA!
©2005, BABY BLUES PARTNERSHIP DIST. BY KING FEATURES SYNDICATE 11-11
HERE. YOU CAN HAVE THE REST OF MY TAPIOCA.
ONE OF THE BENEFITS OF MOTHERHOOD IS THAT AFTER A WHILE NOTHING GROSSES YOU OUT.
KIRKMAN & SCOTT

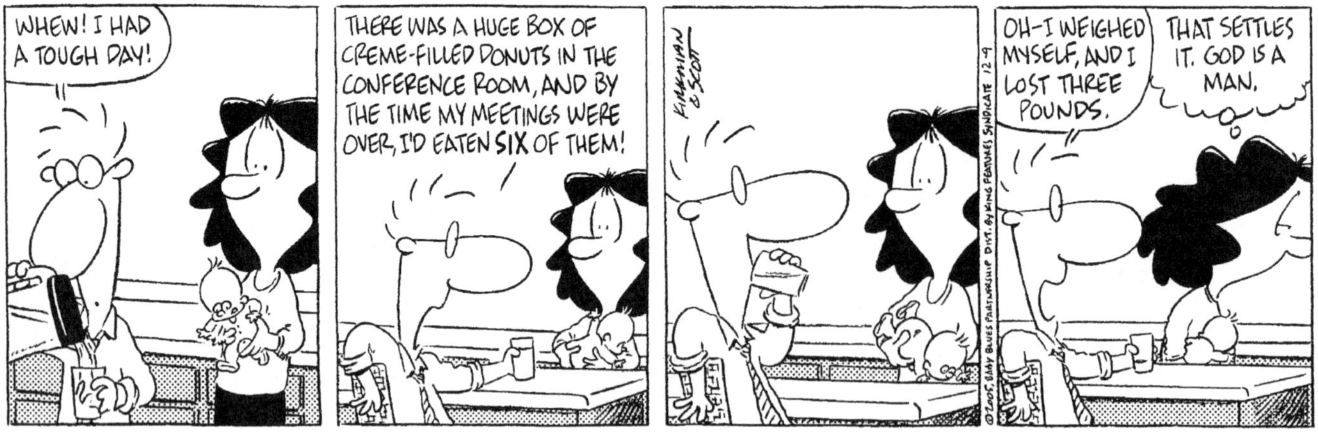
WHEW! I HAD A TOUGH DAY!
THERE WAS A HUGE BOX OF CREME-FILLED DONUTS IN THE CONFERENCE ROOM, AND BY THE TIME MY MEETINGS WERE OVER, I'D EATEN SIX OF THEM!
KIRKMAN & SCOTT
©2005, BABY BLUES PARTNERSHIP DIST. BY KING FEATURES SYNDICATE 12-9
OH-I WEIGHED MYSELF, AND I LOST THREE POUNDS.
THAT SETTLES IT. GOD IS A MAN.

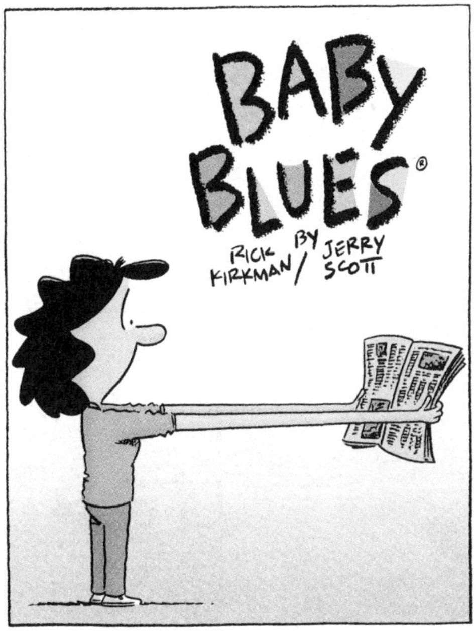
BABY BLUES®
RICK KIRKMAN / BY JERRY SCOTT

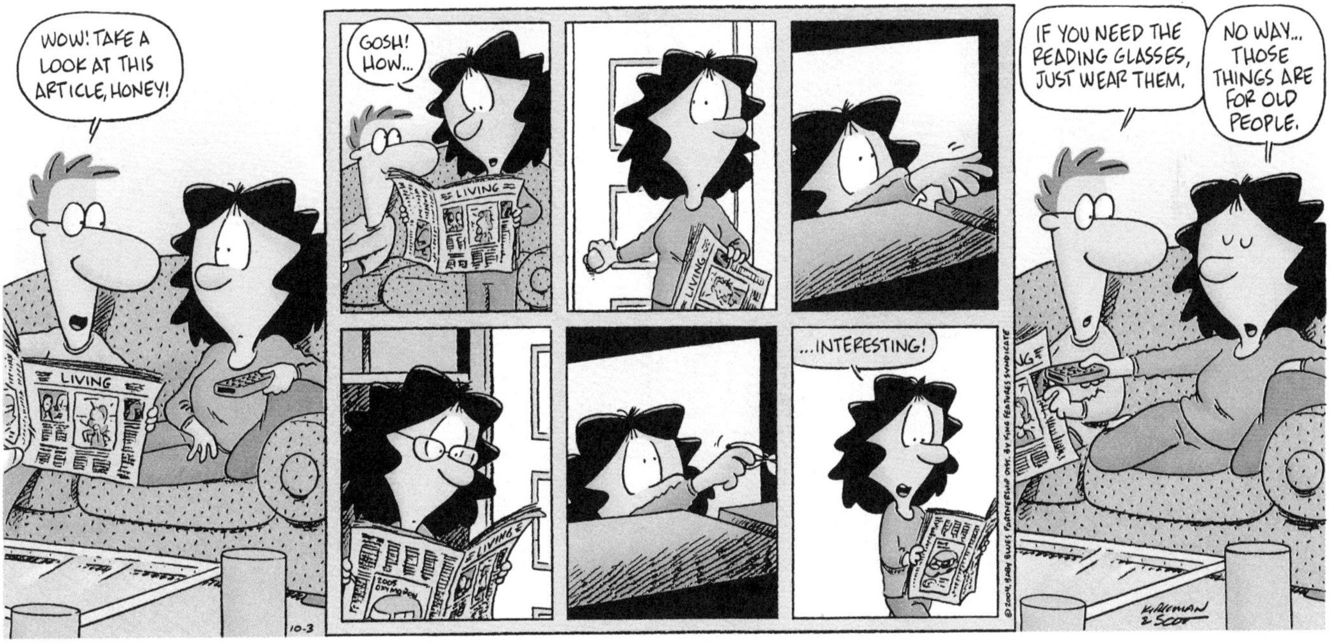
WOW! TAKE A LOOK AT THIS ARTICLE, HONEY!
LIVING
GOSH! HOW...
...INTERESTING!
IF YOU NEED THE READING GLASSES, JUST WEAR THEM.
NO WAY... THOSE THINGS ARE FOR OLD PEOPLE.
10-3
KIRKMAN & SCOTT

I THOUGHT YOU WERE GOING TO WASH THE LASAGNA PAN.
I'M LETTING IT SOAK.

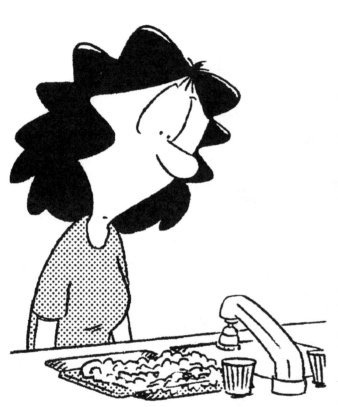

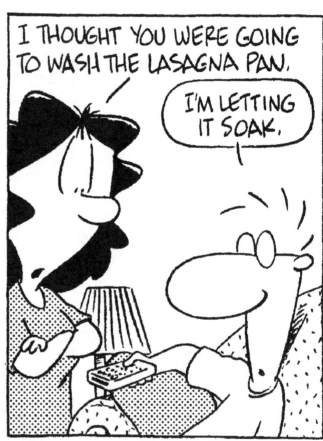

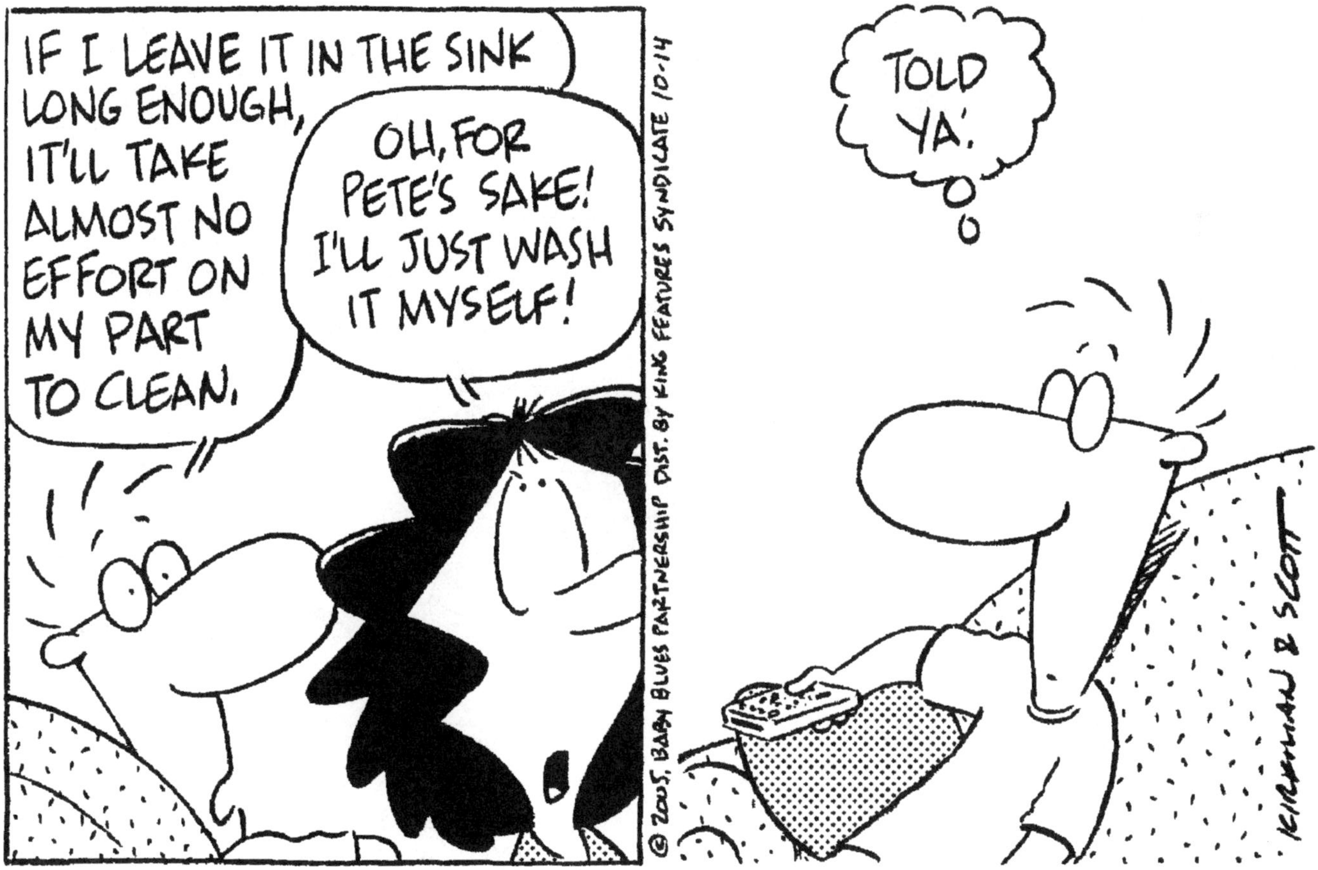
IF I LEAVE IT IN THE SINK LONG ENOUGH, IT'LL TAKE ALMOST NO EFFORT ON MY PART TO CLEAN.
OH, FOR PETE'S SAKE! I'LL JUST WASH IT MYSELF!
© 2005, BABY BLUES PARTNERSHIP DIST. BY KING FEATURES SYNDICATE 10-14
TOLD YA.
KIRKMAN & SCOTT

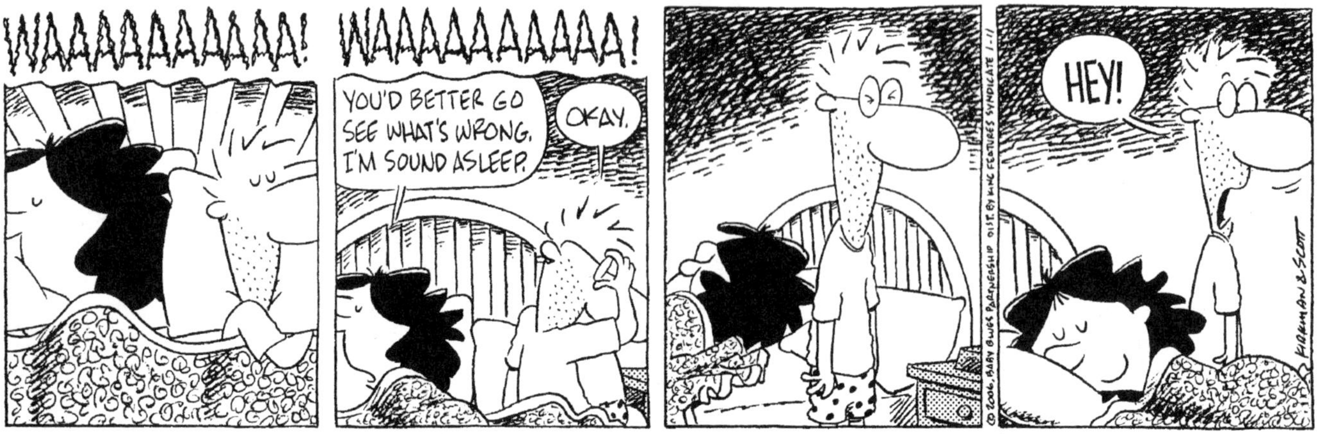
WAAAAAAAAAA!
WAAAAAAAAAA!
YOU'D BETTER GO SEE WHAT'S WRONG. I'M SOUND ASLEEP.
OKAY.
HEY!
KIRKMAN & SCOTT
© 2006, BABY BLUES PARTNERSHIP DIST. BY KING FEATURES SYNDICATE 1-11

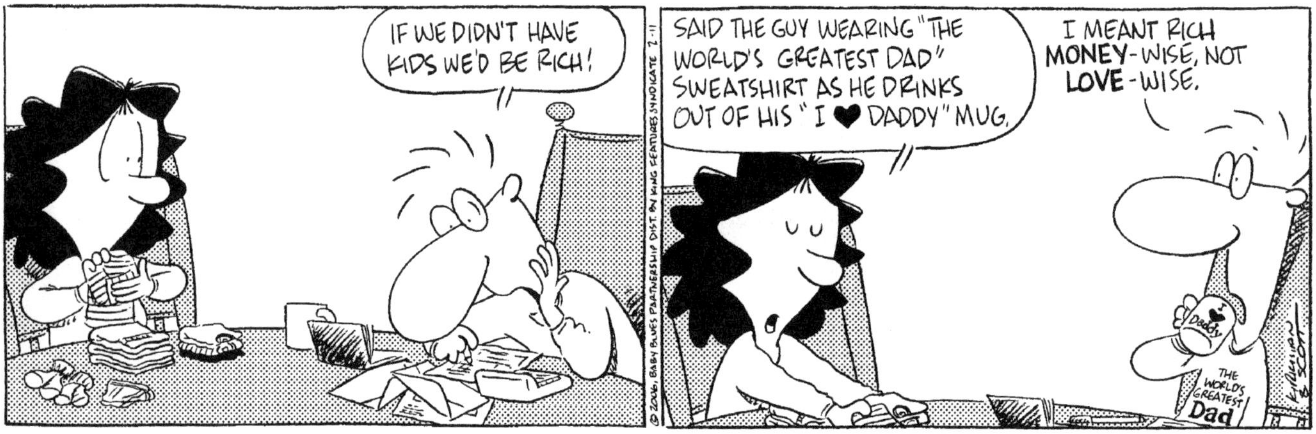
IF WE DIDN'T HAVE KIDS WE'D BE RICH!
SAID THE GUY WEARING "THE WORLD'S GREATEST DAD" SWEATSHIRT AS HE DRINKS OUT OF HIS "I ♥ DADDY" MUG.
I MEANT RICH **MONEY**-WISE, NOT **LOVE**-WISE.
THE WORLD'S GREATEST Dad
© 2006, BABY BLUES PARTNERSHIP DIST. BY KING FEATURES SYNDICATE 2-11

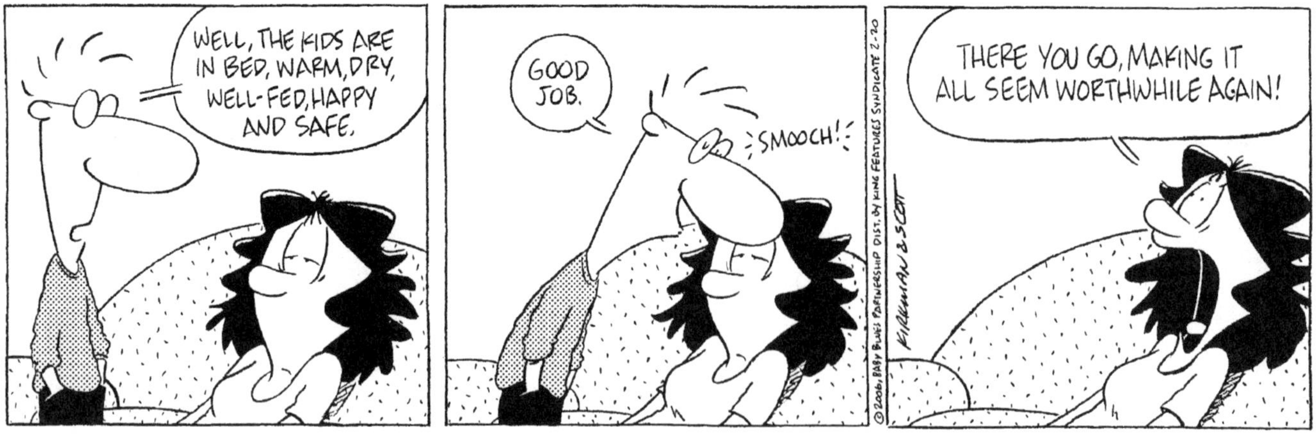
WELL, THE KIDS ARE IN BED, WARM, DRY, WELL-FED, HAPPY AND SAFE.
GOOD JOB.
SMOOCH!
THERE YOU GO, MAKING IT ALL SEEM WORTHWHILE AGAIN!
KIRKMAN & SCOTT
© 2006, BABY BLUES PARTNERSHIP DIST. BY KING FEATURES SYNDICATE 2-20

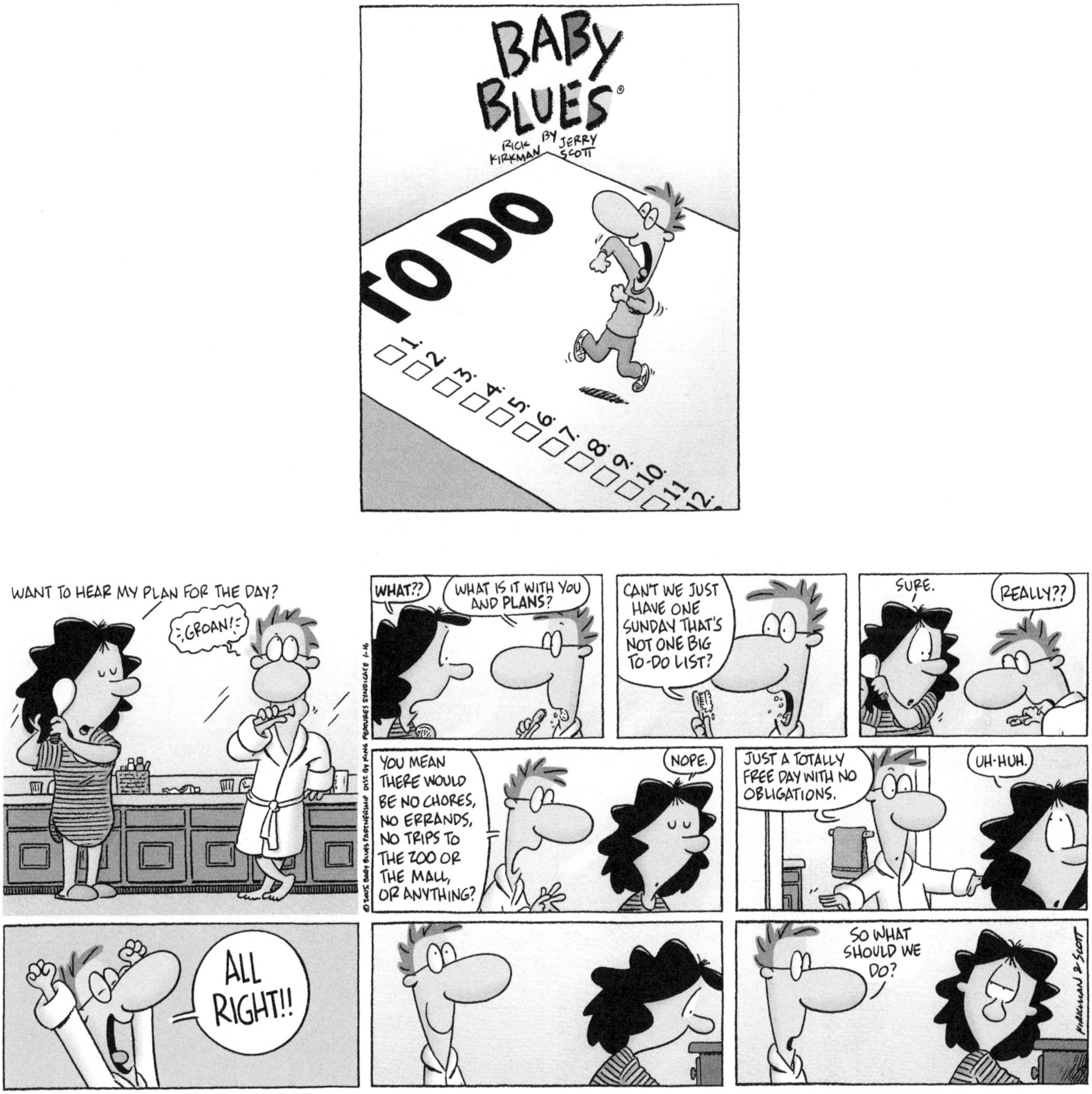
BABY BLUES®
BY RICK KIRKMAN JERRY SCOTT
TO DO
1. 2. 3. 4. 5. 6. 7. 8. 9. 10. 11. 12.
WANT TO HEAR MY PLAN FOR THE DAY?
GROAN!
©2005 BABY BLUES PARTNERSHIP DIST. BY KING FEATURES SYNDICATE 1-16
WHAT??
WHAT IS IT WITH YOU AND PLANS?
CAN'T WE JUST HAVE ONE SUNDAY THAT'S NOT ONE BIG TO-DO LIST?
SURE.
REALLY??
YOU MEAN THERE WOULD BE NO CHORES, NO ERRANDS, NO TRIPS TO THE ZOO OR THE MALL, OR ANYTHING?
NOPE.
JUST A TOTALLY FREE DAY WITH NO OBLIGATIONS.
UH-HUH.
ALL RIGHT!!
SO WHAT SHOULD WE DO?
KIRKMAN & SCOTT

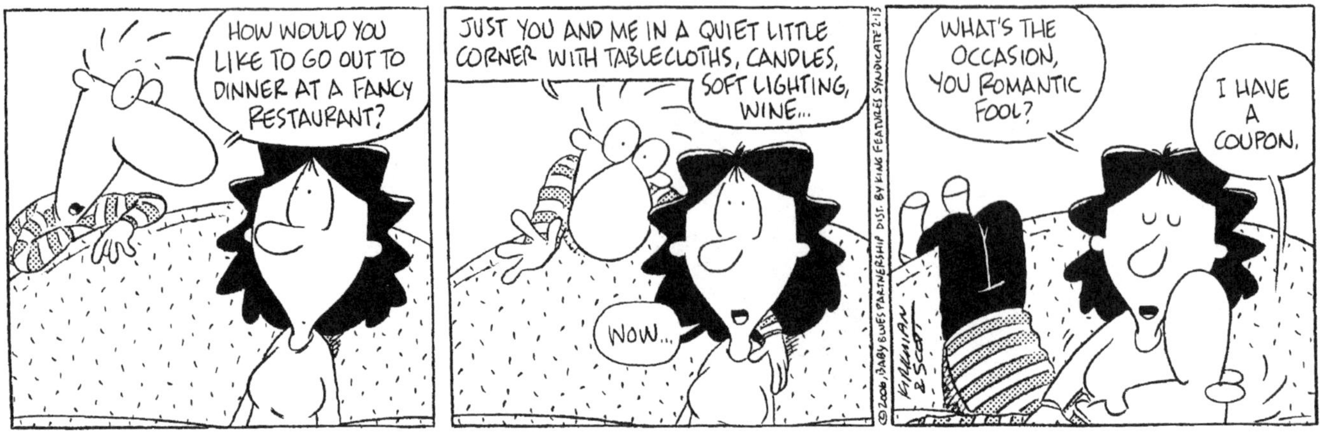
HOW WOULD YOU LIKE TO GO OUT TO DINNER AT A FANCY RESTAURANT?
JUST YOU AND ME IN A QUIET LITTLE CORNER WITH TABLECLOTHS, CANDLES, SOFT LIGHTING, WINE...
WOW...
WHAT'S THE OCCASION, YOU ROMANTIC FOOL?
I HAVE A COUPON.
© 2006, BABY BLUES PARTNERSHIP DIST. BY KING FEATURES SYNDICATE 2-13
KIRKMAN & SCOTT

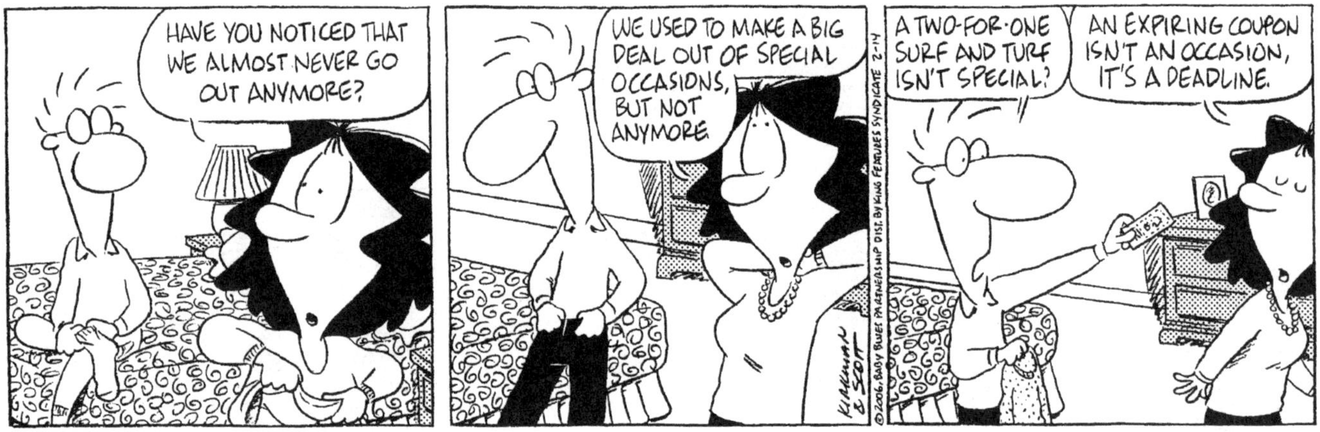
HAVE YOU NOTICED THAT WE ALMOST NEVER GO OUT ANYMORE?
WE USED TO MAKE A BIG DEAL OUT OF SPECIAL OCCASIONS, BUT NOT ANYMORE.
A TWO-FOR-ONE SURF AND TURF ISN'T SPECIAL?
AN EXPIRING COUPON ISN'T AN OCCASION, IT'S A DEADLINE.
© 2006, BABY BLUES PARTNERSHIP DIST. BY KING FEATURES SYNDICATE 2-14
KIRKMAN & SCOTT

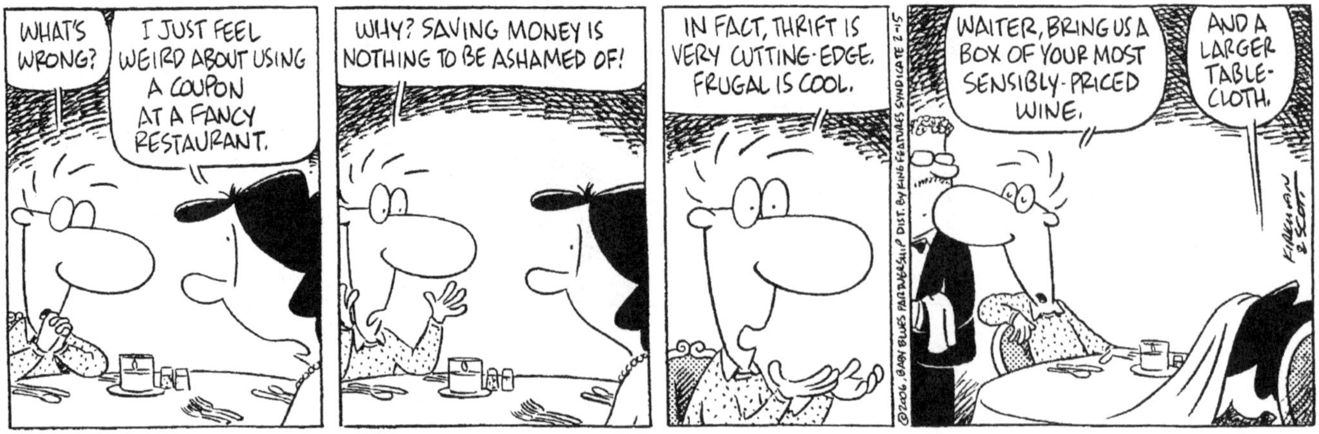
WHAT'S WRONG?
I JUST FEEL WEIRD ABOUT USING A COUPON AT A FANCY RESTAURANT.
WHY? SAVING MONEY IS NOTHING TO BE ASHAMED OF!
IN FACT, THRIFT IS VERY CUTTING-EDGE. FRUGAL IS COOL.
WAITER, BRING US A BOX OF YOUR MOST SENSIBLY-PRICED WINE.
AND A LARGER TABLE-CLOTH.
© 2006, BABY BLUES PARTNERSHIP DIST. BY KING FEATURES SYNDICATE 2-15
KIRKMAN & SCOTT

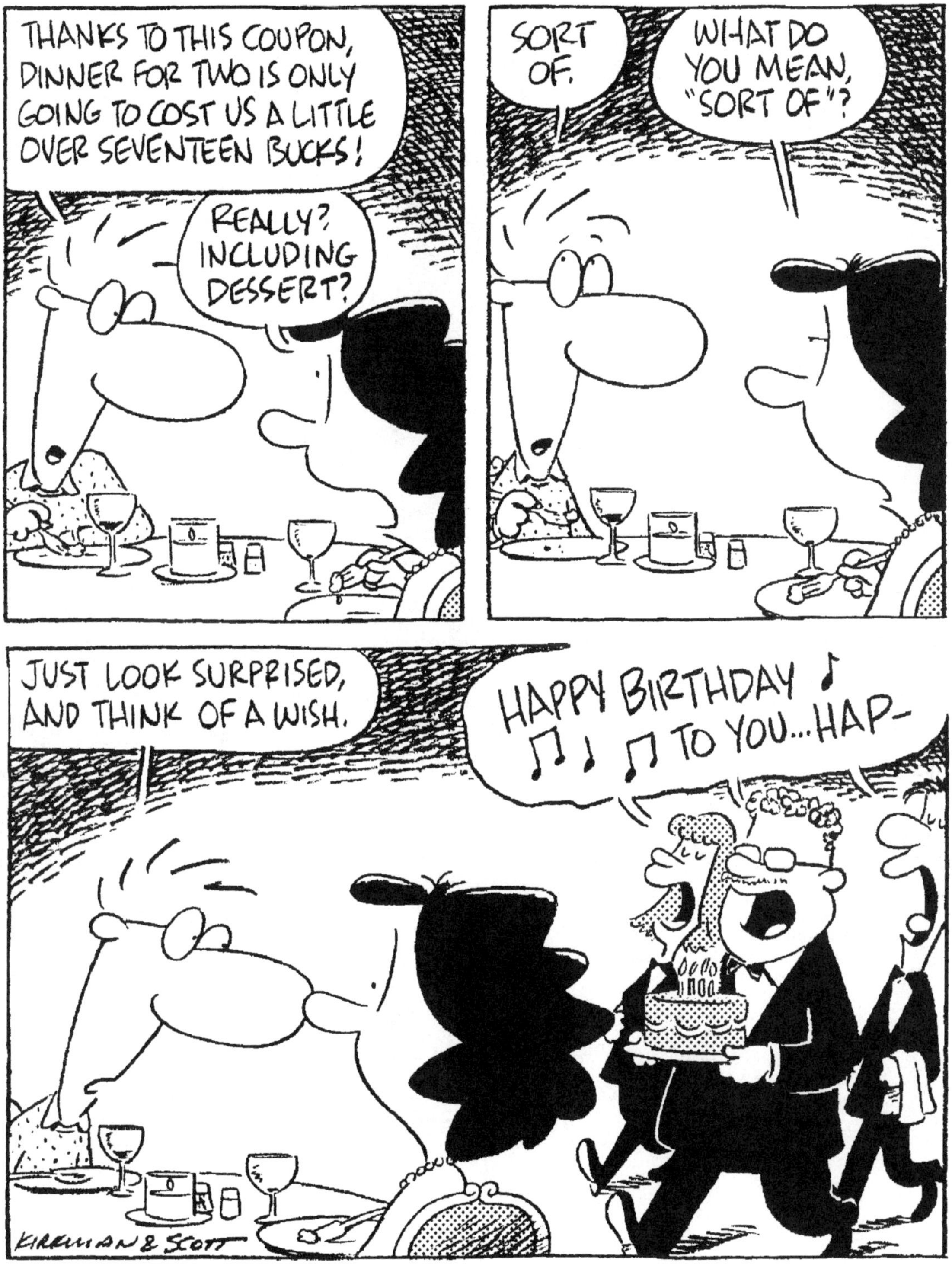
THANKS TO THIS COUPON, DINNER FOR TWO IS ONLY GOING TO COST US A LITTLE OVER SEVENTEEN BUCKS!
REALLY? INCLUDING DESSERT?
SORT OF.
WHAT DO YOU MEAN, "SORT OF"?
JUST LOOK SURPRISED, AND THINK OF A WISH.
HAPPY BIRTHDAY ♪ ♫ ♩ ♫ TO YOU... HAP-
KIRKMAN & SCOTT

BABY BLUES®
BY RICK KIRKMAN / JERRY SCOTT
RECIPE
MARCH
TO DO
24

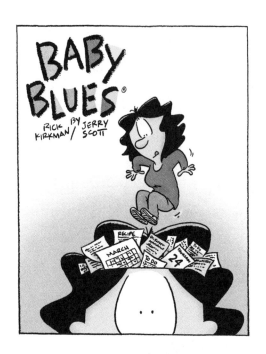

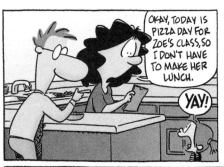

OKAY, TODAY IS PIZZA DAY FOR ZOE'S CLASS, SO I DON'T HAVE TO MAKE HER LUNCH.
YAY!
HAMMIE WANTS THREE SLICES OF BALONEY AND MAYONNAISE ON HIS SANDWICHES, CUT DIAGONALLY. YOU ASKED FOR ROAST BEEF, AND I HAVE SOME OF THOSE SOURDOUGH ROLLS YOU LIKE IN THE FREEZER.
ZOE NEEDS TO TAKE 16 CUPCAKES TO SCHOOL, EIGHT WITH ORANGE FROSTING, AND EIGHT WITH BLUE FROSTING. I CAN DROP THEM OFF AT 9:45 ON MY WAY TO WREN'S DOCTOR APPOINTMENT AT TEN.
WITH ANY LUCK, I'LL BE BACK HERE AT 11:30 TO MEET THE PLUMBER, THEN I PICK UP ZOE AND HAMMIE FROM SCHOOL FIFTEEN MINUTES EARLY SO WE CAN GET TO THEIR DENTIST APPOINTMENTS, AND ON THE WAY HOME WE'LL BUY SOME NEW FURNACE FILTERS AND GET YOUR BROWN JACKET AT THE CLEANERS.
KIRKMAN & SCOTT 3-6
THAT'S AMAZING!
HUH?
HOW DO YOU KEEP ALL THAT INFORMATION IN YOUR HEAD, AND STILL HAVE ROOM FOR ALL THE OTHER STUFF?
WHAT OTHER STUFF?

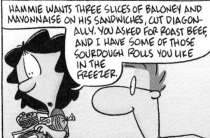

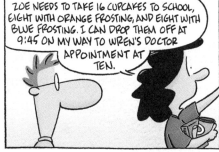

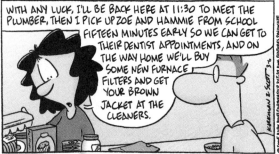

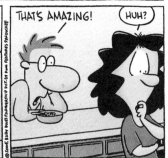

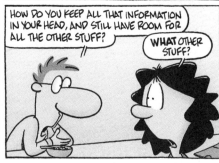

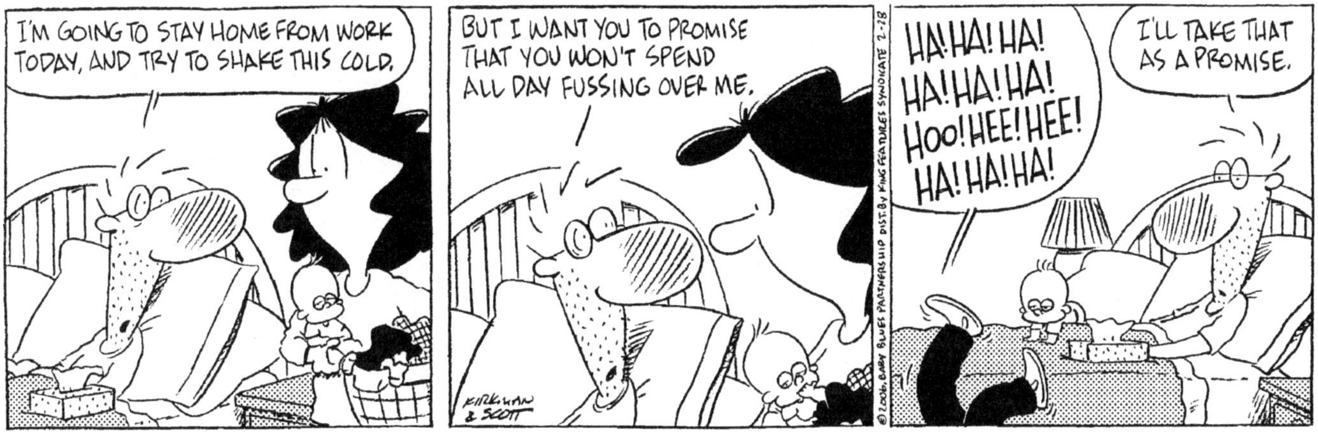
I'M GOING TO STAY HOME FROM WORK TODAY, AND TRY TO SHAKE THIS COLD.
BUT I WANT YOU TO PROMISE THAT YOU WON'T SPEND ALL DAY FUSSING OVER ME.
KIRKMAN & SCOTT
© 2006, BABY BLUES PARTNERSHIP DIST. BY KING FEATURES SYNDICATE 2-28
HA! HA! HA! HA! HA! HA! HOO! HEE! HEE! HA! HA! HA!
I'LL TAKE THAT AS A PROMISE.

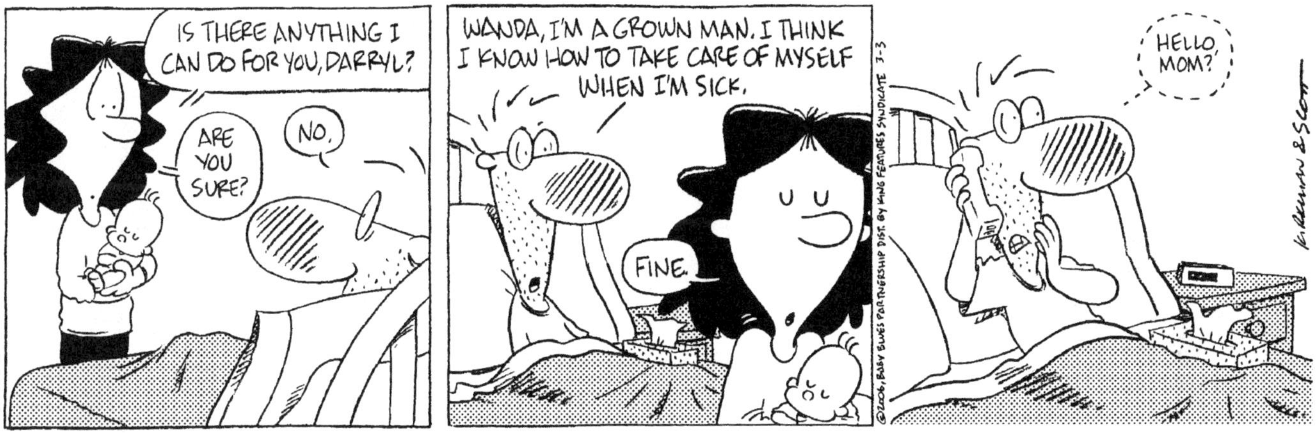
IS THERE ANYTHING I CAN DO FOR YOU, DARRYL?
ARE YOU SURE?
NO.
WANDA, I'M A GROWN MAN. I THINK I KNOW HOW TO TAKE CARE OF MYSELF WHEN I'M SICK.
FINE.
© 2006, BABY BLUES PARTNERSHIP DIST. BY KING FEATURES SYNDICATE 3-3
HELLO, MOM?
KIRKMAN & SCOTT

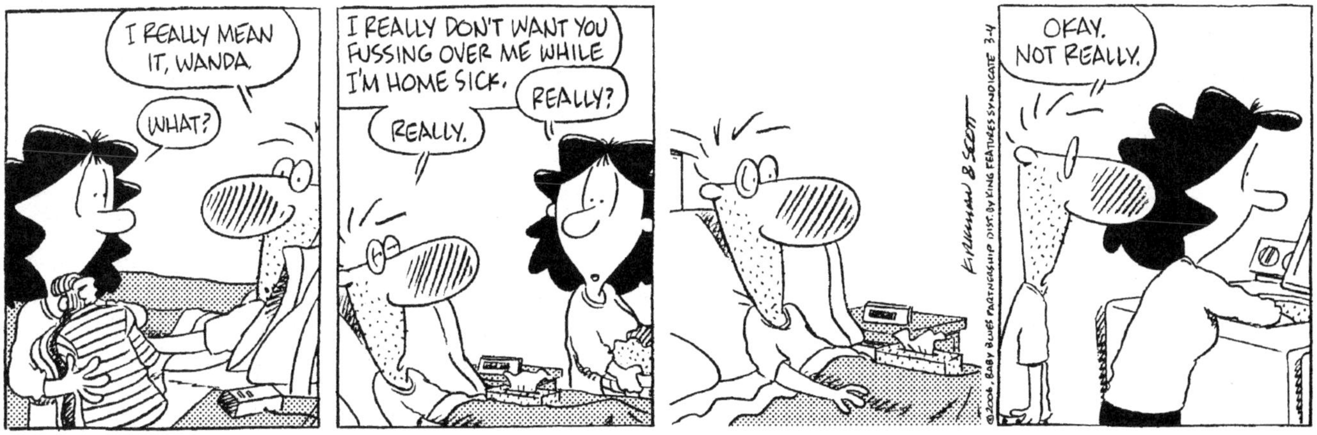
I REALLY MEAN IT, WANDA.
WHAT?
I REALLY DON'T WANT YOU FUSSING OVER ME WHILE I'M HOME SICK.
REALLY.
REALLY?
KIRKMAN & SCOTT
© 2006, BABY BLUES PARTNERSHIP DIST. BY KING FEATURES SYNDICATE 3-4
OKAY. NOT REALLY.

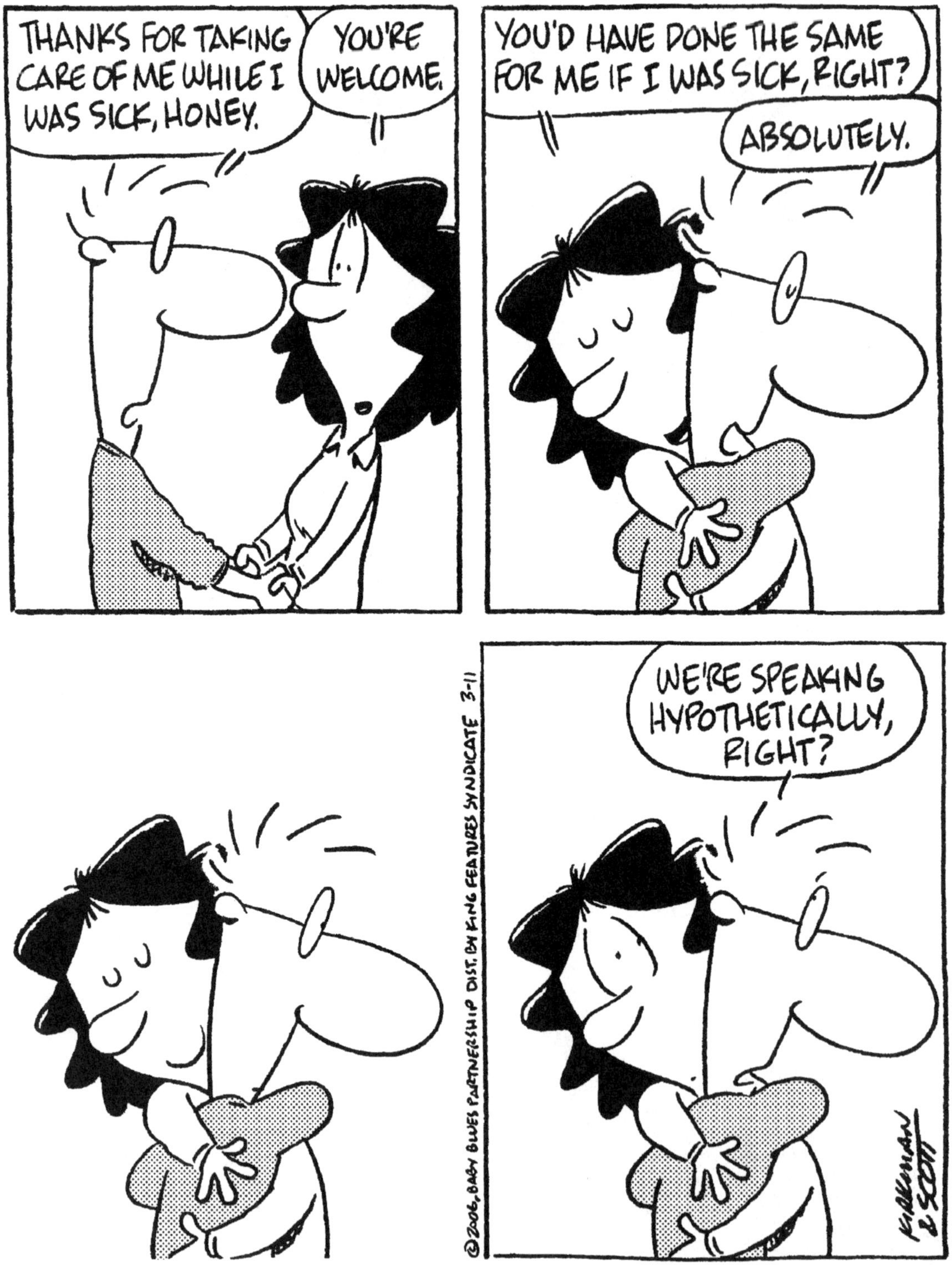
THANKS FOR TAKING CARE OF ME WHILE I WAS SICK, HONEY.
YOU'RE WELCOME.
YOU'D HAVE DONE THE SAME FOR ME IF I WAS SICK, RIGHT?
ABSOLUTELY.
WE'RE SPEAKING HYPOTHETICALLY, RIGHT?
©2006, BABY BLUES PARTNERSHIP DIST. BY KING FEATURES SYNDICATE 3-11
KIRKMAN & SCOTT

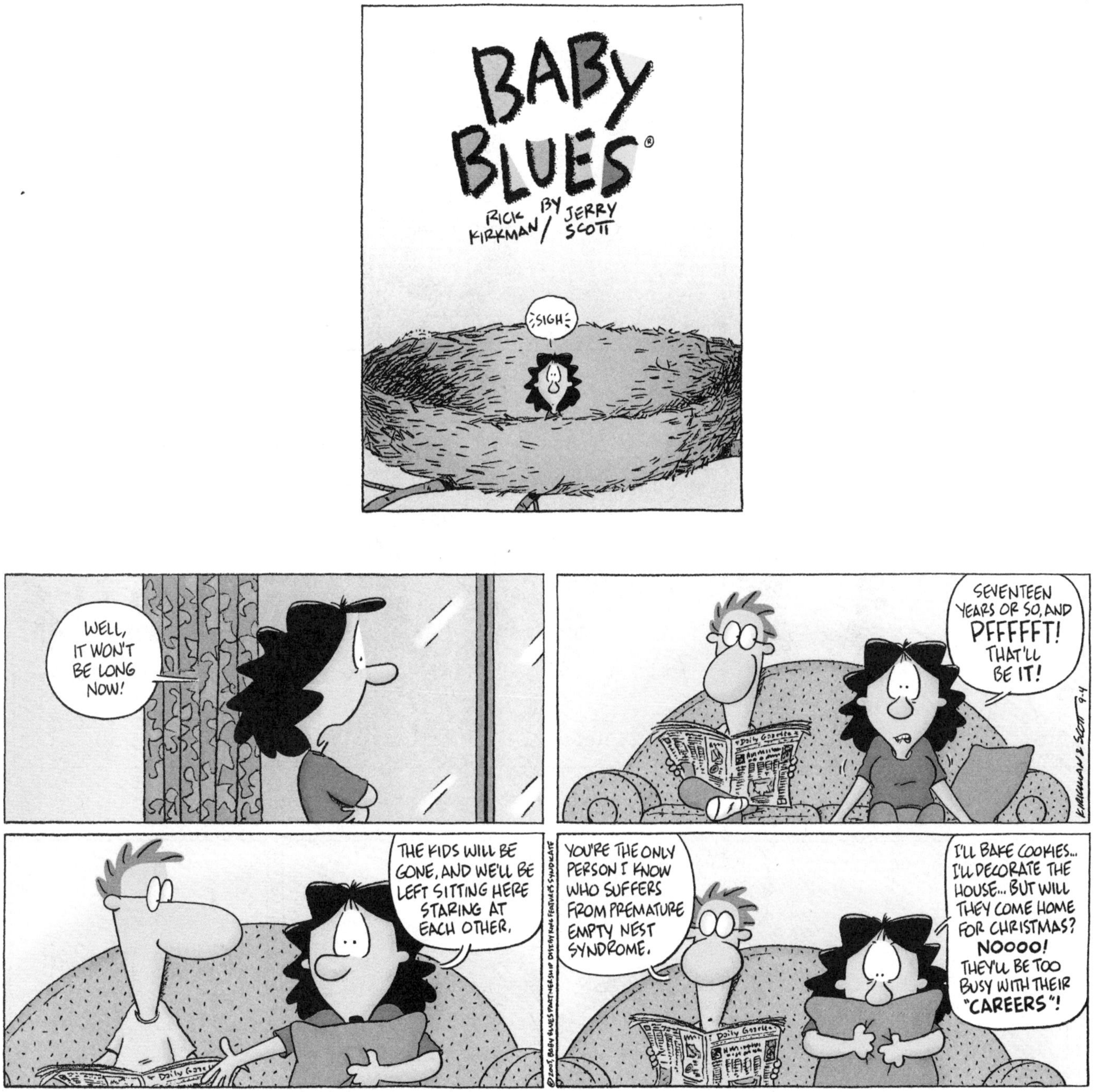
BABY BLUES®
BY RICK KIRKMAN / JERRY SCOTT
SIGH
WELL, IT WON'T BE LONG NOW!
SEVENTEEN YEARS OR SO, AND PFFFFFT! THAT'LL BE IT!
KIRKMAN & SCOTT 9-4
THE KIDS WILL BE GONE, AND WE'LL BE LEFT SITTING HERE STARING AT EACH OTHER.
YOU'RE THE ONLY PERSON I KNOW WHO SUFFERS FROM PREMATURE EMPTY NEST SYNDROME.
I'LL BAKE COOKIES... I'LL DECORATE THE HOUSE... BUT WILL THEY COME HOME FOR CHRISTMAS? NOOOO! THEY'LL BE TOO BUSY WITH THEIR "CAREERS"!

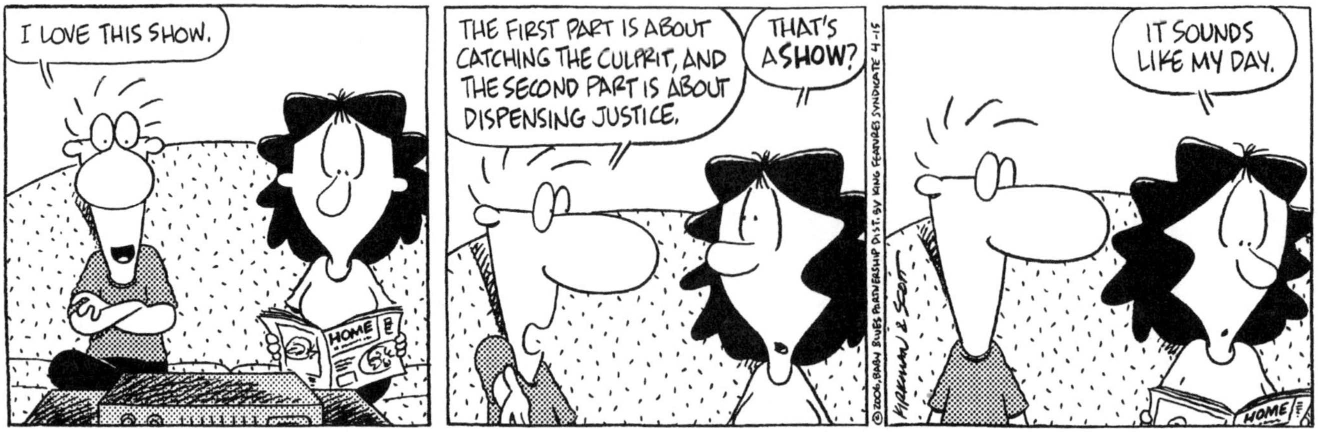
I LOVE THIS SHOW.
THE FIRST PART IS ABOUT CATCHING THE CULPRIT, AND THE SECOND PART IS ABOUT DISPENSING JUSTICE.
THAT'S A SHOW?
IT SOUNDS LIKE MY DAY.
HOME

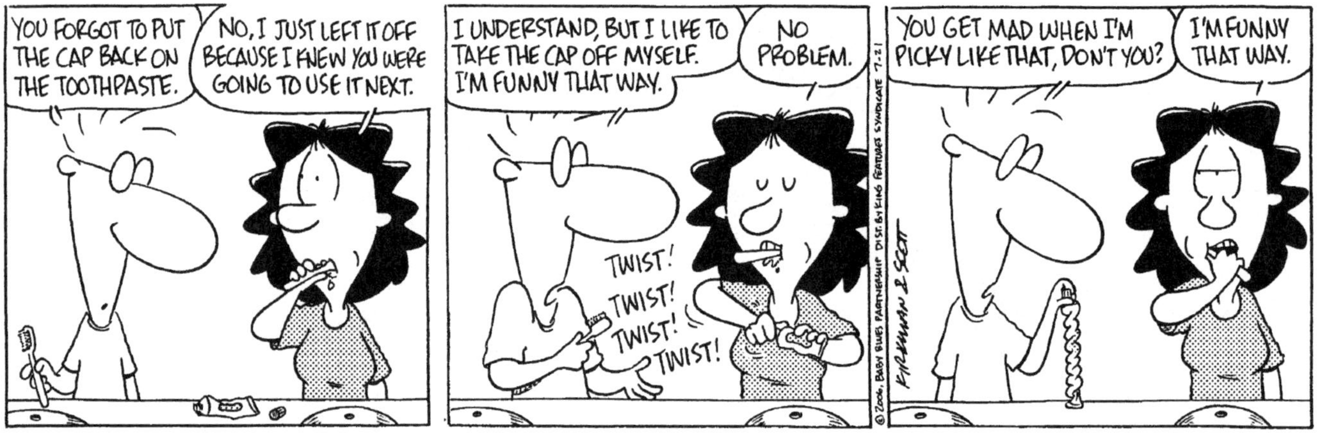
YOU FORGOT TO PUT THE CAP BACK ON THE TOOTHPASTE.
NO, I JUST LEFT IT OFF BECAUSE I KNEW YOU WERE GOING TO USE IT NEXT.
I UNDERSTAND, BUT I LIKE TO TAKE THE CAP OFF MYSELF. I'M FUNNY THAT WAY.
NO PROBLEM.
TWIST! TWIST! TWIST! TWIST!
YOU GET MAD WHEN I'M PICKY LIKE THAT, DON'T YOU?
I'M FUNNY THAT WAY.

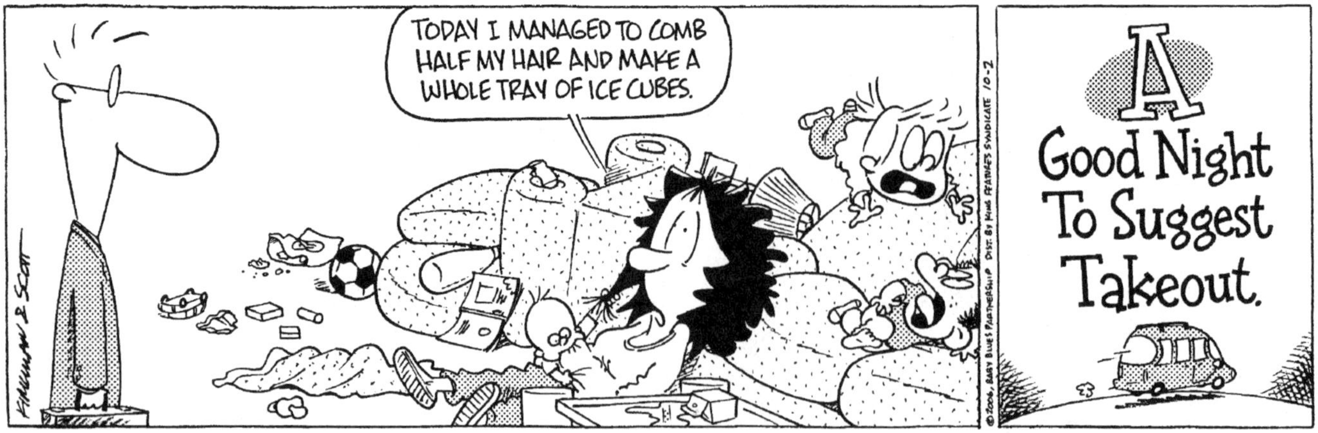
TODAY I MANAGED TO COMB HALF MY HAIR AND MAKE A WHOLE TRAY OF ICE CUBES.
A Good Night To Suggest Takeout.

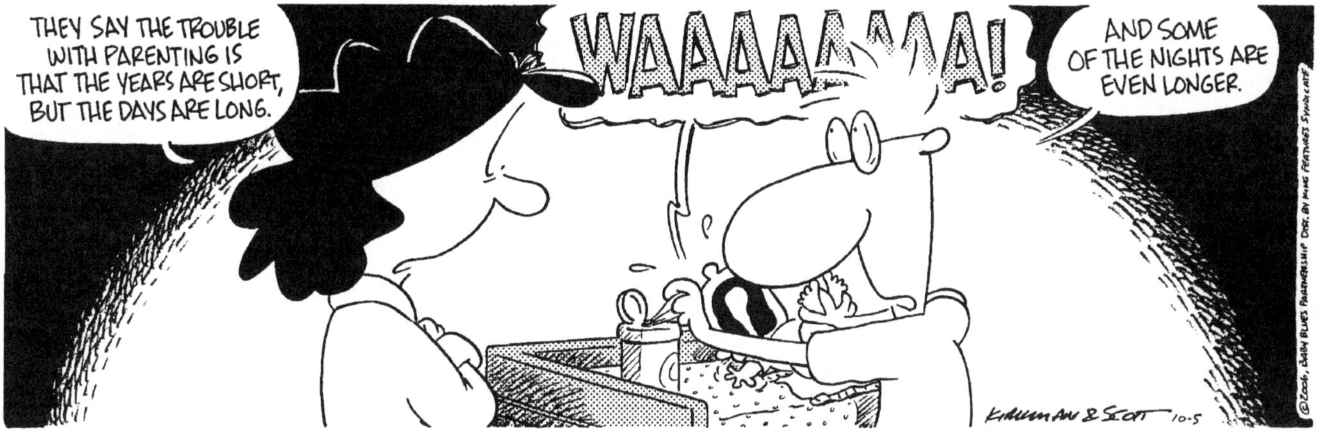
THEY SAY THE TROUBLE WITH PARENTING IS THAT THE YEARS ARE SHORT, BUT THE DAYS ARE LONG.
WAAAAAAAA!
AND SOME OF THE NIGHTS ARE EVEN LONGER.
KIRKMAN & SCOTT 10-5
©2006, BABY BLUES PARTNERSHIP DIST. BY KING FEATURES SYNDICATE

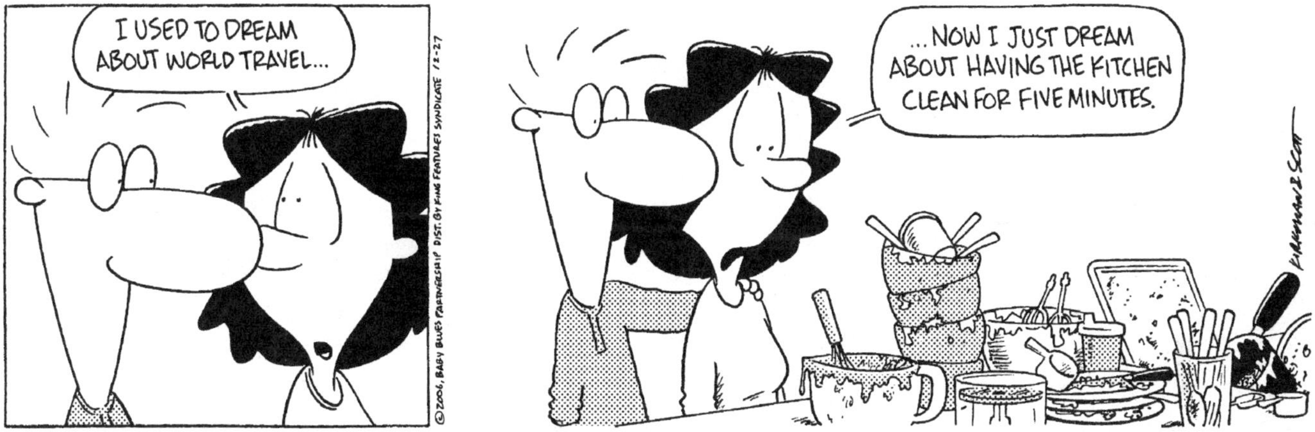
I USED TO DREAM ABOUT WORLD TRAVEL...
©2006, BABY BLUES PARTNERSHIP DIST. BY KING FEATURES SYNDICATE 12-27
...NOW I JUST DREAM ABOUT HAVING THE KITCHEN CLEAN FOR FIVE MINUTES.
KIRKMAN & SCOTT

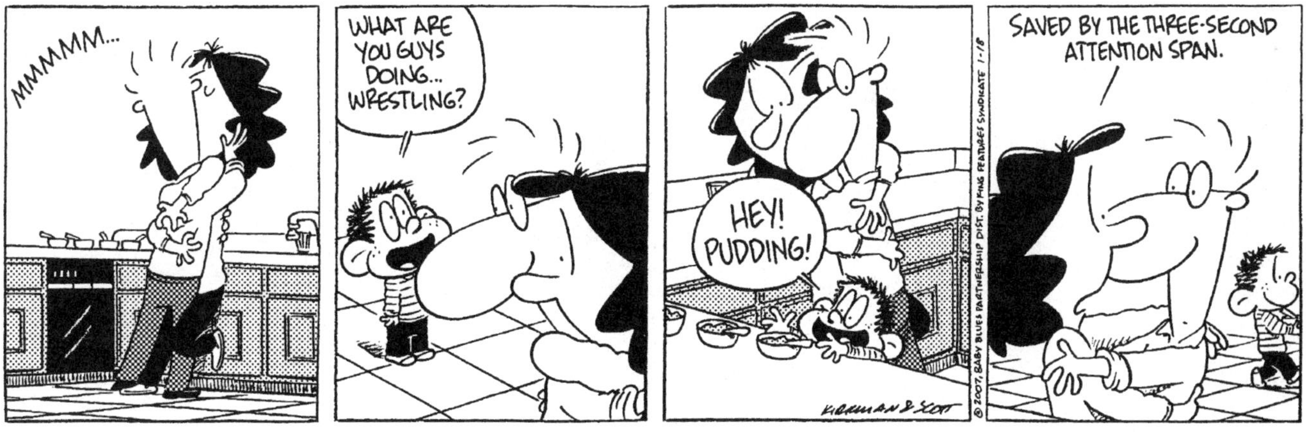
MMMMMM...
WHAT ARE YOU GUYS DOING... WRESTLING?
HEY! PUDDING!
KIRKMAN & SCOTT
©2007, BABY BLUES PARTNERSHIP DIST. BY KING FEATURES SYNDICATE 1-18
SAVED BY THE THREE-SECOND ATTENTION SPAN.

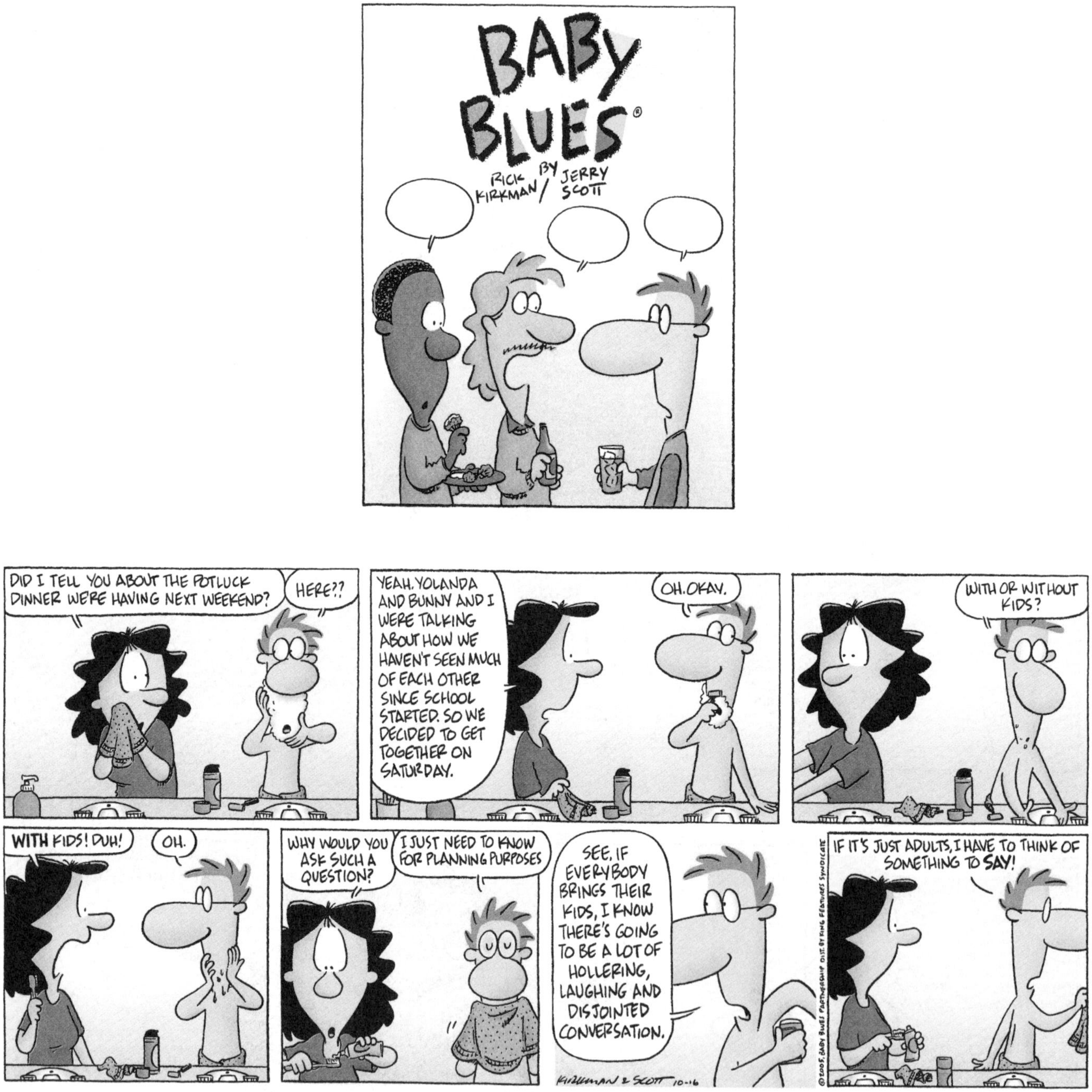
BABY BLUES®
BY RICK KIRKMAN / JERRY SCOTT
DID I TELL YOU ABOUT THE POTLUCK DINNER WE'RE HAVING NEXT WEEKEND?
HERE??
YEAH. YOLANDA AND BUNNY AND I WERE TALKING ABOUT HOW WE HAVEN'T SEEN MUCH OF EACH OTHER SINCE SCHOOL STARTED. SO WE DECIDED TO GET TOGETHER ON SATURDAY.
OH. OKAY.
WITH OR WITHOUT KIDS?
WITH KIDS! DUH!
OH.
WHY WOULD YOU ASK SUCH A QUESTION?
I JUST NEED TO KNOW FOR PLANNING PURPOSES
SEE, IF EVERYBODY BRINGS THEIR KIDS, I KNOW THERE'S GOING TO BE A LOT OF HOLLERING, LAUGHING AND DISJOINTED CONVERSATION.
KIRKMAN & SCOTT 10-16
IF IT'S JUST ADULTS, I HAVE TO THINK OF SOMETHING TO SAY!

THE WINDOW OF CONVERSATIONAL OPPORTUNITY CONTINUES TO SHRINK...

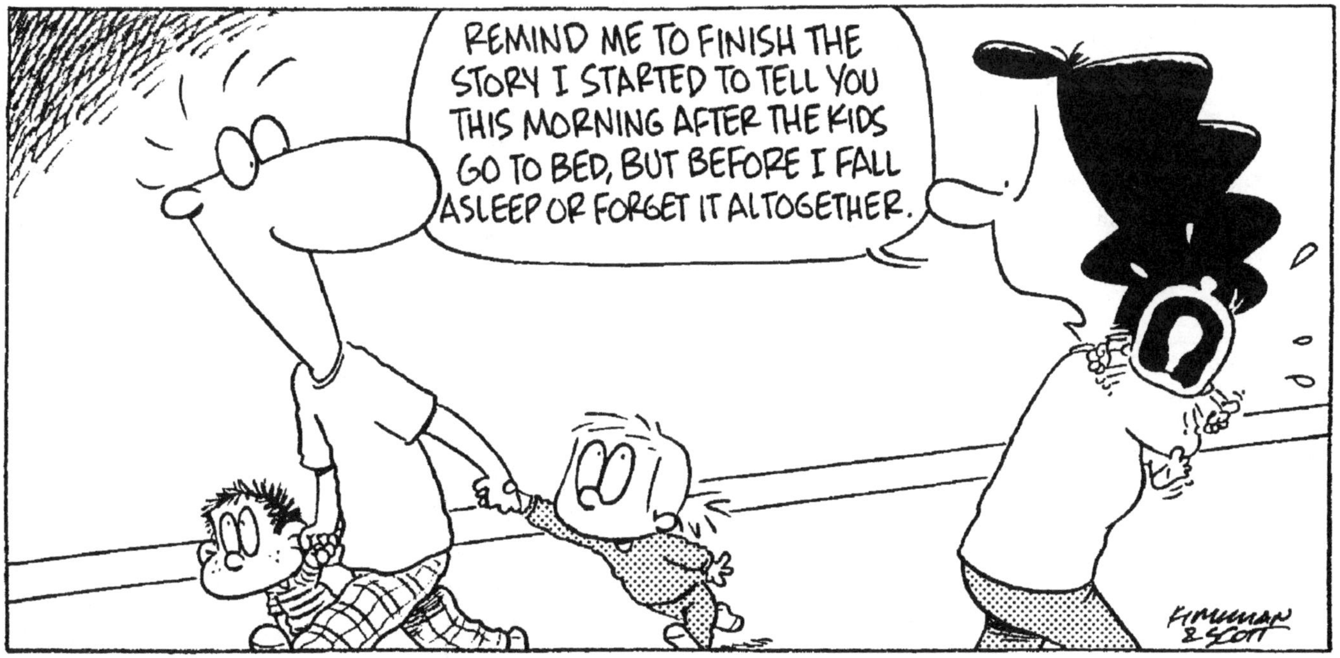
REMIND ME TO FINISH THE STORY I STARTED TO TELL YOU THIS MORNING AFTER THE KIDS GO TO BED, BUT BEFORE I FALL ASLEEP OR FORGET IT ALTOGETHER.
KIRKMAN & SCOTT

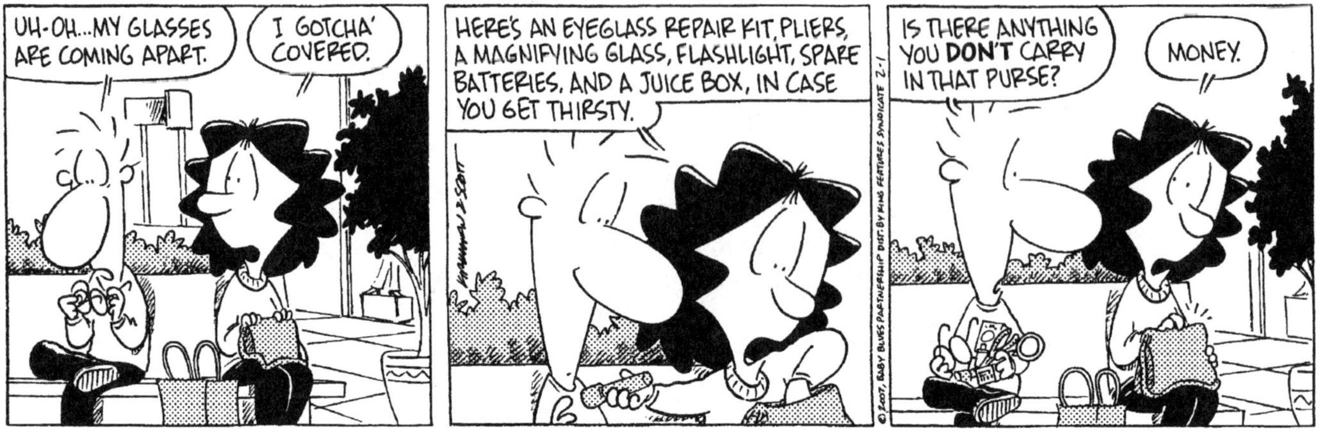
UH-OH...MY GLASSES ARE COMING APART.
I GOTCHA' COVERED.
HERE'S AN EYEGLASS REPAIR KIT, PLIERS, A MAGNIFYING GLASS, FLASHLIGHT, SPARE BATTERIES, AND A JUICE BOX, IN CASE YOU GET THIRSTY.
IS THERE ANYTHING YOU **DON'T** CARRY IN THAT PURSE?
MONEY.
© 2007, BABY BLUES PARTNERSHIP DIST. BY KING FEATURES SYNDICATE 2-1

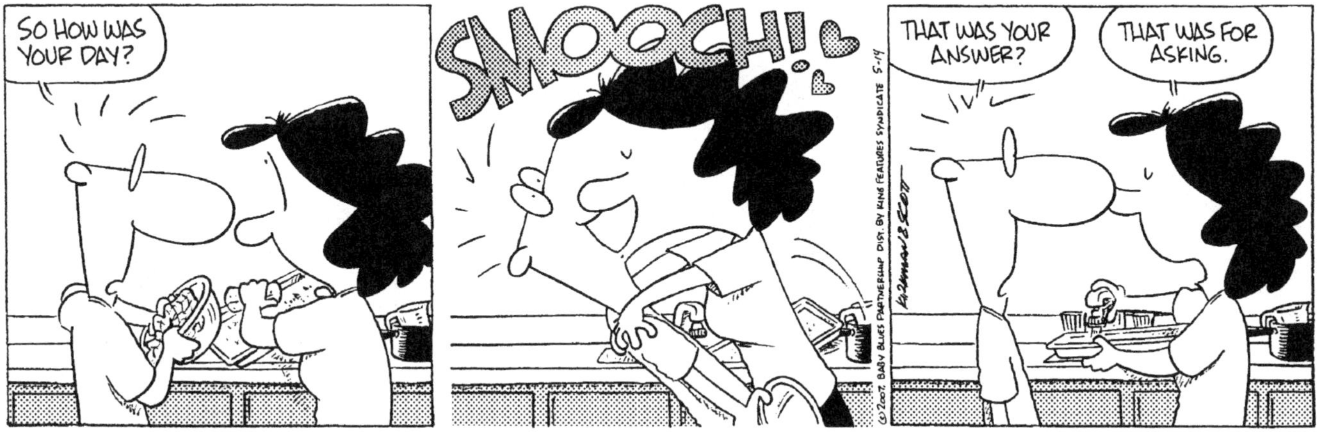
SO HOW WAS YOUR DAY?
SMOOCH!
THAT WAS YOUR ANSWER?
THAT WAS FOR ASKING.
© 2007, BABY BLUES PARTNERSHIP DIST. BY KING FEATURES SYNDICATE 5-19

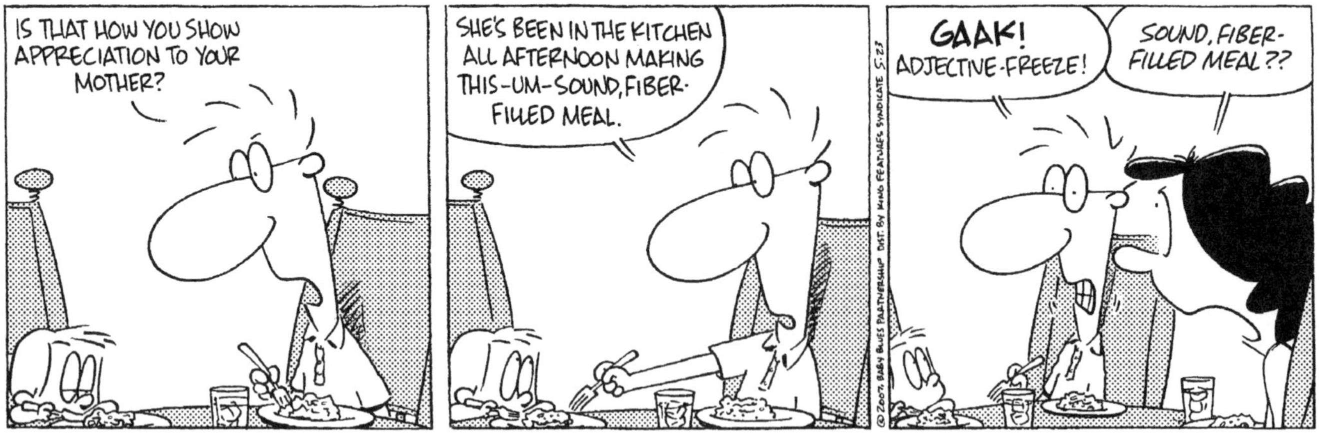
IS THAT HOW YOU SHOW APPRECIATION TO YOUR MOTHER?
SHE'S BEEN IN THE KITCHEN ALL AFTERNOON MAKING THIS-UM-SOUND, FIBER-FILLED MEAL.
GAAK! ADJECTIVE-FREEZE!
SOUND, FIBER-FILLED MEAL??
© 2007, BABY BLUES PARTNERSHIP DIST. BY KING FEATURES SYNDICATE 5-23

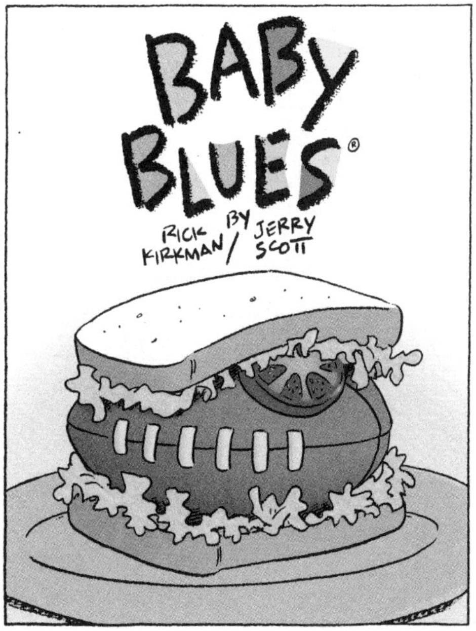
BABY BLUES®
BY RICK KIRKMAN / JERRY SCOTT

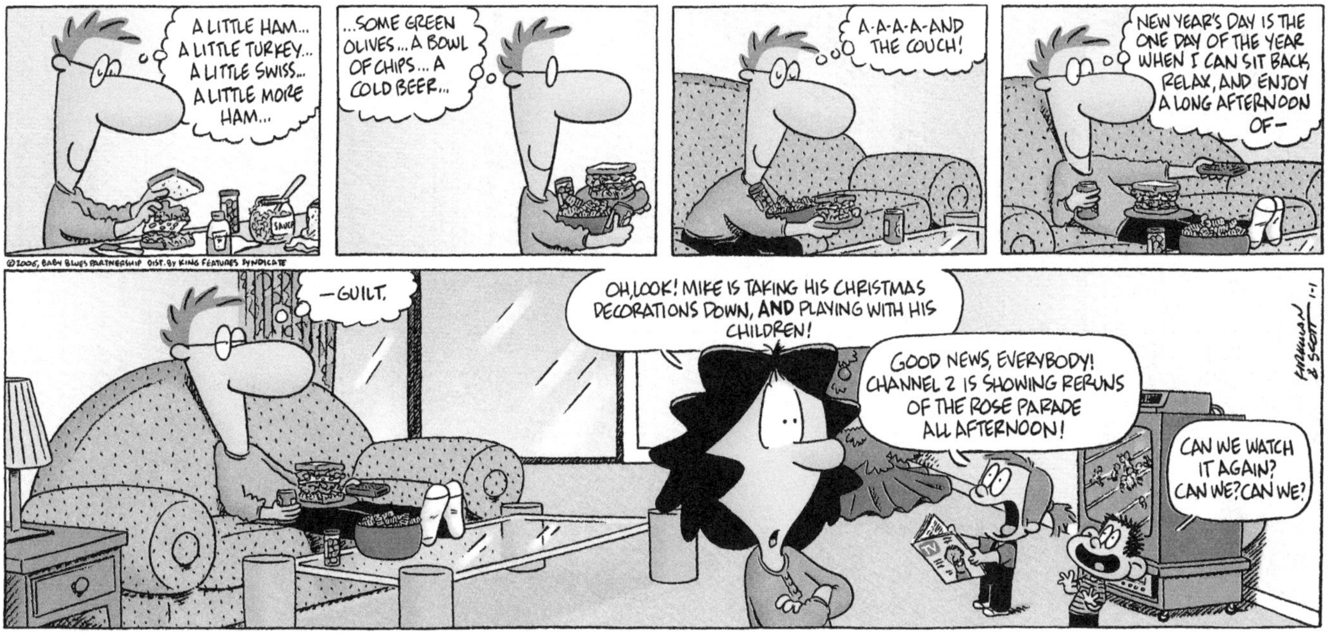
A LITTLE HAM... A LITTLE TURKEY... A LITTLE SWISS... A LITTLE MORE HAM...
SAUCE
...SOME GREEN OLIVES... A BOWL OF CHIPS... A COLD BEER...
A-A-A-A-AND THE COUCH!
NEW YEAR'S DAY IS THE ONE DAY OF THE YEAR WHEN I CAN SIT BACK, RELAX, AND ENJOY A LONG AFTERNOON OF—
©2006, BABY BLUES PARTNERSHIP DIST. BY KING FEATURES SYNDICATE
—GUILT.
OH, LOOK! MIKE IS TAKING HIS CHRISTMAS DECORATIONS DOWN, AND PLAYING WITH HIS CHILDREN!
GOOD NEWS, EVERYBODY! CHANNEL 2 IS SHOWING RERUNS OF THE ROSE PARADE ALL AFTERNOON!
CAN WE WATCH IT AGAIN? CAN WE? CAN WE?
TV
KIRKMAN & SCOTT 1-1

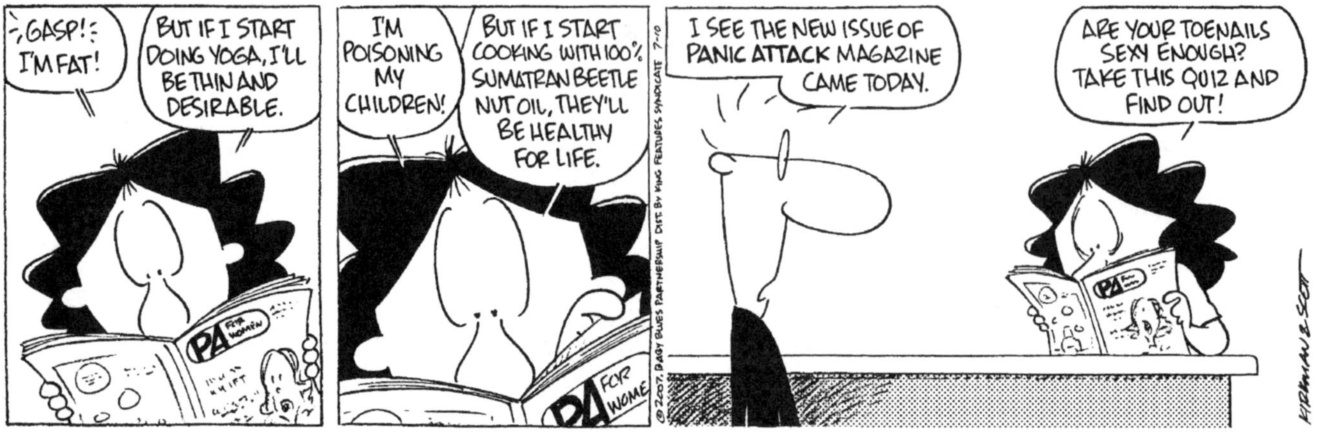
GASP! I'M FAT!
BUT IF I START DOING YOGA, I'LL BE THIN AND DESIRABLE.
I'M POISONING MY CHILDREN!
BUT IF I START COOKING WITH 100% SUMATRAN BEETLE NUT OIL, THEY'LL BE HEALTHY FOR LIFE.
© 2007, BABY BLUES PARTNERSHIP DIST. BY KING FEATURES SYNDICATE 7-10
I SEE THE NEW ISSUE OF PANIC ATTACK MAGAZINE CAME TODAY.
ARE YOUR TOENAILS SEXY ENOUGH? TAKE THIS QUIZ AND FIND OUT!
KIRKMAN & SCOTT

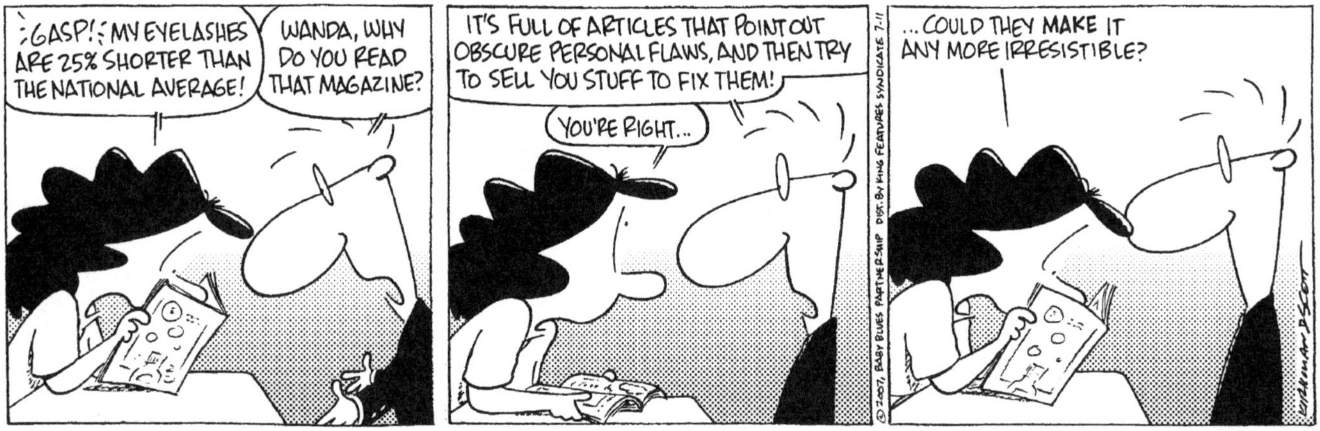
GASP! MY EYELASHES ARE 25% SHORTER THAN THE NATIONAL AVERAGE!
WANDA, WHY DO YOU READ THAT MAGAZINE?
IT'S FULL OF ARTICLES THAT POINT OUT OBSCURE PERSONAL FLAWS, AND THEN TRY TO SELL YOU STUFF TO FIX THEM!
YOU'RE RIGHT...
© 2007, BABY BLUES PARTNERSHIP DIST. BY KING FEATURES SYNDICATE 7-11
...COULD THEY MAKE IT ANY MORE IRRESISTIBLE?
KIRKMAN & SCOTT

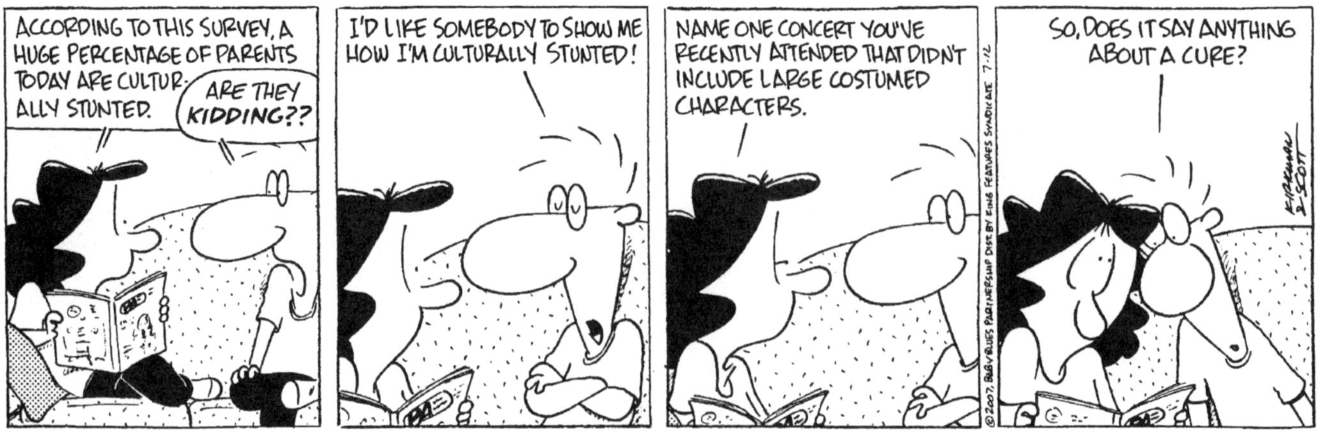
ACCORDING TO THIS SURVEY, A HUGE PERCENTAGE OF PARENTS TODAY ARE CULTURALLY STUNTED.
ARE THEY KIDDING??
I'D LIKE SOMEBODY TO SHOW ME HOW I'M CULTURALLY STUNTED!
NAME ONE CONCERT YOU'VE RECENTLY ATTENDED THAT DIDN'T INCLUDE LARGE COSTUMED CHARACTERS.
© 2007, BABY BLUES PARTNERSHIP DIST. BY KING FEATURES SYNDICATE 7-12
SO, DOES IT SAY ANYTHING ABOUT A CURE?
KIRKMAN & SCOTT

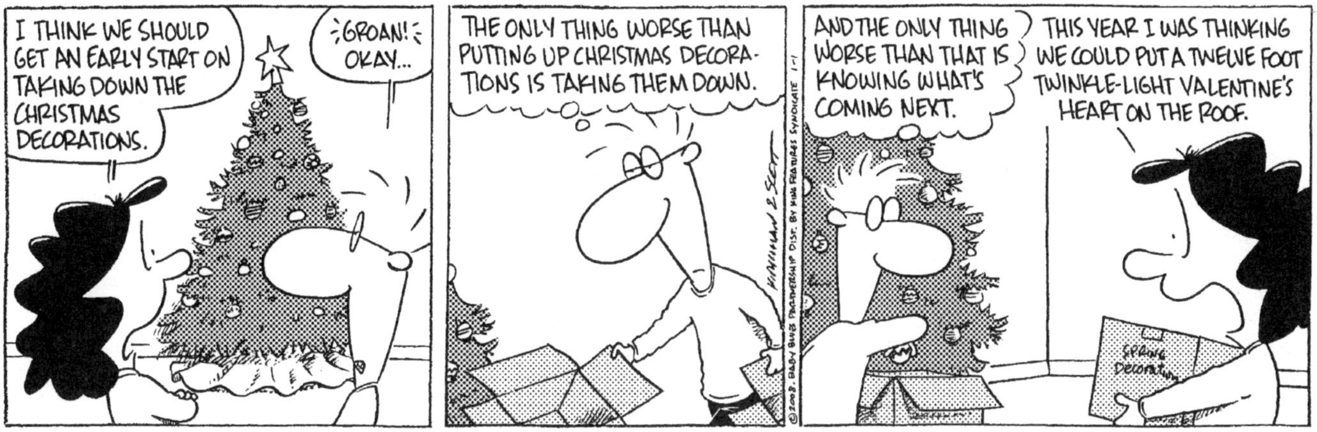
I THINK WE SHOULD GET AN EARLY START ON TAKING DOWN THE CHRISTMAS DECORATIONS.
GROAN! OKAY...
THE ONLY THING WORSE THAN PUTTING UP CHRISTMAS DECORATIONS IS TAKING THEM DOWN.
AND THE ONLY THING WORSE THAN THAT IS KNOWING WHAT'S COMING NEXT.
THIS YEAR I WAS THINKING WE COULD PUT A TWELVE FOOT TWINKLE-LIGHT VALENTINE'S HEART ON THE ROOF.
SPRING DECORAT...
©2008, BABY BLUES PARTNERSHIP DIST. BY KING FEATURES SYNDICATE 1-1
KIRKMAN & SCOTT

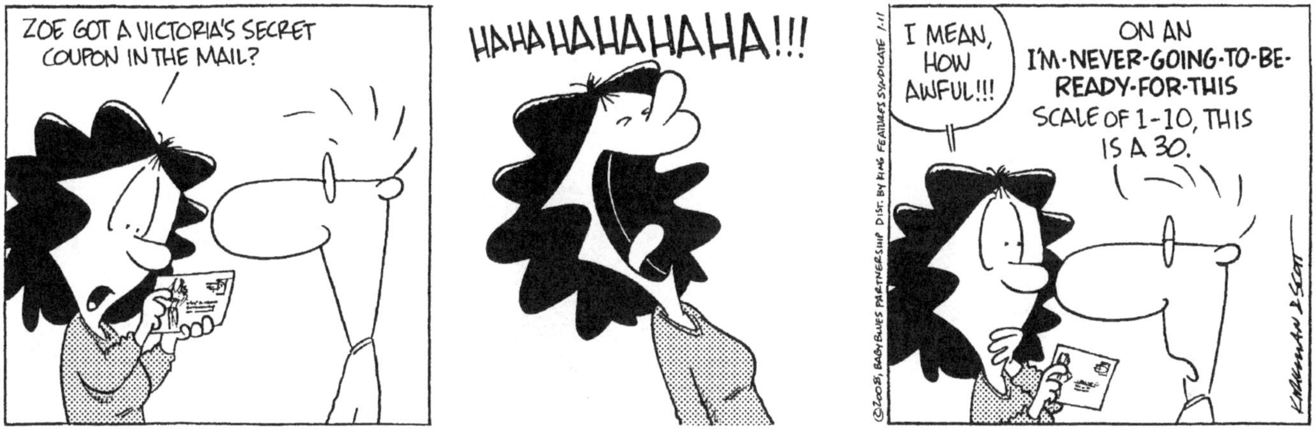
ZOE GOT A VICTORIA'S SECRET COUPON IN THE MAIL?
HAHAHAHAHAHAHA!!!
I MEAN, HOW AWFUL!!!
ON AN I'M-NEVER-GOING-TO-BE-READY-FOR-THIS SCALE OF 1-10, THIS IS A 30.
©2008, BABY BLUES PARTNERSHIP DIST. BY KING FEATURES SYNDICATE 1-11
KIRKMAN & SCOTT

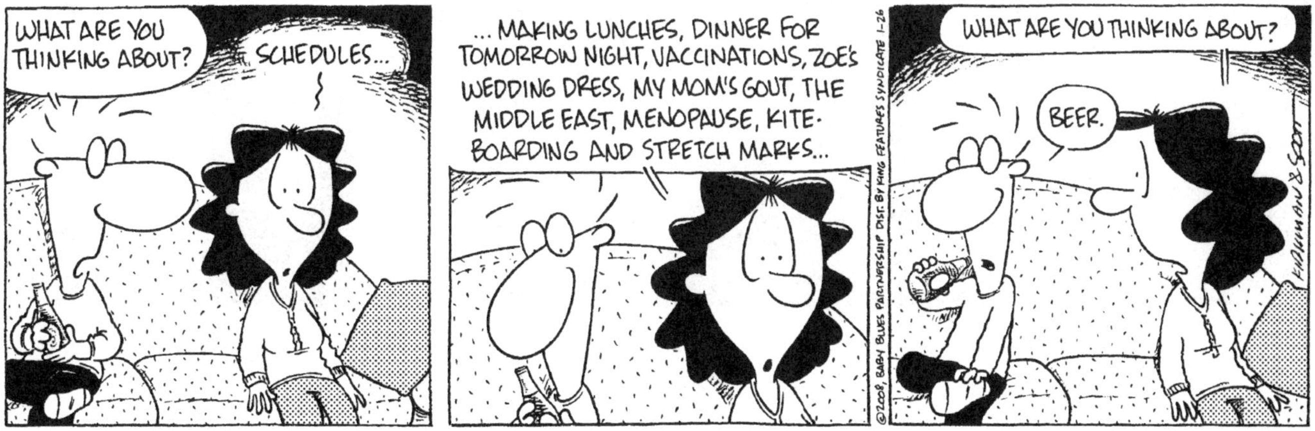
WHAT ARE YOU THINKING ABOUT?
SCHEDULES...
... MAKING LUNCHES, DINNER FOR TOMORROW NIGHT, VACCINATIONS, ZOE'S WEDDING DRESS, MY MOM'S GOUT, THE MIDDLE EAST, MENOPAUSE, KITE-BOARDING AND STRETCH MARKS...
WHAT ARE YOU THINKING ABOUT?
BEER.
©2008, BABY BLUES PARTNERSHIP DIST. BY KING FEATURES SYNDICATE 1-26
KIRKMAN & SCOTT

BABY BLUES®
BY RICK KIRKMAN / JERRY SCOTT

YOU KNOW... THE KIDS ARE ALL ASLEEP, AND IT'S ONLY 10 O'CLOCK.
IS THAT SO?
YEAH. DOES THAT GIVE YOU ANY IDEAS?
IT SURE DOES.
WILL YOU EXCUSE ME WHILE I GO SLIP INTO SOMETHING MORE COMFORTABLE?
YOU BET
Z
I SHOULD HAVE SEEN THAT ONE COMING.
KIRKMAN & SCOTT 1-22 ©2006, BABY BLUES PARTNERSHIP DIST. BY KING FEATURES SYNDICATE

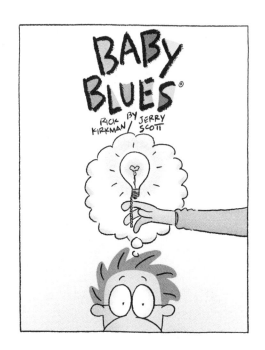

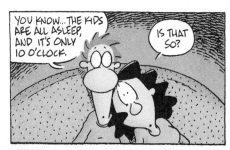

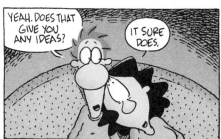

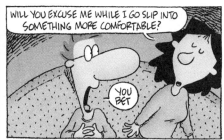

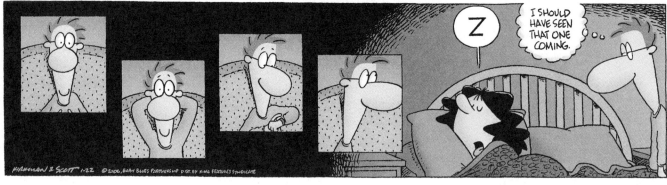

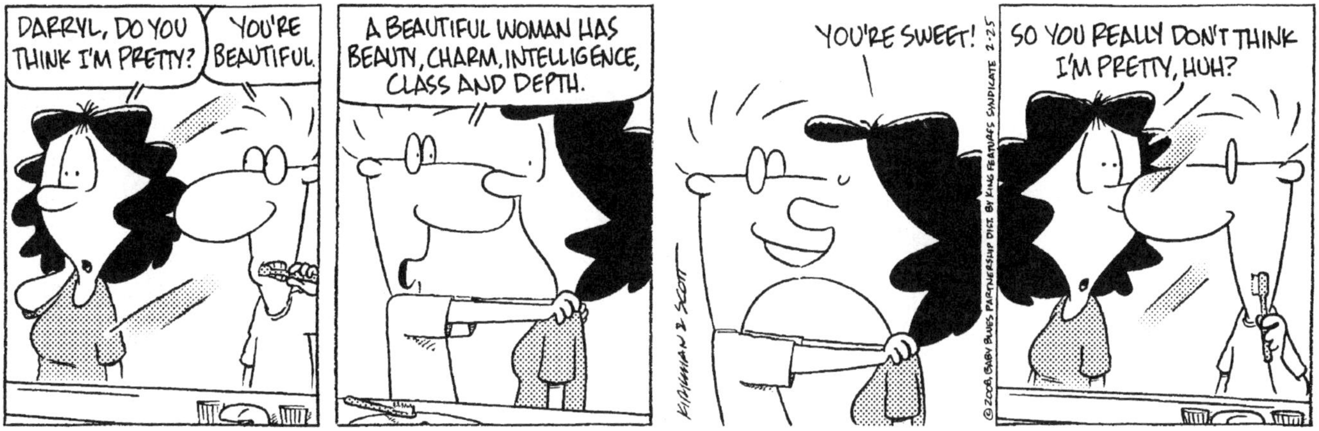
DARRYL, DO YOU THINK I'M PRETTY?
YOU'RE BEAUTIFUL.
A BEAUTIFUL WOMAN HAS BEAUTY, CHARM, INTELLIGENCE, CLASS AND DEPTH.
KIRKMAN & SCOTT
YOU'RE SWEET!
©2008, BABY BLUES PARTNERSHIP DIST. BY KING FEATURES SYNDICATE 2-25
SO YOU REALLY DON'T THINK I'M PRETTY, HUH?

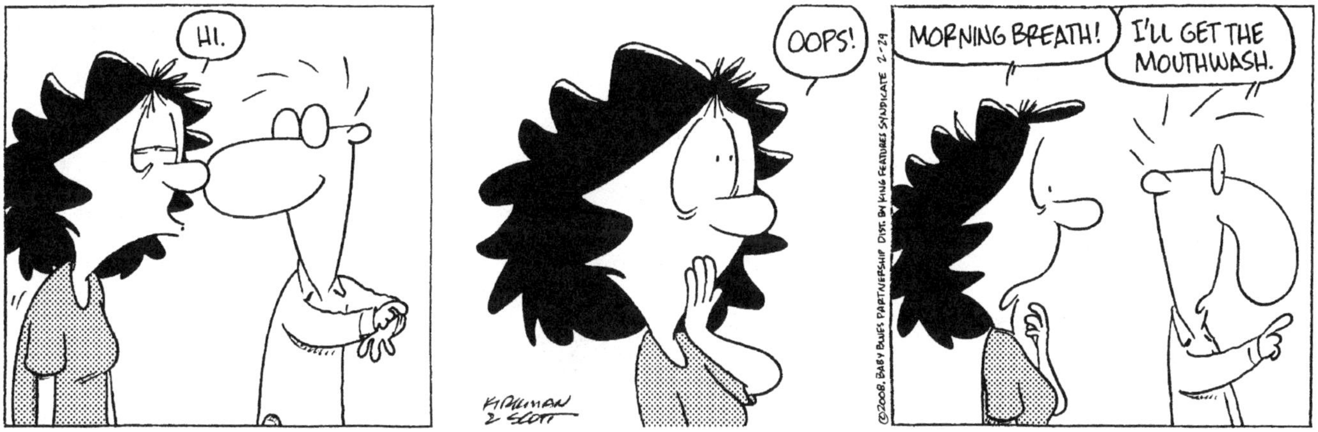
HI.
KIRKMAN & SCOTT
OOPS!
©2008, BABY BLUES PARTNERSHIP DIST. BY KING FEATURES SYNDICATE 2-29
MORNING BREATH!
I'LL GET THE MOUTHWASH.

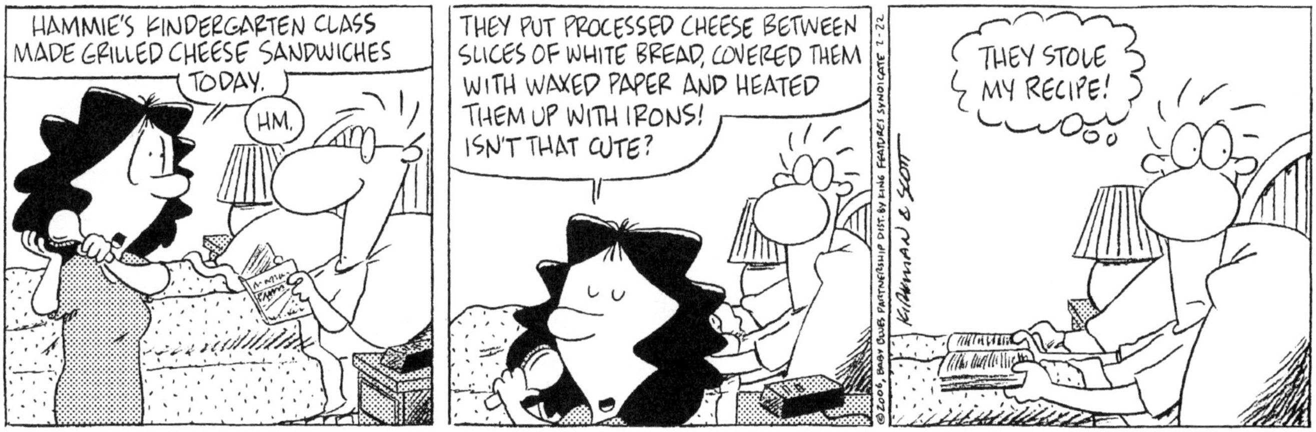
HAMMIE'S KINDERGARTEN CLASS MADE GRILLED CHEESE SANDWICHES TODAY.
HM.
THEY PUT PROCESSED CHEESE BETWEEN SLICES OF WHITE BREAD, COVERED THEM WITH WAXED PAPER AND HEATED THEM UP WITH IRONS! ISN'T THAT CUTE?
©2008, BABY BLUES PARTNERSHIP DIST. BY KING FEATURES SYNDICATE 2-22
KIRKMAN & SCOTT
THEY STOLE MY RECIPE!

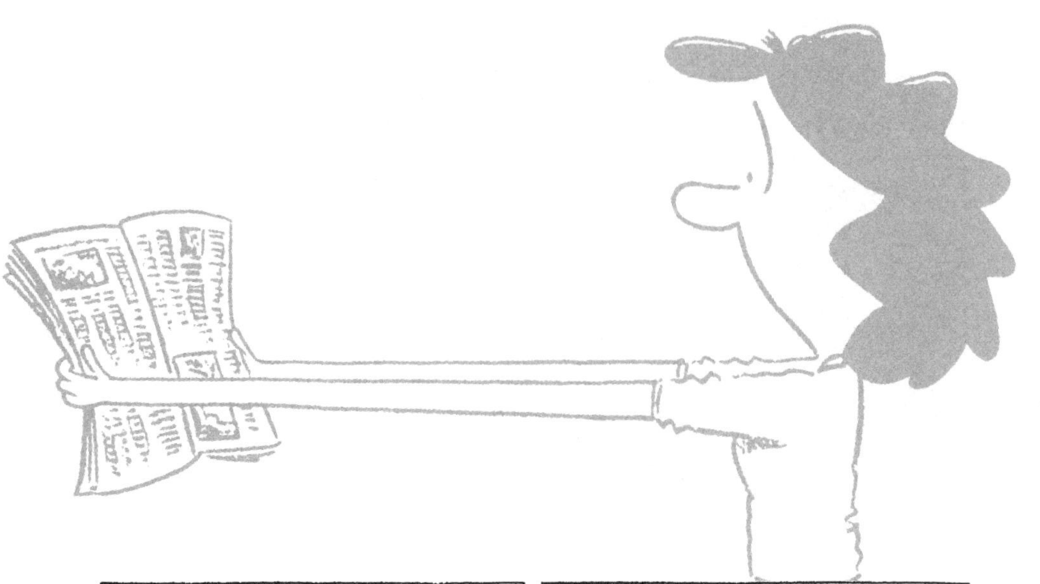

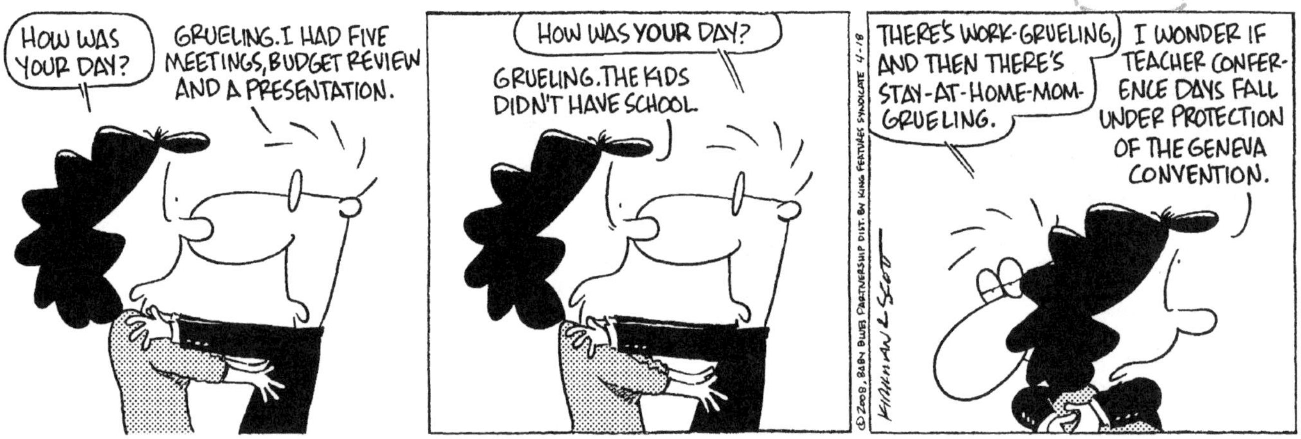

HOW WAS YOUR DAY?
GRUELING. I HAD FIVE MEETINGS, BUDGET REVIEW AND A PRESENTATION.
HOW WAS YOUR DAY?
GRUELING. THE KIDS DIDN'T HAVE SCHOOL.
© 2008, BABY BLUES PARTNERSHIP DIST. BY KING FEATURES SYNDICATE 4-18
KIRKMAN & SCOTT
THERE'S WORK-GRUELING, AND THEN THERE'S STAY-AT-HOME-MOM-GRUELING.
I WONDER IF TEACHER CONFERENCE DAYS FALL UNDER PROTECTION OF THE GENEVA CONVENTION.

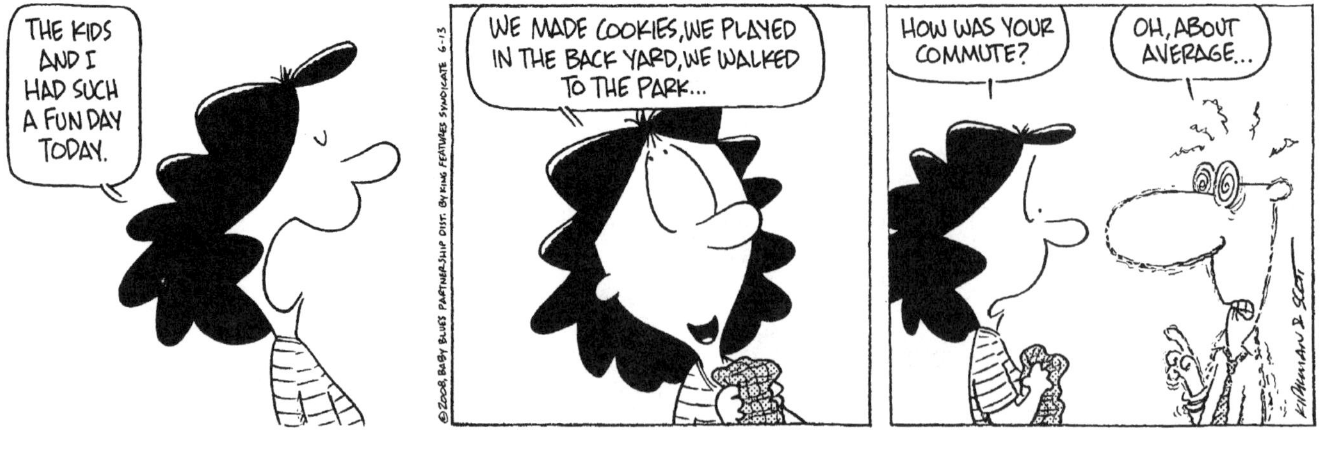

THE KIDS AND I HAD SUCH A FUN DAY TODAY.
© 2008, BABY BLUES PARTNERSHIP DIST. BY KING FEATURES SYNDICATE 6-13
WE MADE COOKIES, WE PLAYED IN THE BACK YARD, WE WALKED TO THE PARK...
HOW WAS YOUR COMMUTE?
OH, ABOUT AVERAGE...
KIRKMAN & SCOTT

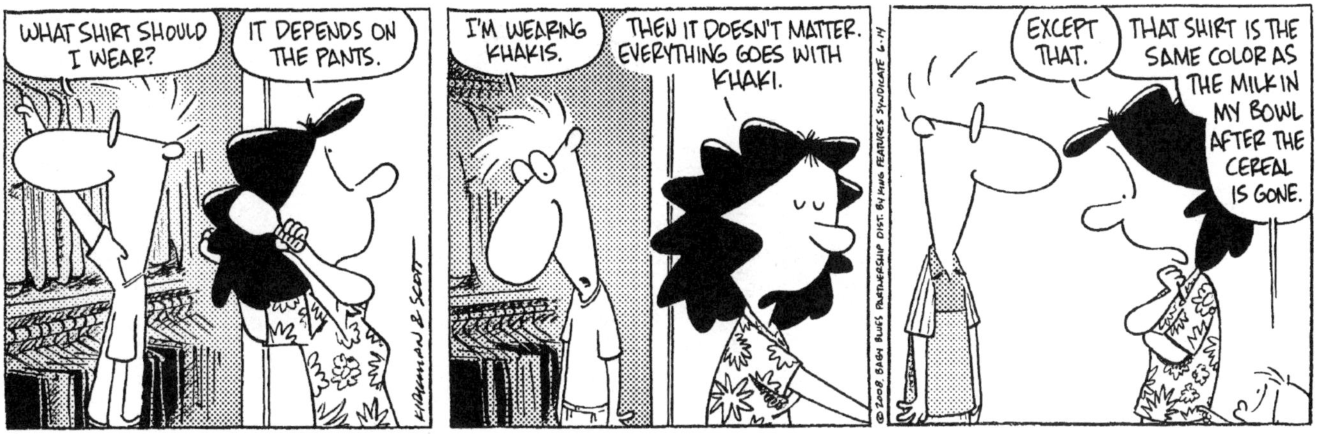
WHAT SHIRT SHOULD I WEAR?
IT DEPENDS ON THE PANTS.
KIRKMAN & SCOTT
I'M WEARING KHAKIS.
THEN IT DOESN'T MATTER. EVERYTHING GOES WITH KHAKI.
© 2008, BABY BLUES PARTNERSHIP DIST. BY KING FEATURES SYNDICATE 6-14
EXCEPT THAT.
THAT SHIRT IS THE SAME COLOR AS THE MILK IN MY BOWL AFTER THE CEREAL IS GONE.

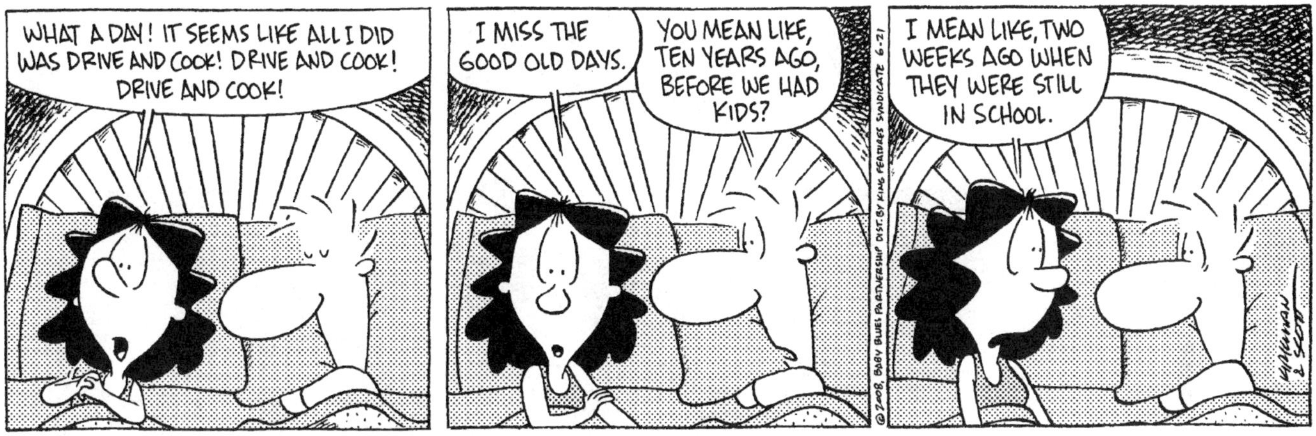
WHAT A DAY! IT SEEMS LIKE ALL I DID WAS DRIVE AND COOK! DRIVE AND COOK! DRIVE AND COOK!
I MISS THE GOOD OLD DAYS.
YOU MEAN LIKE, TEN YEARS AGO, BEFORE WE HAD KIDS?
© 2008, BABY BLUES PARTNERSHIP DIST. BY KING FEATURES SYNDICATE 6-21
I MEAN LIKE, TWO WEEKS AGO WHEN THEY WERE STILL IN SCHOOL.
KIRKMAN & SCOTT

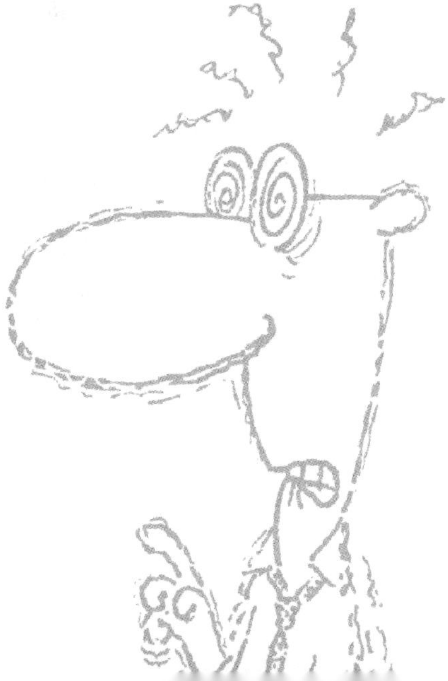

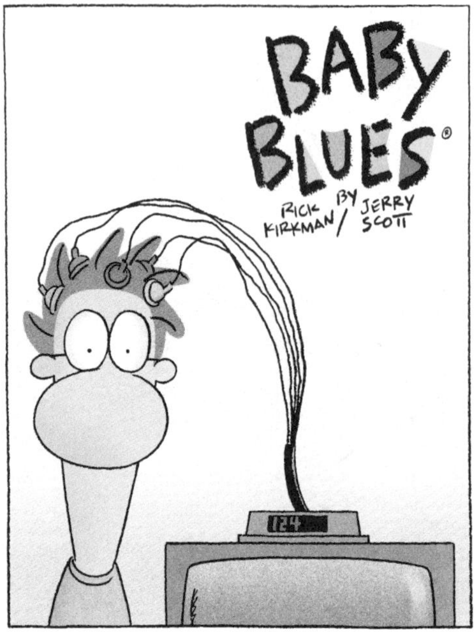
BABY BLUES®
RICK KIRKMAN / BY JERRY SCOTT
1:24

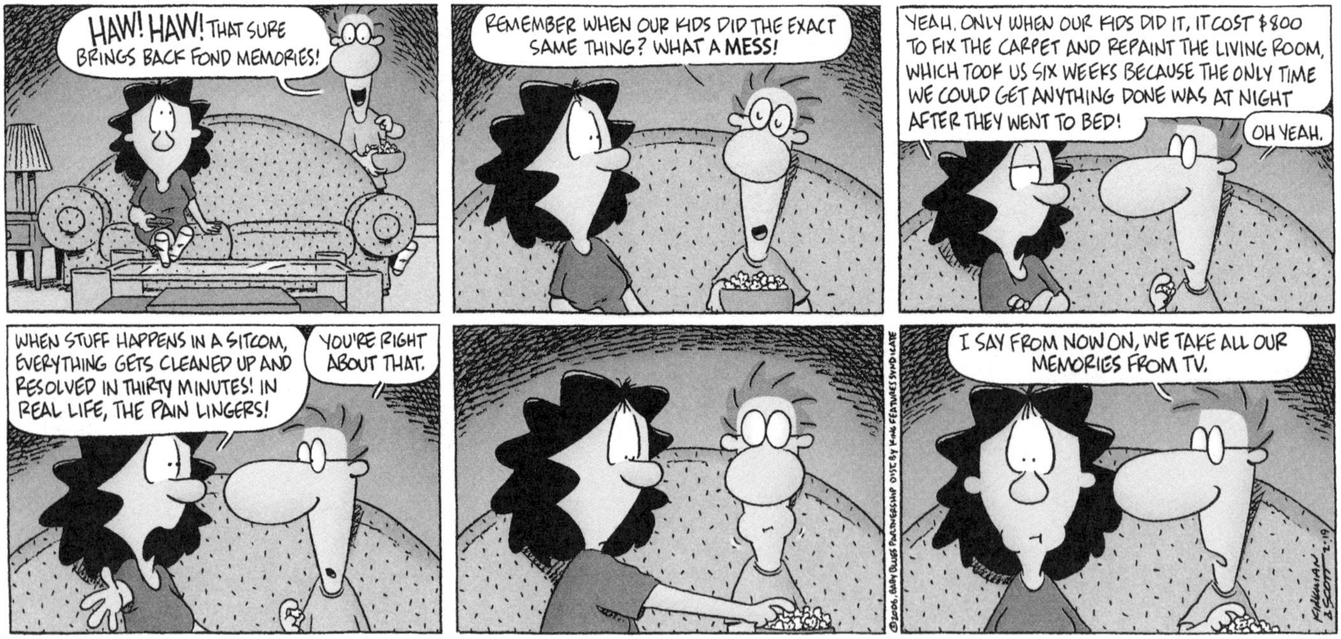
HAW! HAW! THAT SURE BRINGS BACK FOND MEMORIES!
REMEMBER WHEN OUR KIDS DID THE EXACT SAME THING? WHAT A MESS!
YEAH. ONLY WHEN OUR KIDS DID IT, IT COST $800 TO FIX THE CARPET AND REPAINT THE LIVING ROOM, WHICH TOOK US SIX WEEKS BECAUSE THE ONLY TIME WE COULD GET ANYTHING DONE WAS AT NIGHT AFTER THEY WENT TO BED!
OH YEAH.
WHEN STUFF HAPPENS IN A SITCOM, EVERYTHING GETS CLEANED UP AND RESOLVED IN THIRTY MINUTES! IN REAL LIFE, THE PAIN LINGERS!
YOU'RE RIGHT ABOUT THAT.
©2006, BABY BLUES PARTNERSHIP DIST. BY KING FEATURES SYNDICATE
I SAY FROM NOW ON, WE TAKE ALL OUR MEMORIES FROM TV.
KIRKMAN & SCOTT

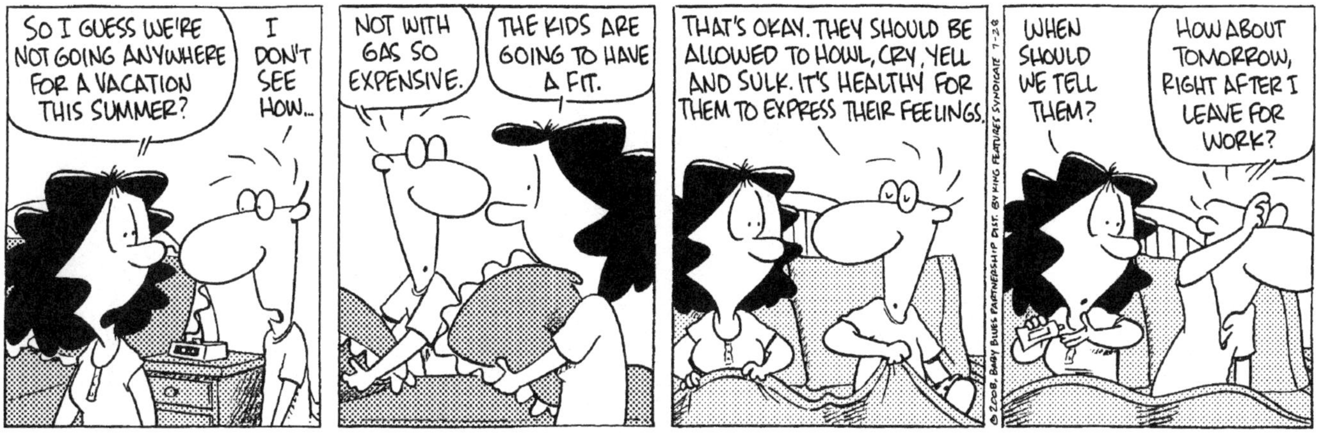
SO I GUESS WE'RE NOT GOING ANYWHERE FOR A VACATION THIS SUMMER?
I DON'T SEE HOW...
NOT WITH GAS SO EXPENSIVE.
THE KIDS ARE GOING TO HAVE A FIT.
THAT'S OKAY. THEY SHOULD BE ALLOWED TO HOWL, CRY, YELL AND SULK. IT'S HEALTHY FOR THEM TO EXPRESS THEIR FEELINGS.
© 2008, BABY BLUES PARTNERSHIP DIST. BY KING FEATURES SYNDICATE 7-28
WHEN SHOULD WE TELL THEM?
HOW ABOUT TOMORROW, RIGHT AFTER I LEAVE FOR WORK?

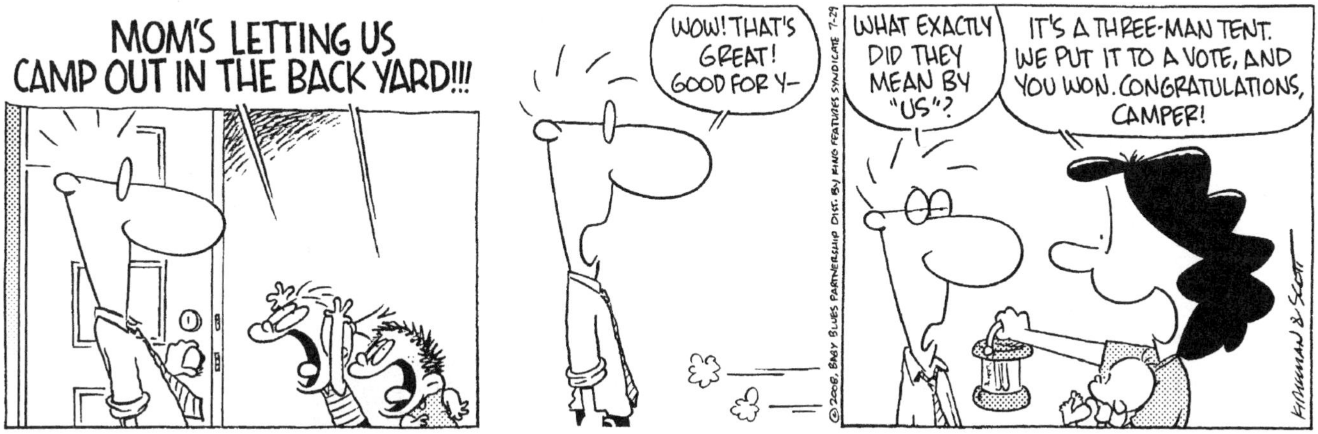
MOM'S LETTING US CAMP OUT IN THE BACK YARD!!!
WOW! THAT'S GREAT! GOOD FOR Y-
© 2008, BABY BLUES PARTNERSHIP DIST. BY KING FEATURES SYNDICATE 7-29
WHAT EXACTLY DID THEY MEAN BY "US"?
IT'S A THREE-MAN TENT. WE PUT IT TO A VOTE, AND YOU WON. CONGRATULATIONS, CAMPER!
KIRKMAN & SCOTT

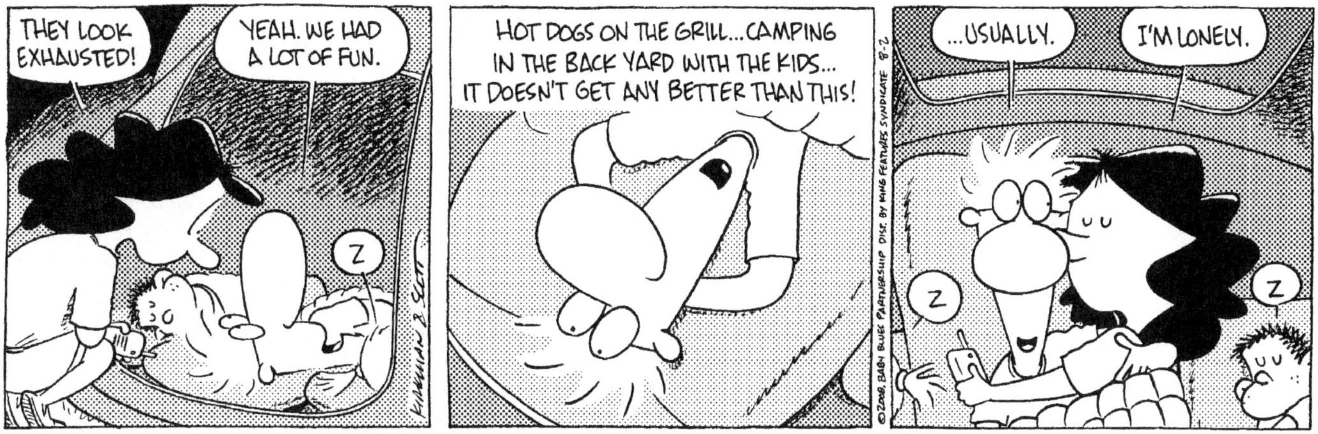
THEY LOOK EXHAUSTED!
YEAH. WE HAD A LOT OF FUN.
Z
KIRKMAN & SCOTT
HOT DOGS ON THE GRILL... CAMPING IN THE BACK YARD WITH THE KIDS... IT DOESN'T GET ANY BETTER THAN THIS!
© 2008, BABY BLUES PARTNERSHIP DIST. BY KING FEATURES SYNDICATE 8-2
...USUALLY.
I'M LONELY.
Z
Z

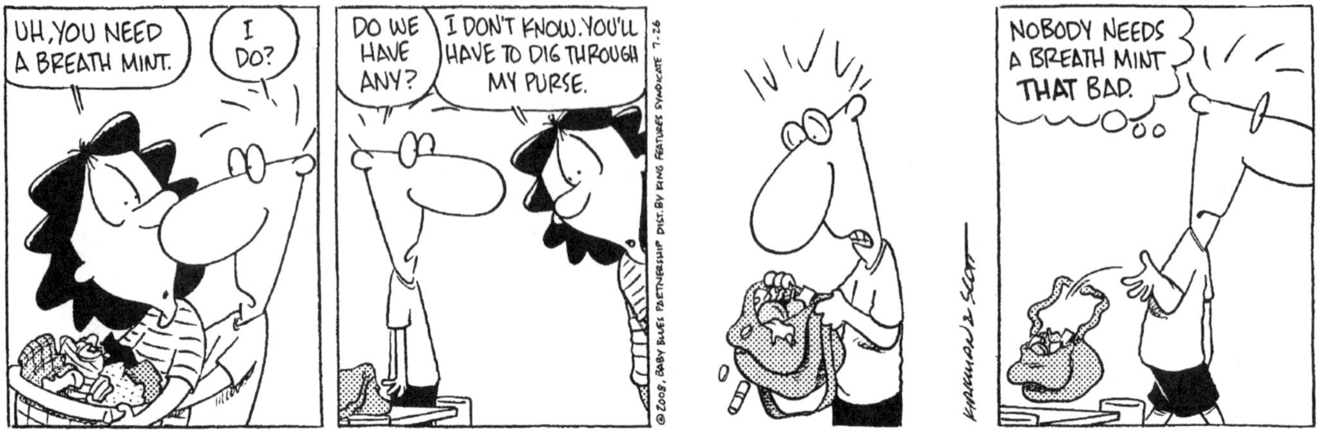
UH, YOU NEED A BREATH MINT.
I DO?
DO WE HAVE ANY?
I DON'T KNOW. YOU'LL HAVE TO DIG THROUGH MY PURSE.
NOBODY NEEDS A BREATH MINT THAT BAD.

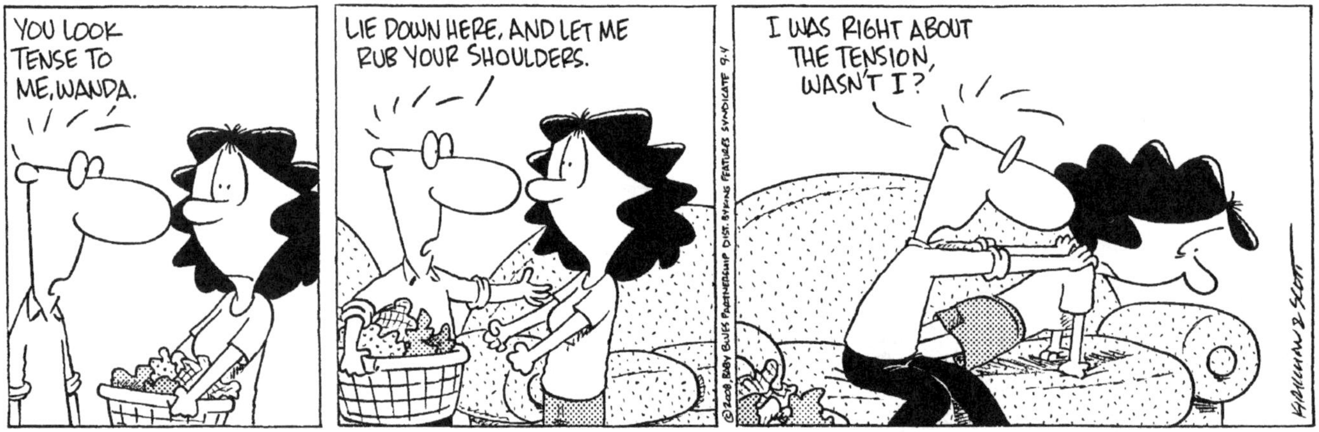
YOU LOOK TENSE TO ME, WANDA.
LIE DOWN HERE, AND LET ME RUB YOUR SHOULDERS.
I WAS RIGHT ABOUT THE TENSION, WASN'T I?

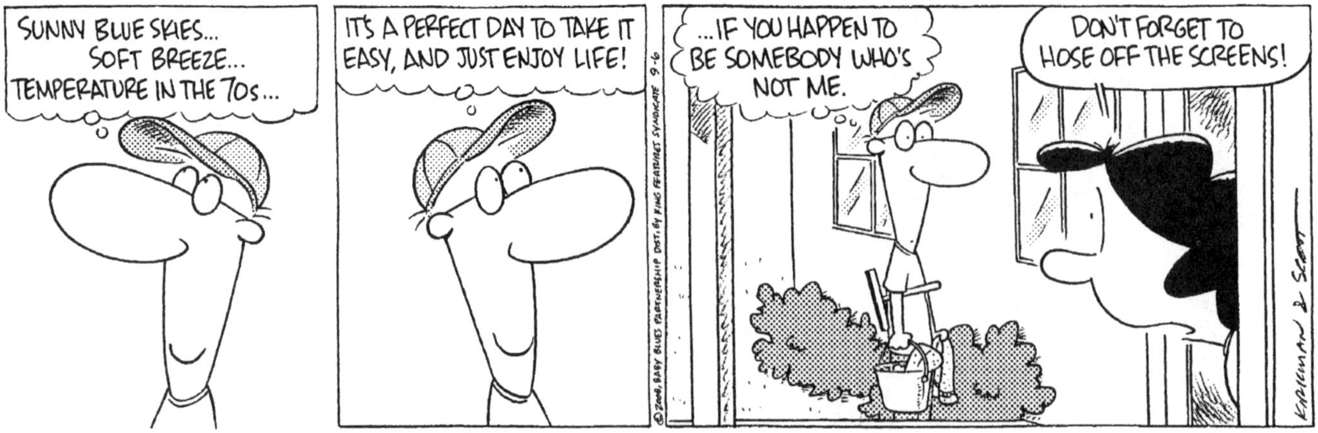
SUNNY BLUE SKIES... SOFT BREEZE... TEMPERATURE IN THE 70s...
IT'S A PERFECT DAY TO TAKE IT EASY, AND JUST ENJOY LIFE!
...IF YOU HAPPEN TO BE SOMEBODY WHO'S NOT ME.
DON'T FORGET TO HOSE OFF THE SCREENS!

BABY BLUES®
BY RICK KIRKMAN / JERRY SCOTT

SO, YOU'LL TAKE ZOE AND HAMMIE TO THE STORE AND PICK UP THESE THREE THINGS. RIGHT.

HAVE THE FIRST ONE GIFT-WRAPPED, THEN DROP OFF IT AND HAMMIE AT THE ADDRESS AT THE BOTTOM. OKAY.

THEN CIRCLE BACK HERE, AND I'LL WRAP THE SECOND ITEM WHILE YOU CHANGE WREN'S CLOTHES. UH-HUH.

AT THAT POINT, IT'LL BE TIME TO WALK ZOE OVER TO KEESHA'S WITH WRAPPED ITEM #2. GOTCHA.

BY THE TIME YOU GET BACK, WREN AND I WILL BE AT PHOEBE'S PARTY. YOU'LL HAVE TO PICK UP HAMMIE BY FOUR. YEAH.

MAKE SURE HAMMIE SAYS THANK YOU, AND I'LL MEET YOU BACK HERE AT 4:30 SO WE CAN ALL GO PICK UP ZOE TOGETHER. ANY QUESTIONS? NO.

I BET NAPOLEON NEVER DID THIS MUCH STRATEGIZING. YEAH, WELL, NAPOLEON DIDN'T HAVE THREE KIDS WITH THREE DIFFERENT BIRTHDAY PARTIES ON THE SAME DAY, EITHER.

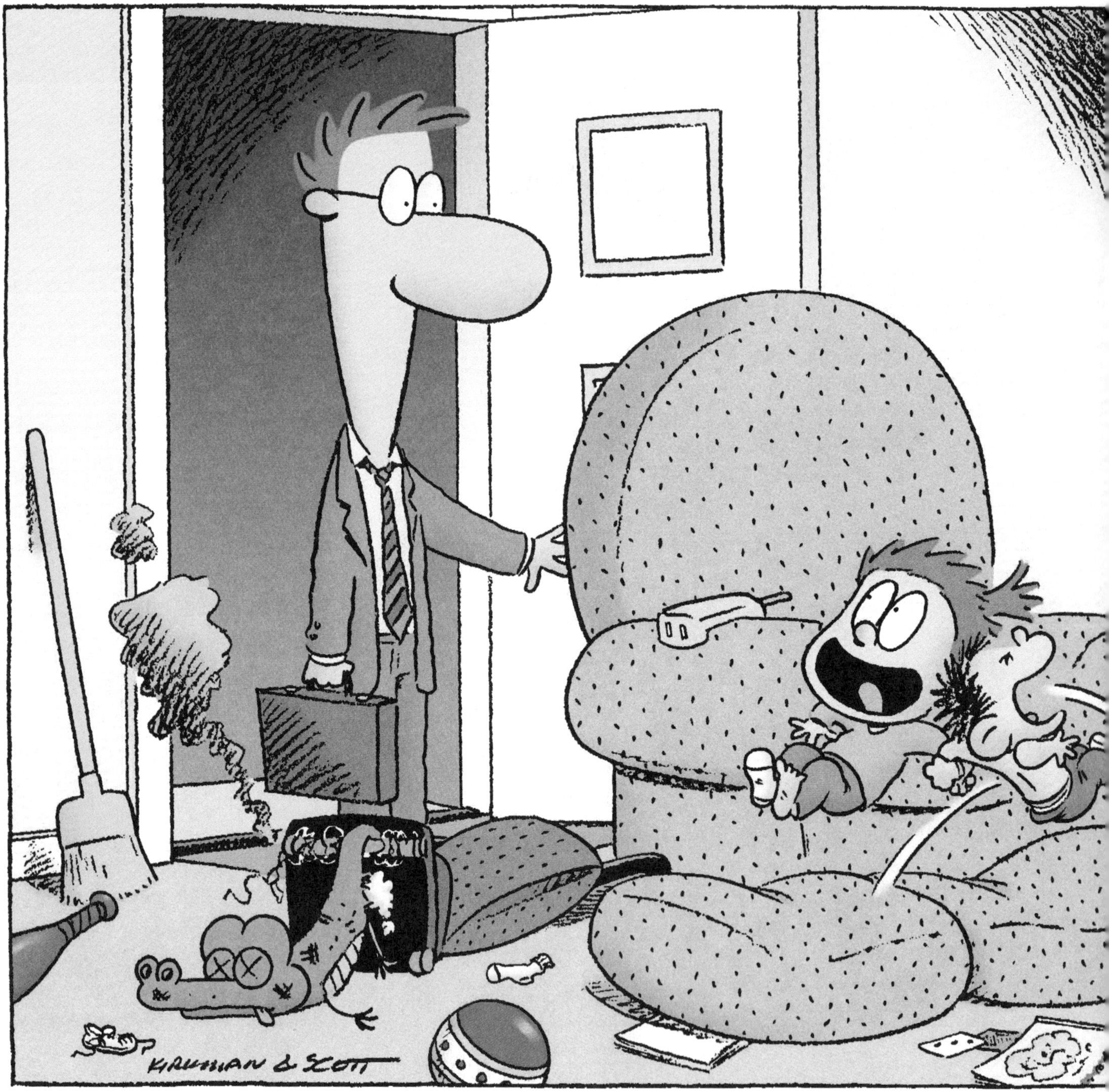
KIRKMAN & SCOTT

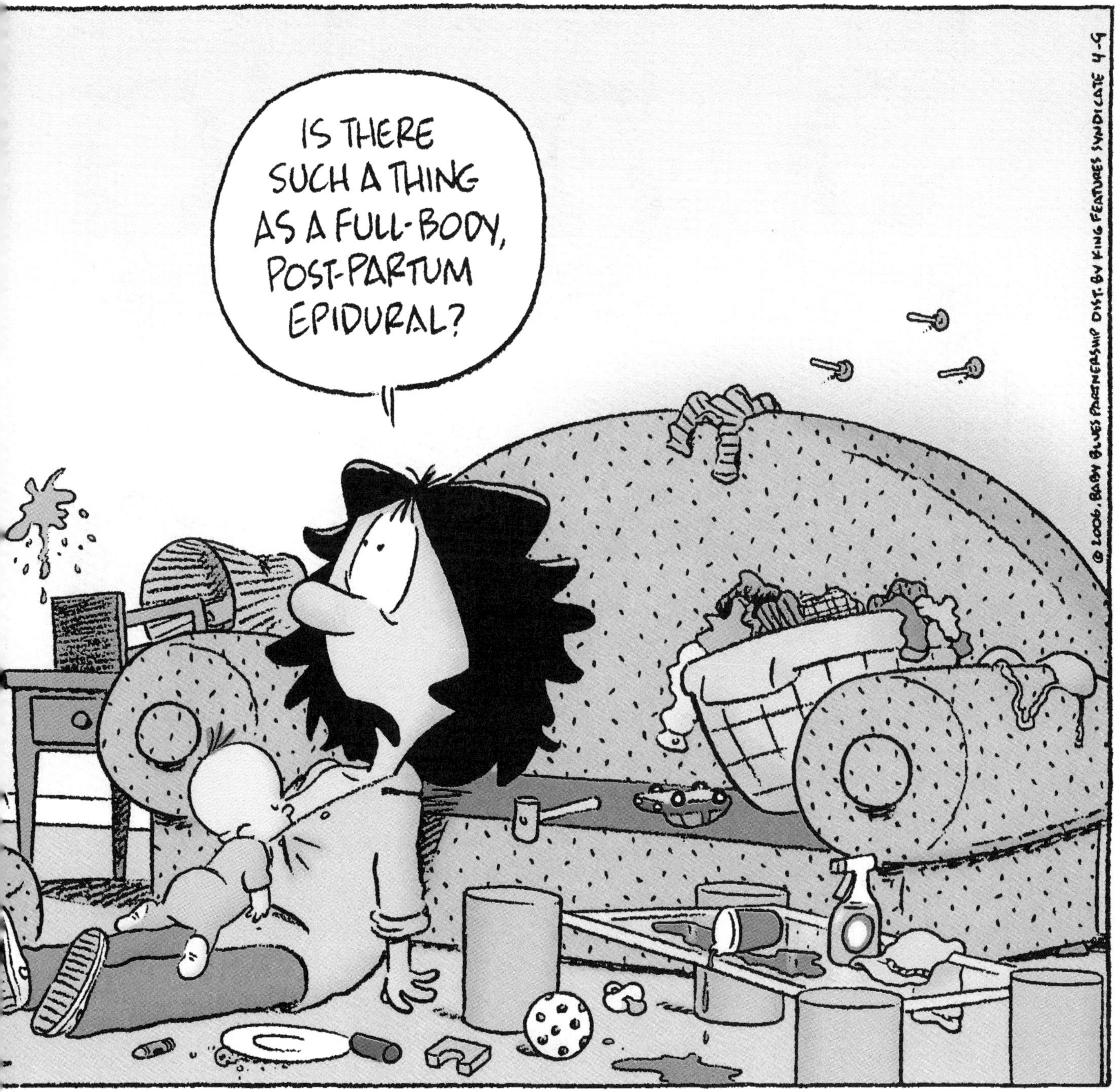
IS THERE SUCH A THING AS A FULL-BODY, POST-PARTUM EPIDURAL?
© 2006, BABY BLUES PARTNERSHIP DIST. BY KING FEATURES SYNDICATE 4-9

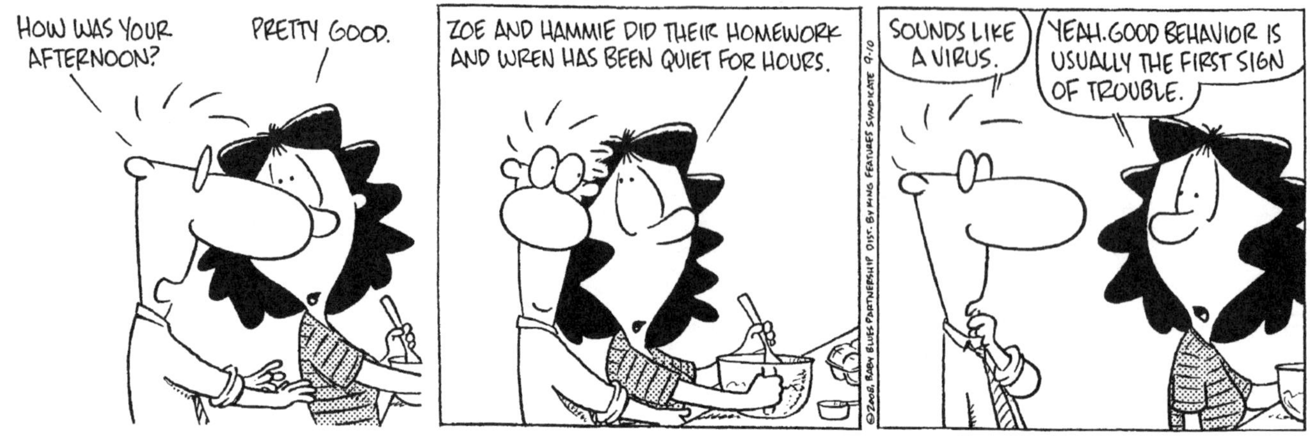
HOW WAS YOUR AFTERNOON?
PRETTY GOOD.
ZOE AND HAMMIE DID THEIR HOMEWORK AND WREN HAS BEEN QUIET FOR HOURS.
©2008, BABY BLUES PARTNERSHIP DIST. BY KING FEATURES SYNDICATE 9-10
SOUNDS LIKE A VIRUS.
YEAH. GOOD BEHAVIOR IS USUALLY THE FIRST SIGN OF TROUBLE.

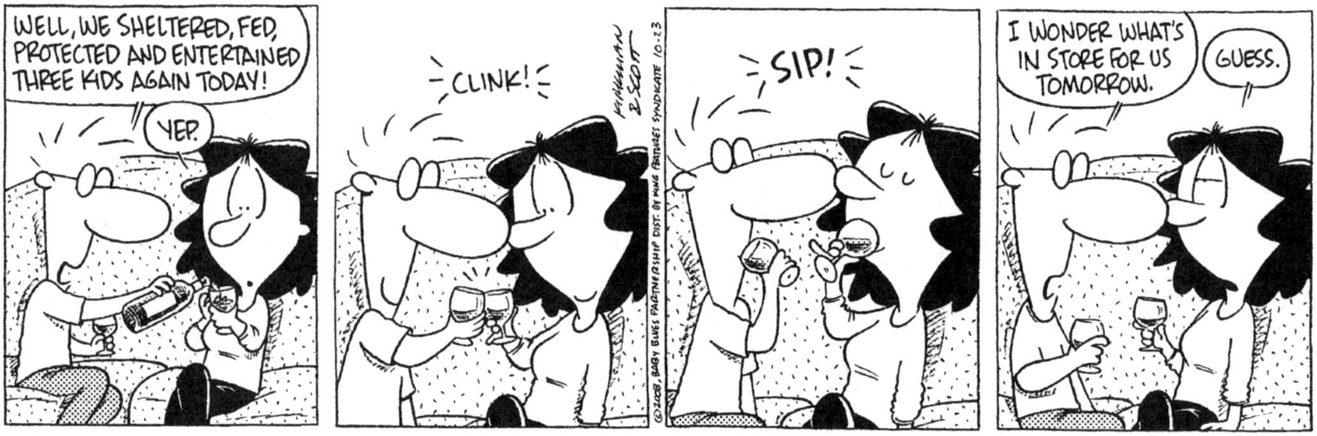
WELL, WE SHELTERED, FED, PROTECTED AND ENTERTAINED THREE KIDS AGAIN TODAY!
YEP.
CLINK!
KIRKMAN & SCOTT
©2008, BABY BLUES PARTNERSHIP DIST. BY KING FEATURES SYNDICATE 10-23
SIP!
I WONDER WHAT'S IN STORE FOR US TOMORROW.
GUESS.

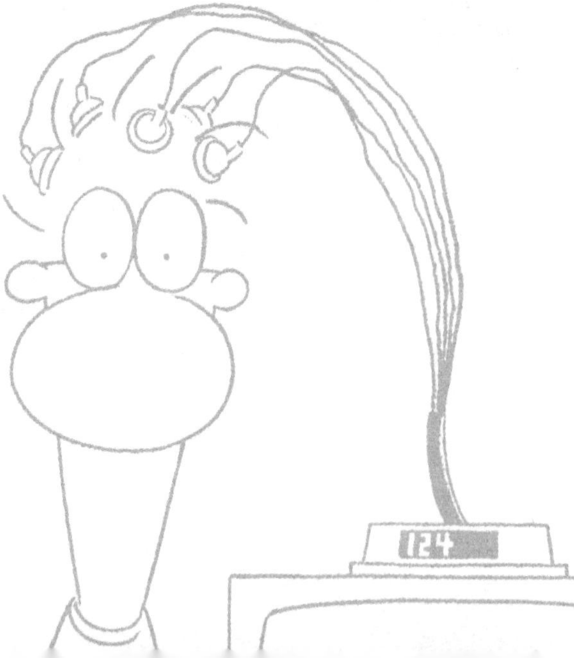
124

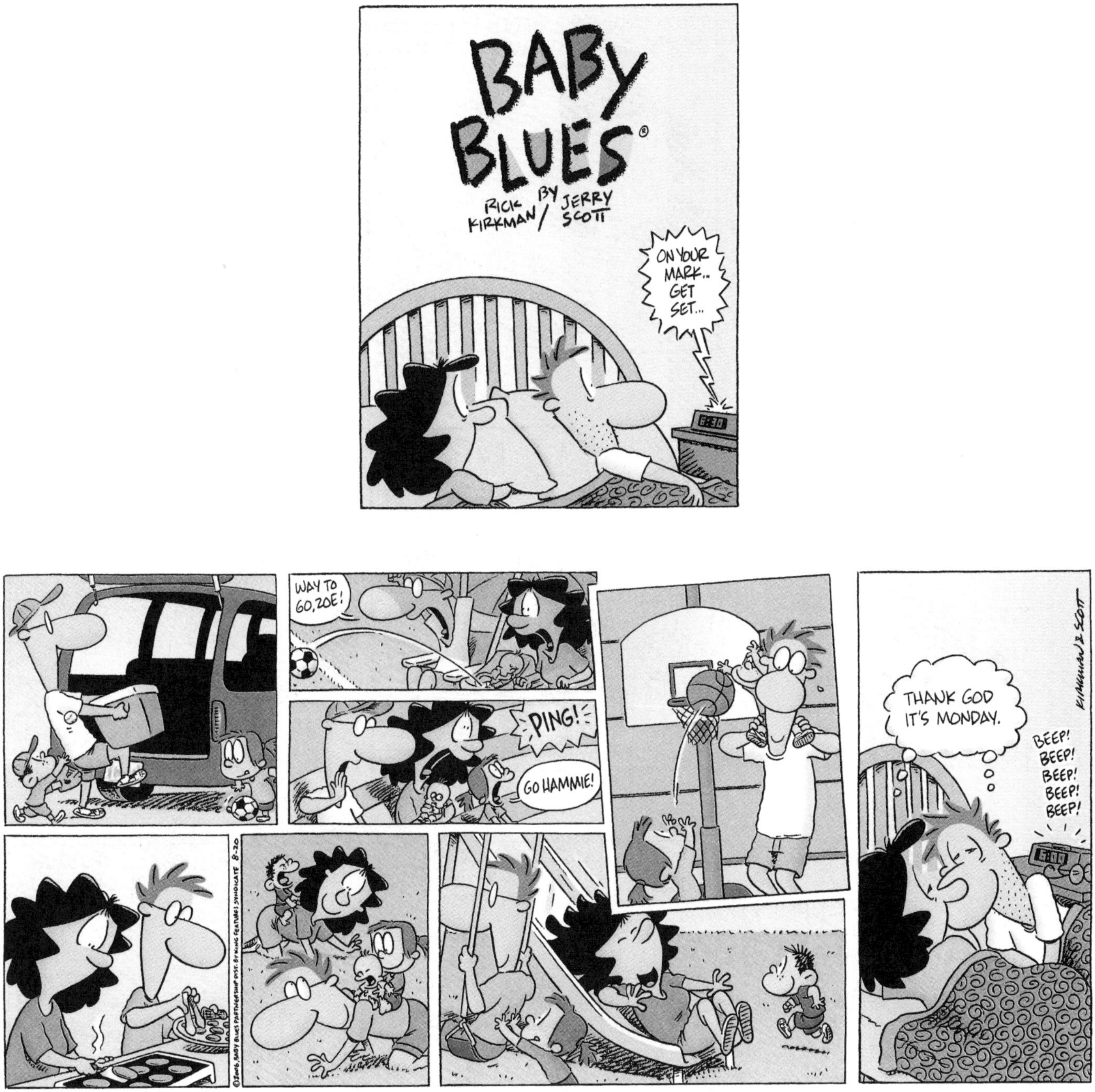
BABY BLUES®
BY RICK KIRKMAN / JERRY SCOTT
ON YOUR MARK.. GET SET...
WAY TO GO, ZOE!
PING!
GO HAMMIE!
©2006, BABY BLUES PARTNERSHIP DIST. BY KING FEATURES SYNDICATE 8-20
KIRKMAN & SCOTT
THANK GOD IT'S MONDAY.
BEEP! BEEP! BEEP! BEEP! BEEP!

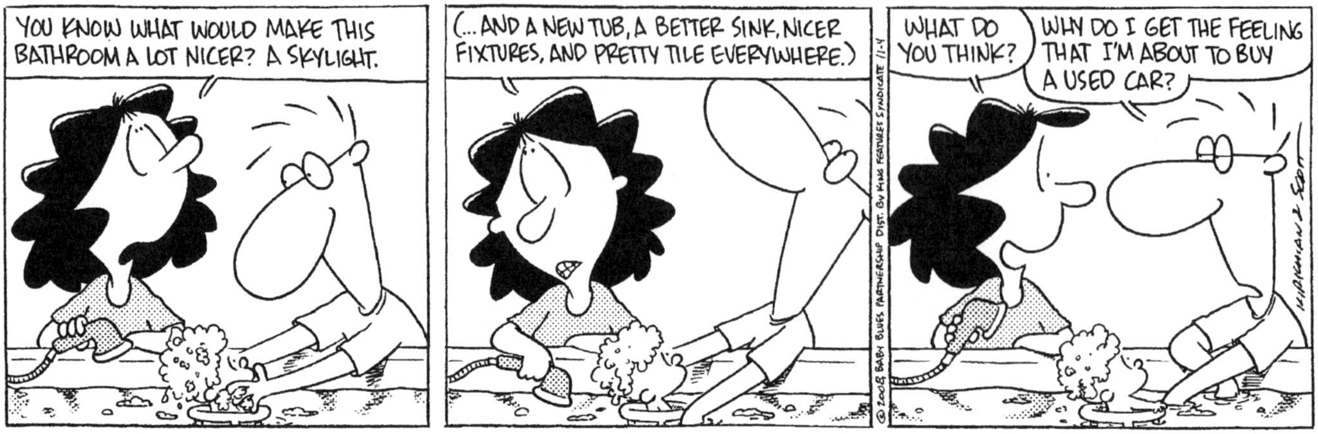
YOU KNOW WHAT WOULD MAKE THIS BATHROOM A LOT NICER? A SKYLIGHT.
(...AND A NEW TUB, A BETTER SINK, NICER FIXTURES, AND PRETTY TILE EVERYWHERE.)
© 2008 BABY BLUES PARTNERSHIP DIST. BY KING FEATURES SYNDICATE 11-4
WHAT DO YOU THINK?
WHY DO I GET THE FEELING THAT I'M ABOUT TO BUY A USED CAR?
KIRKMAN & SCOTT

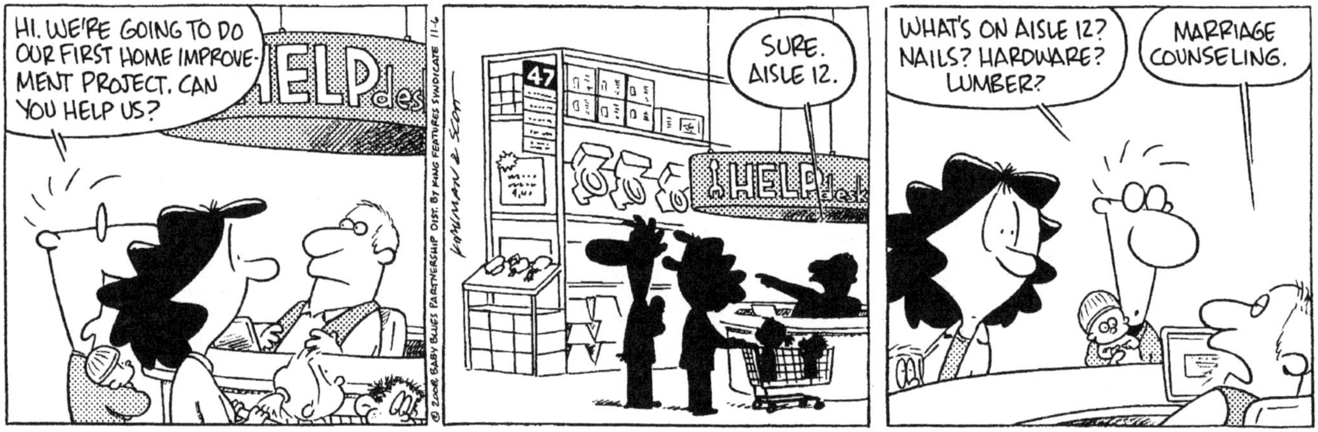
HI. WE'RE GOING TO DO OUR FIRST HOME IMPROVEMENT PROJECT. CAN YOU HELP US?
HELP des
© 2008 BABY BLUES PARTNERSHIP DIST. BY KING FEATURES SYNDICATE 11-6
KIRKMAN & SCOTT
47
SURE. AISLE 12.
HELP desk
WHAT'S ON AISLE 12? NAILS? HARDWARE? LUMBER?
MARRIAGE COUNSELING.

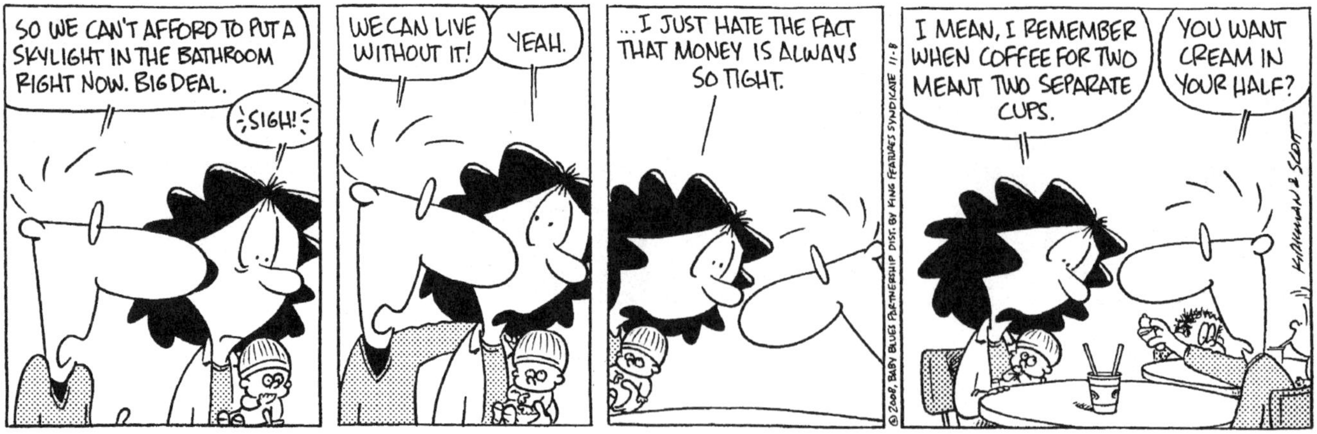
SO WE CAN'T AFFORD TO PUT A SKYLIGHT IN THE BATHROOM RIGHT NOW. BIG DEAL.
SIGH!
WE CAN LIVE WITHOUT IT!
YEAH.
...I JUST HATE THE FACT THAT MONEY IS ALWAYS SO TIGHT.
© 2008, BABY BLUES PARTNERSHIP DIST. BY KING FEATURES SYNDICATE 11-8
I MEAN, I REMEMBER WHEN COFFEE FOR TWO MEANT TWO SEPARATE CUPS.
YOU WANT CREAM IN YOUR HALF?
KIRKMAN & SCOTT

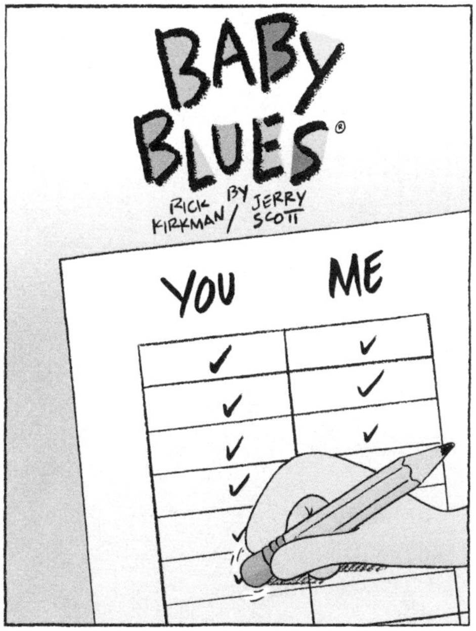

BABY BLUES®
BY RICK KIRKMAN / JERRY SCOTT
YOU
ME

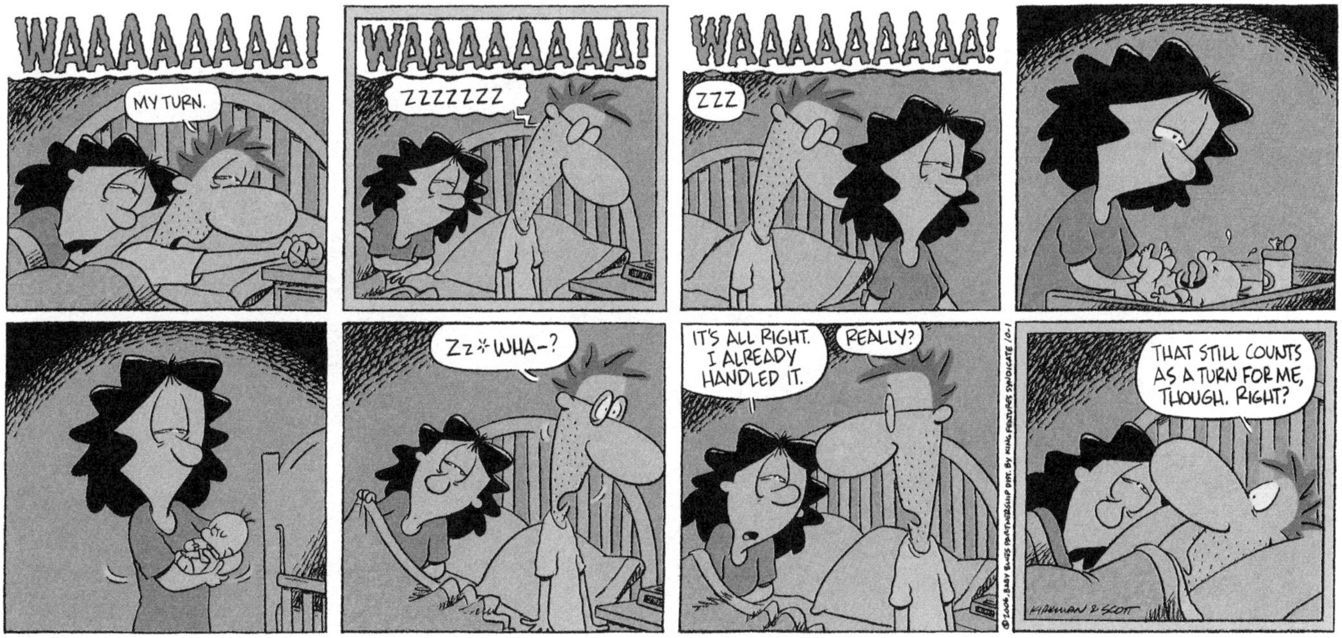

WAAAAAAAA!
MY TURN.
WAAAAAAAAA!
ZZZZZZZ
WAAAAAAAAA!
ZZZ
Zz✳WHA-?
IT'S ALL RIGHT. I ALREADY HANDLED IT.
REALLY?
THAT STILL COUNTS AS A TURN FOR ME, THOUGH. RIGHT?
© 2006, BABY BLUES PARTNERSHIP DIST. BY KING FEATURES SYNDICATE 10-1
KIRKMAN & SCOTT

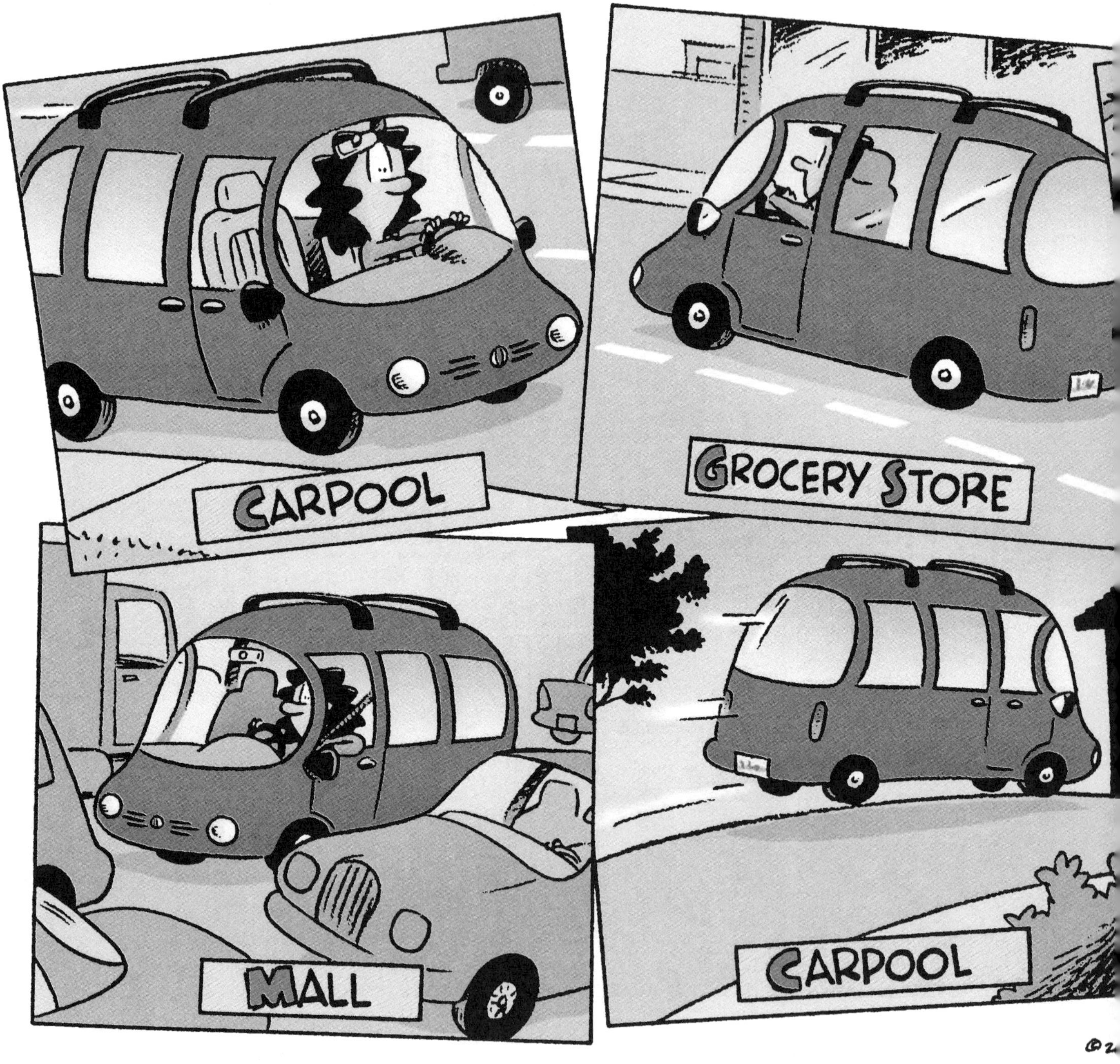
CARPOOL
GROCERY STORE
MALL
CARPOOL

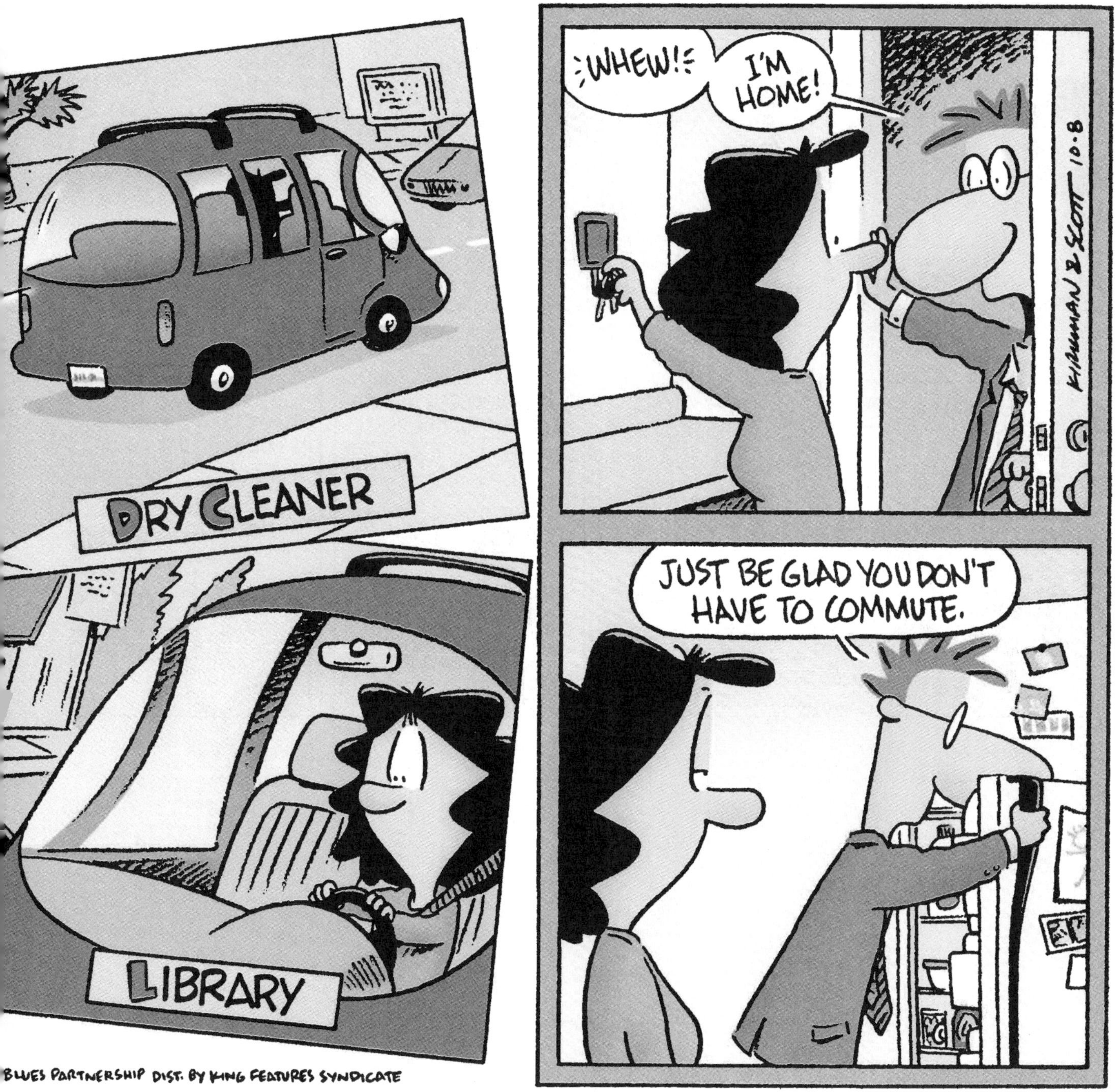
DRY CLEANER
LIBRARY
WHEW!
I'M HOME!
KIRKMAN & SCOTT 10-8
JUST BE GLAD YOU DON'T HAVE TO COMMUTE.
BLUES PARTNERSHIP DIST. BY KING FEATURES SYNDICATE

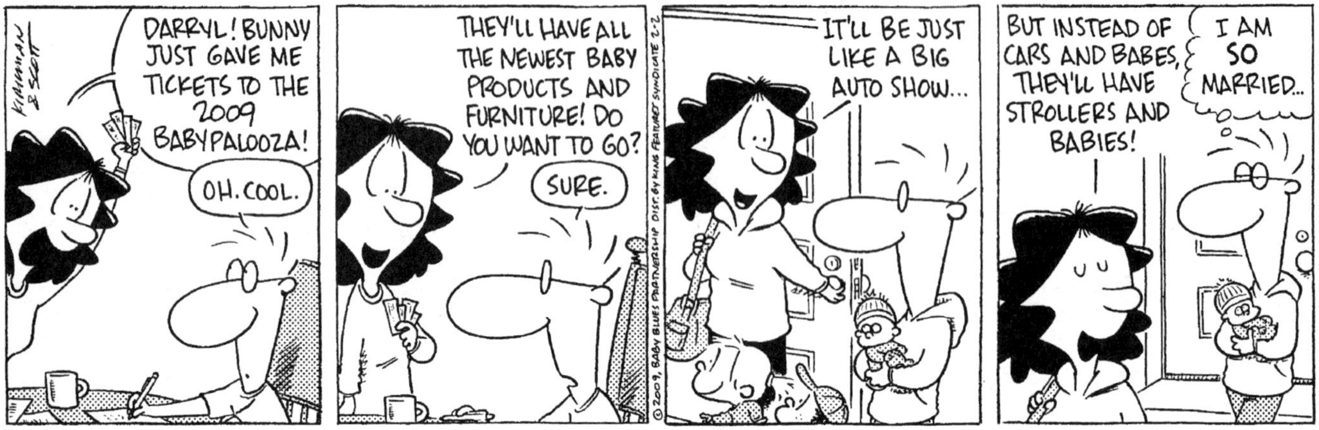
KIRKMAN & SCOTT
DARRYL! BUNNY JUST GAVE ME TICKETS TO THE 2009 BABYPALOOZA!
OH. COOL.
THEY'LL HAVE ALL THE NEWEST BABY PRODUCTS AND FURNITURE! DO YOU WANT TO GO?
SURE.
© 2009, BABY BLUES PARTNERSHIP DIST. BY KING FEATURES SYNDICATE 2-2
IT'LL BE JUST LIKE A BIG AUTO SHOW...
BUT INSTEAD OF CARS AND BABES, THEY'LL HAVE STROLLERS AND BABIES!
I AM SO MARRIED...

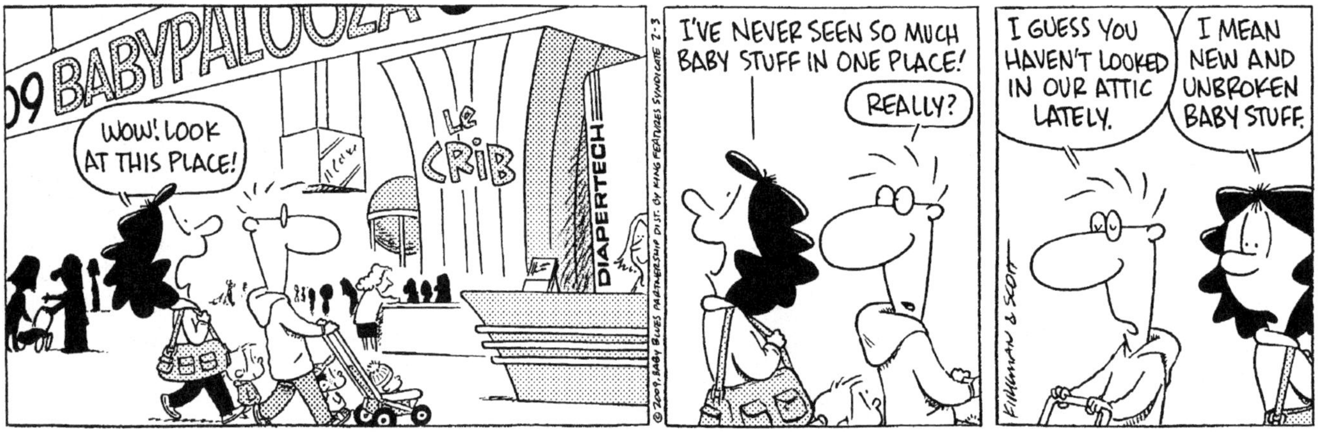
09 BABYPALOOZA
WOW! LOOK AT THIS PLACE!
LE CRIB
DIAPERTECH
© 2009, BABY BLUES PARTNERSHIP DIST. BY KING FEATURES SYNDICATE 2-3
I'VE NEVER SEEN SO MUCH BABY STUFF IN ONE PLACE!
REALLY?
I GUESS YOU HAVEN'T LOOKED IN OUR ATTIC LATELY.
I MEAN NEW AND UNBROKEN BABY STUFF.
KIRKMAN & SCOTT

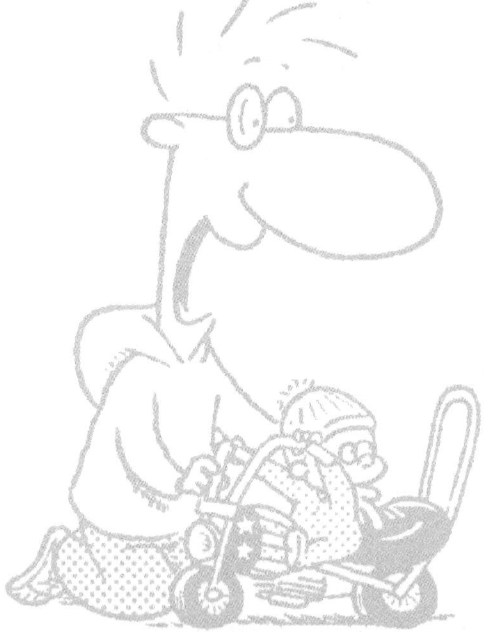

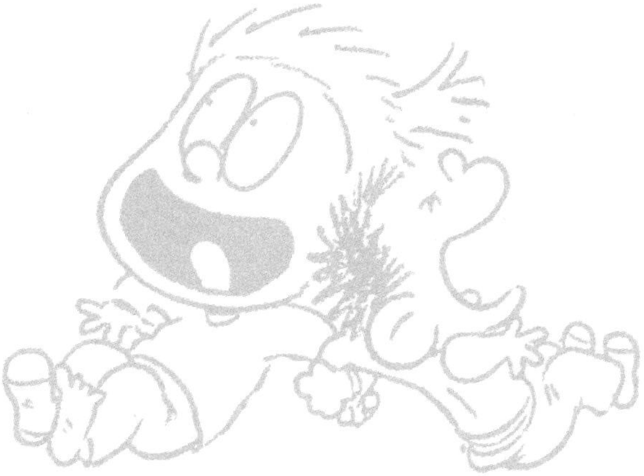

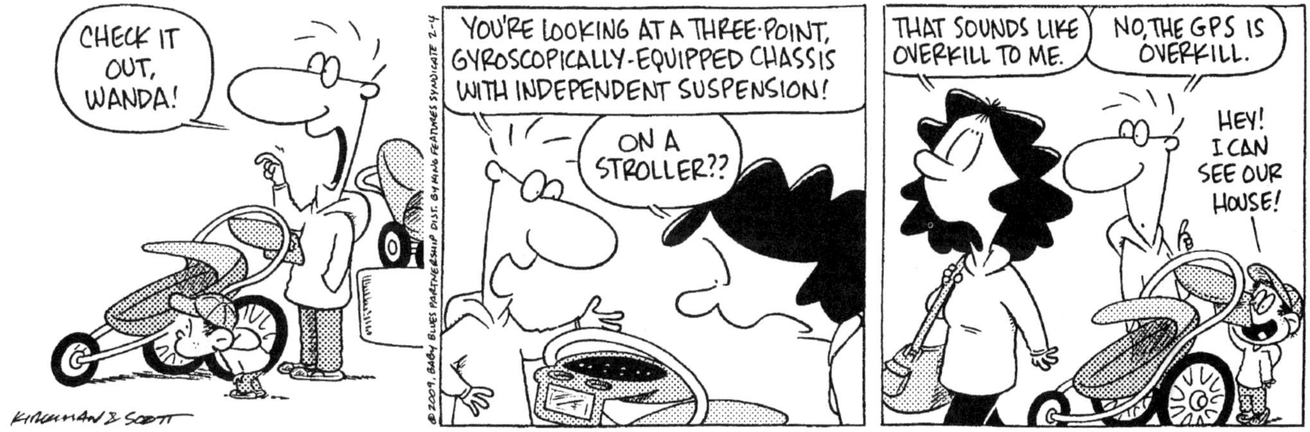

CHECK IT OUT, WANDA!
KIRKMAN & SCOTT
© 2009, BABY BLUES PARTNERSHIP DIST. BY KING FEATURES SYNDICATE 2-4
YOU'RE LOOKING AT A THREE-POINT, GYROSCOPICALLY-EQUIPPED CHASSIS WITH INDEPENDENT SUSPENSION!
ON A STROLLER??
THAT SOUNDS LIKE OVERKILL TO ME.
NO, THE GPS IS OVERKILL.
HEY! I CAN SEE OUR HOUSE!

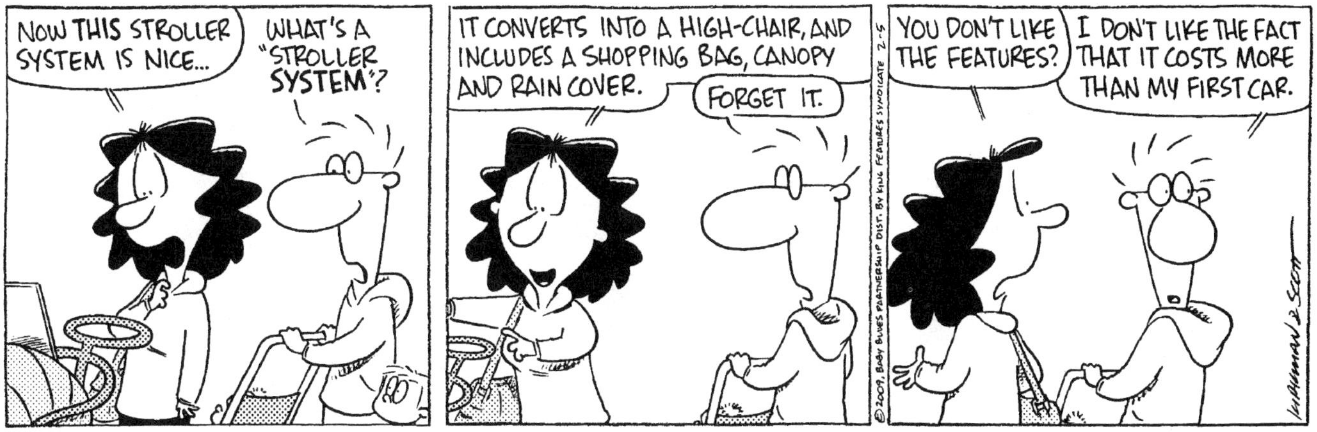

NOW THIS STROLLER SYSTEM IS NICE...
WHAT'S A "STROLLER SYSTEM"?
IT CONVERTS INTO A HIGH-CHAIR, AND INCLUDES A SHOPPING BAG, CANOPY AND RAIN COVER.
FORGET IT.
© 2009, BABY BLUES PARTNERSHIP DIST. BY KING FEATURES SYNDICATE 2-5
YOU DON'T LIKE THE FEATURES?
I DON'T LIKE THE FACT THAT IT COSTS MORE THAN MY FIRST CAR.
KIRKMAN & SCOTT

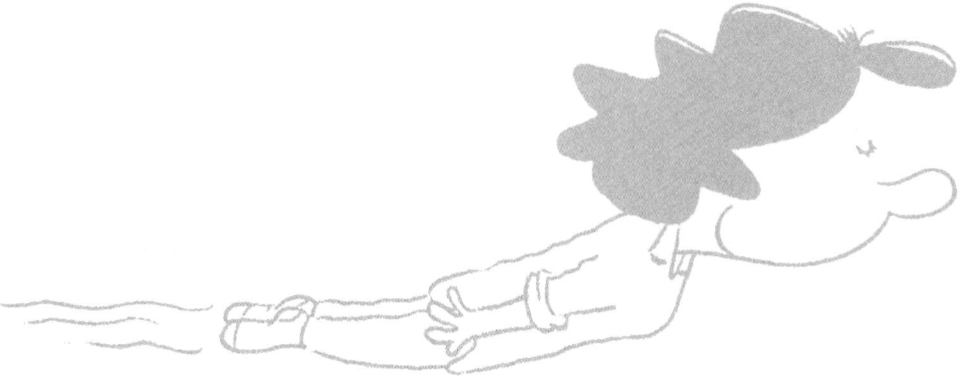

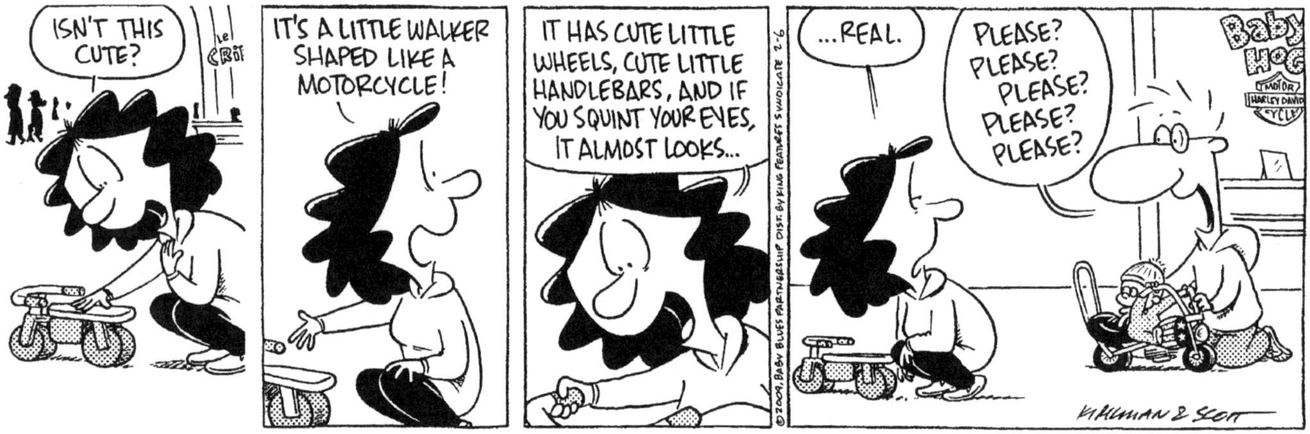

ISN'T THIS CUTE?
IT'S A LITTLE WALKER SHAPED LIKE A MOTORCYCLE!
IT HAS CUTE LITTLE WHEELS, CUTE LITTLE HANDLEBARS, AND IF YOU SQUINT YOUR EYES, IT ALMOST LOOKS...
...REAL.
PLEASE? PLEASE? PLEASE? PLEASE? PLEASE?
Baby HOG
KIRKMAN & SCOTT

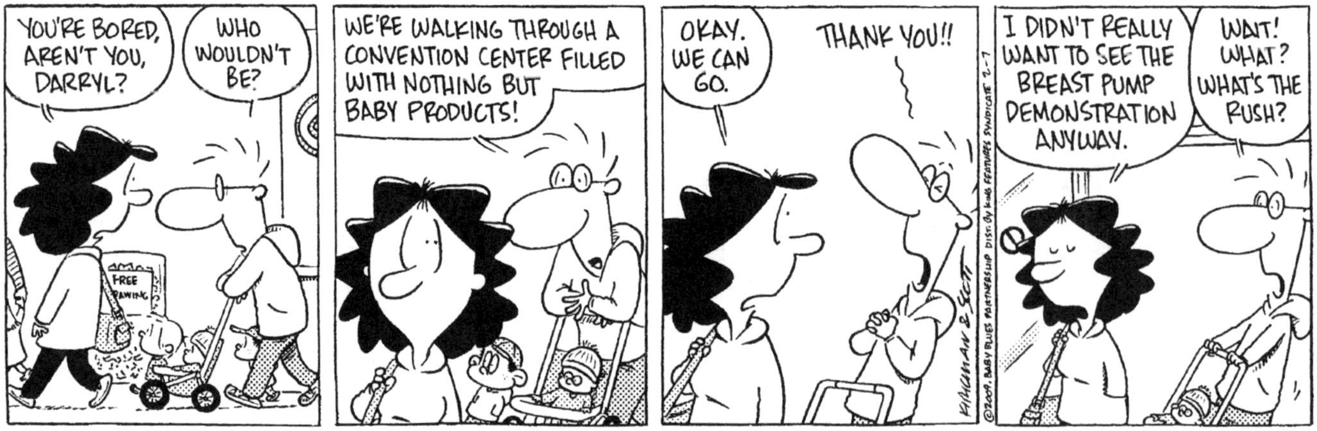

YOU'RE BORED, AREN'T YOU, DARRYL?
WHO WOULDN'T BE?
WE'RE WALKING THROUGH A CONVENTION CENTER FILLED WITH NOTHING BUT BABY PRODUCTS!
OKAY. WE CAN GO.
THANK YOU!!
I DIDN'T REALLY WANT TO SEE THE BREAST PUMP DEMONSTRATION ANYWAY.
WAIT! WHAT? WHAT'S THE RUSH?
KIRKMAN & SCOTT

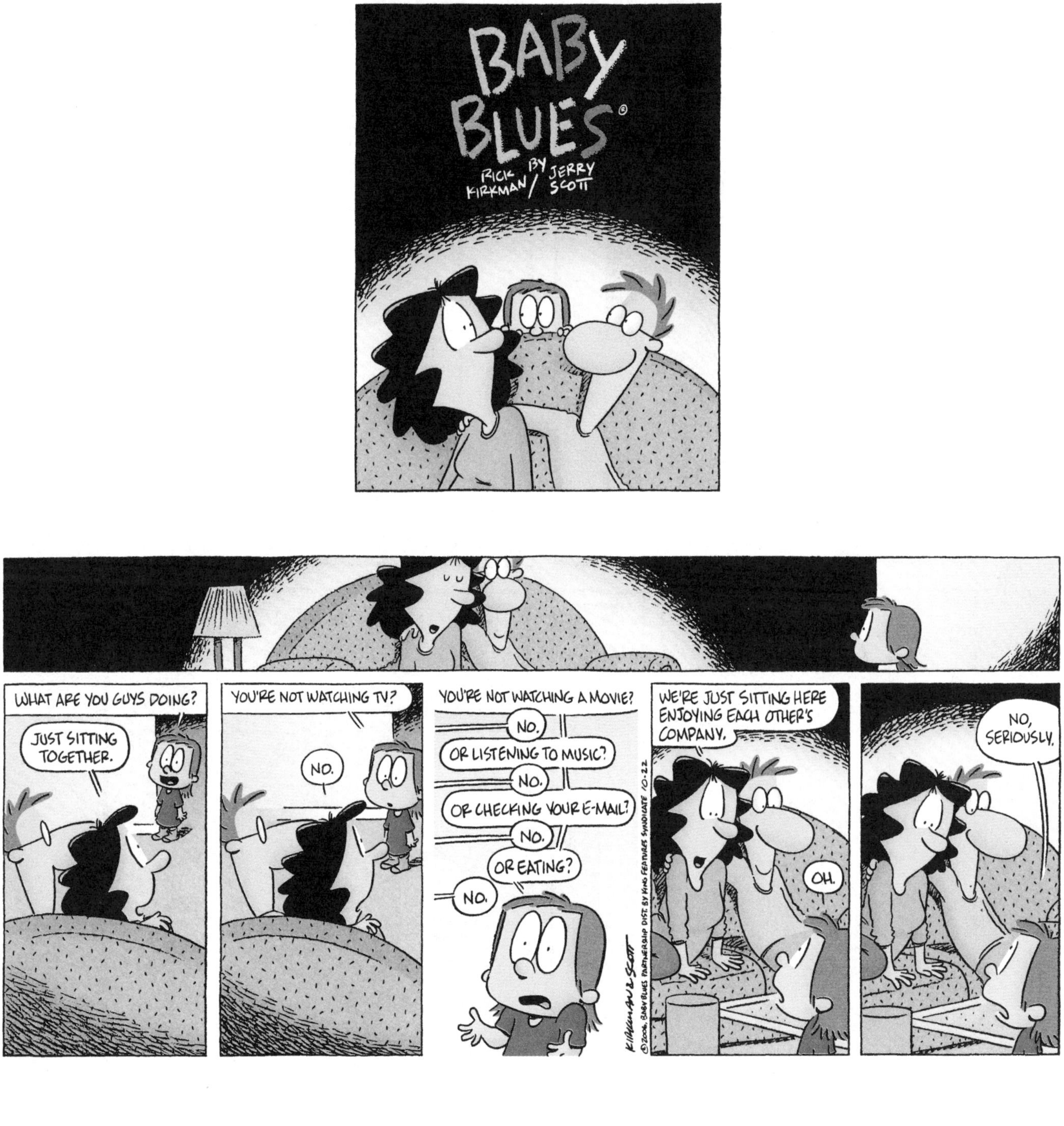
BABY BLUES®
BY RICK KIRKMAN / JERRY SCOTT
WHAT ARE YOU GUYS DOING?
JUST SITTING TOGETHER.
YOU'RE NOT WATCHING TV?
NO.
YOU'RE NOT WATCHING A MOVIE?
NO.
OR LISTENING TO MUSIC?
NO.
OR CHECKING YOUR E-MAIL?
NO.
OR EATING?
NO.
KIRKMAN & SCOTT
©2006, BABY BLUES PARTNERSHIP DIST. BY KING FEATURES SYNDICATE 10-22
WE'RE JUST SITTING HERE ENJOYING EACH OTHER'S COMPANY.
OH.
NO, SERIOUSLY.

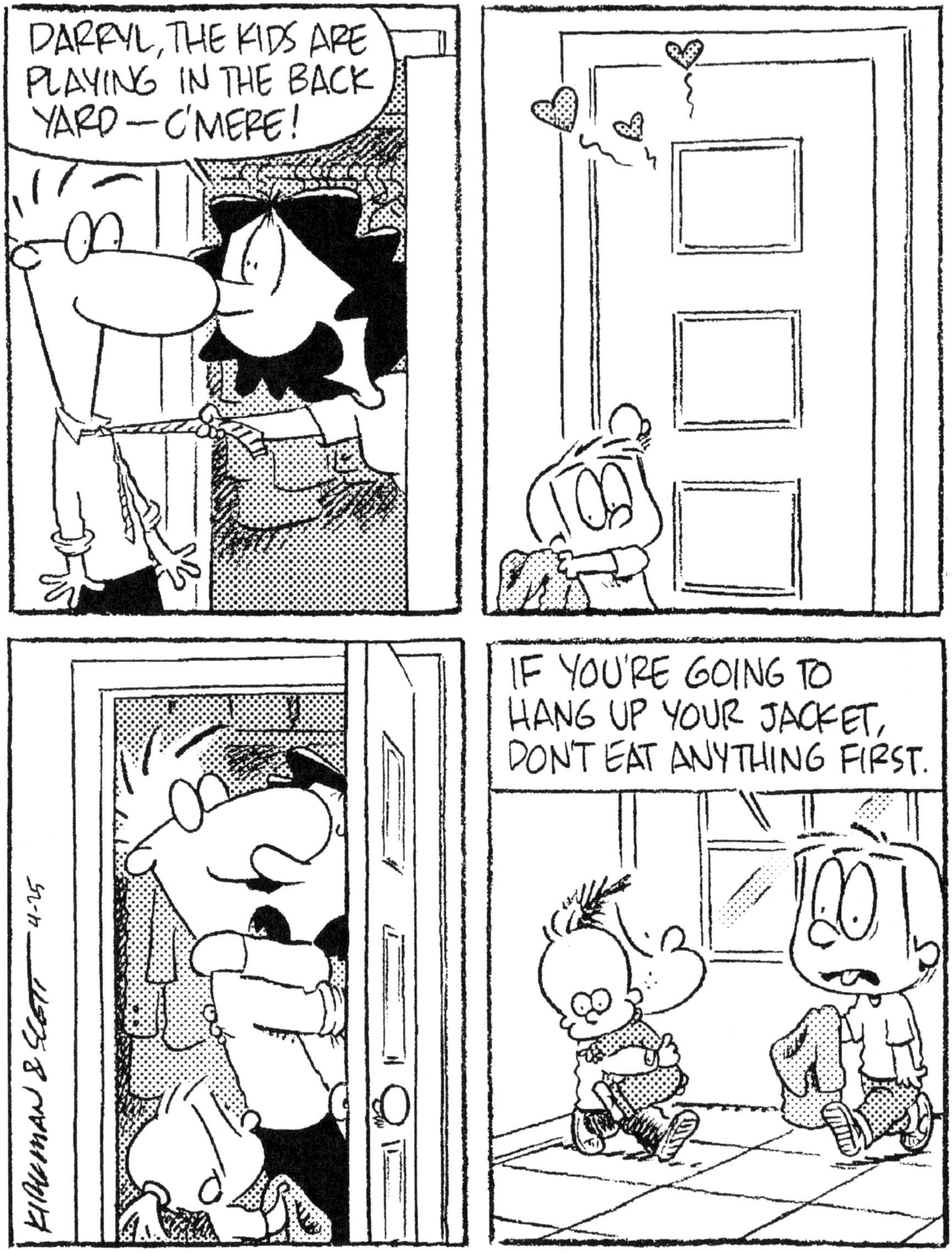
DARRYL, THE KIDS ARE PLAYING IN THE BACK YARD—C'MERE!
IF YOU'RE GOING TO HANG UP YOUR JACKET, DON'T EAT ANYTHING FIRST.
KIRKMAN & SCOTT 4-25

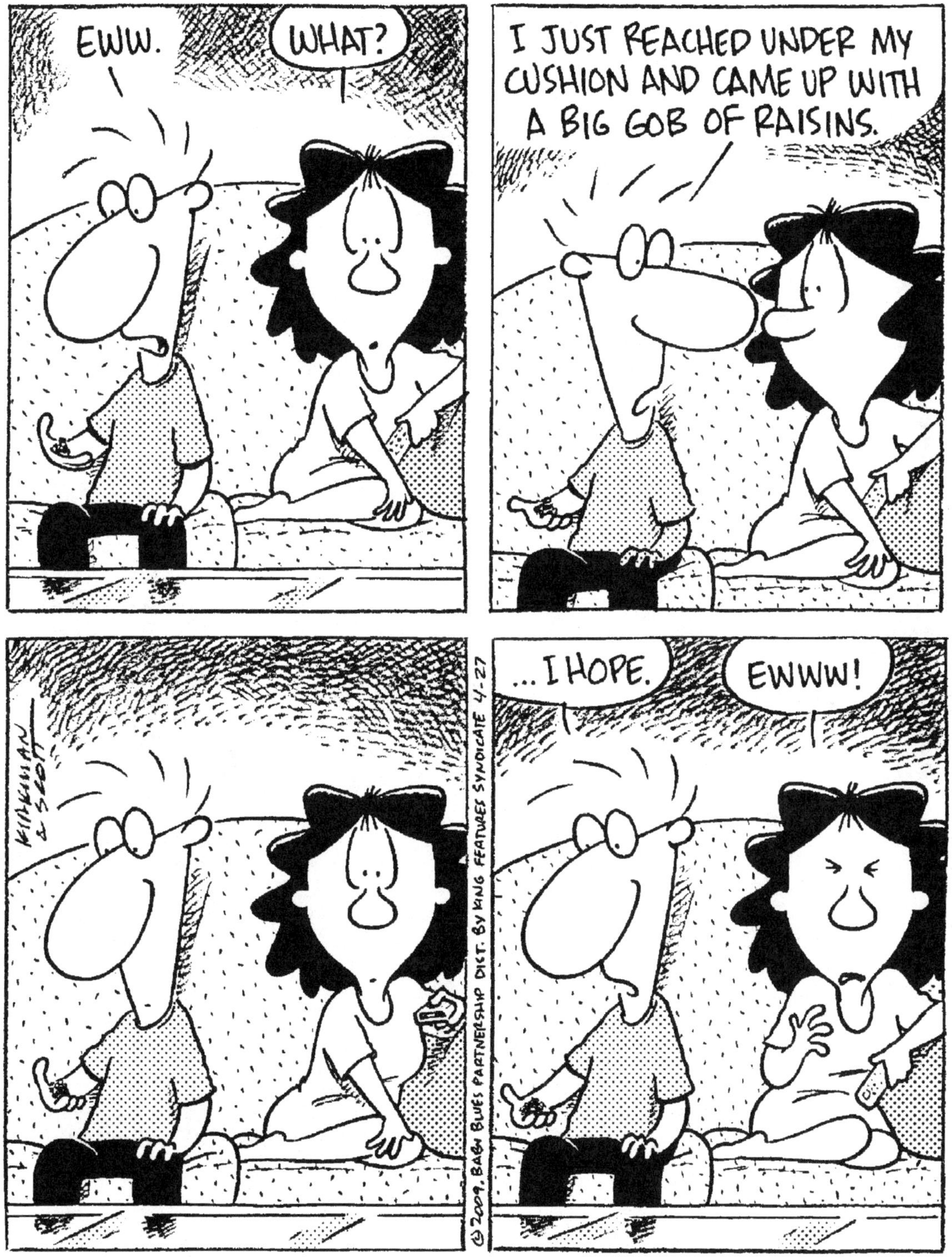
EWW.
WHAT?
I JUST REACHED UNDER MY CUSHION AND CAME UP WITH A BIG GOB OF RAISINS.
KIRKMAN & SCOTT
© 2009, BABY BLUES PARTNERSHIP DIST. BY KING FEATURES SYNDICATE 4-27
...I HOPE.
EWWW!

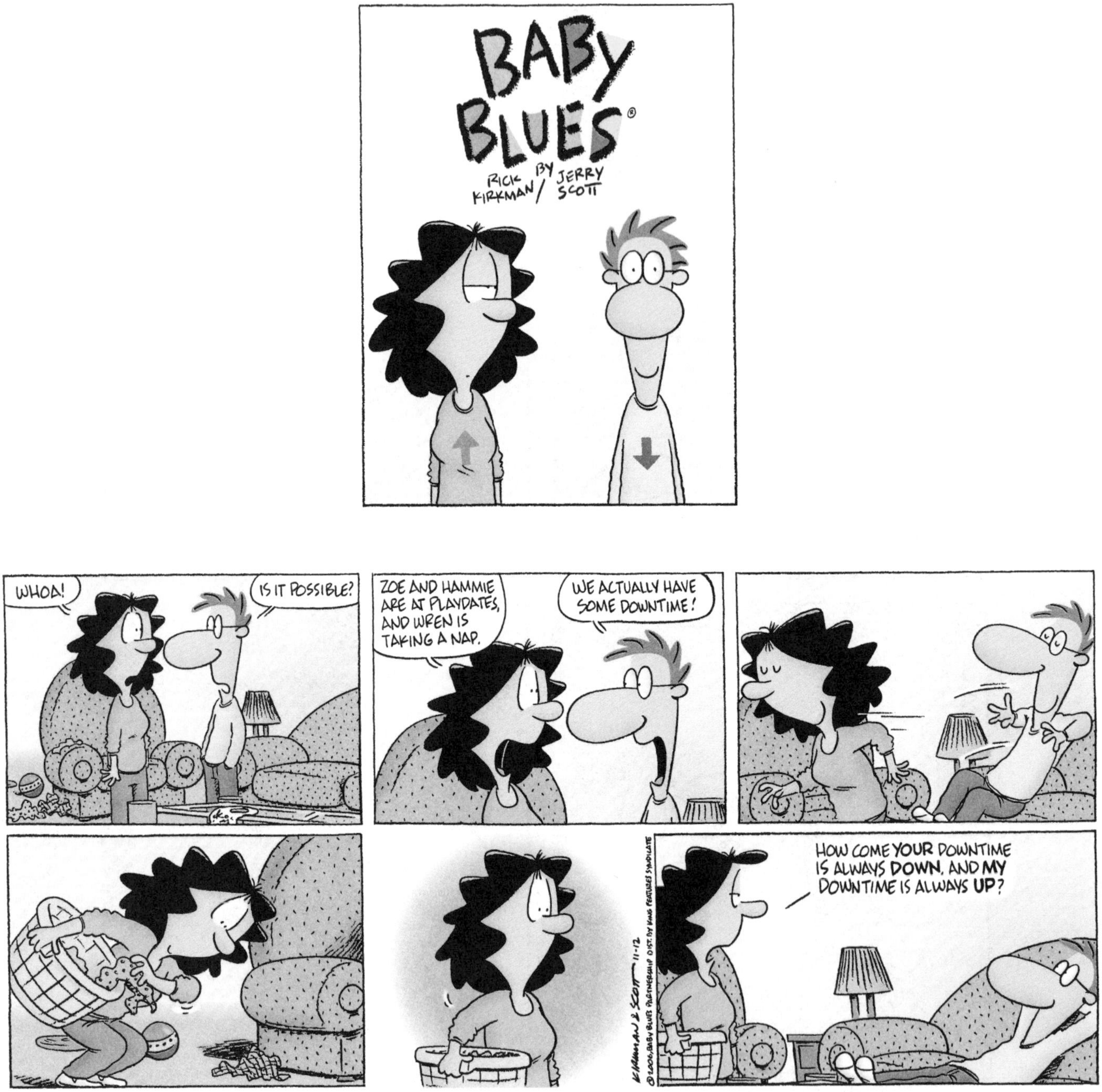

BABY BLUES®
BY RICK KIRKMAN / JERRY SCOTT
WHOA!
IS IT POSSIBLE?
ZOE AND HAMMIE ARE AT PLAYDATES, AND WREN IS TAKING A NAP.
WE ACTUALLY HAVE SOME DOWNTIME!
KIRKMAN & SCOTT 11-12
© 2006, BABY BLUES PARTNERSHIP DIST. BY KING FEATURES SYNDICATE
HOW COME **YOUR** DOWNTIME IS ALWAYS **DOWN**, AND **MY** DOWNTIME IS ALWAYS **UP**?

NOW PLAYING BABY BLUES® IN COLOR
NOW PLAYING BABY BLUES® IN COLOR

IT'S TRUE... WE DO SAVE A FORTUNE ON BABYSITTERS.
AND IT DOESN'T TAKE ANY GAS.
AND WE DON'T HAVE TO BUY TICKETS.
OR PAY FOR PARKING.
HI.
HI.
KIRKMAN & SCOTT 12-10
BUT TRADING HOUSES WITH THE NEIGHBORS TO WATCH A DVD ISN'T THE SAME THING AS A DATE.
HEY, GOING OUT IS GOING OUT.

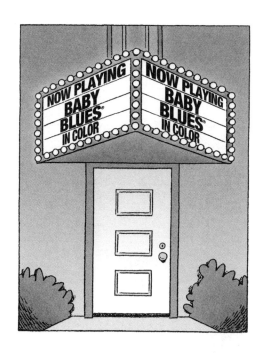

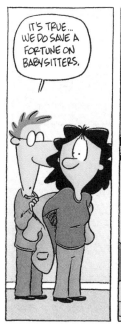

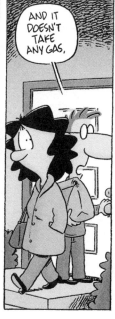

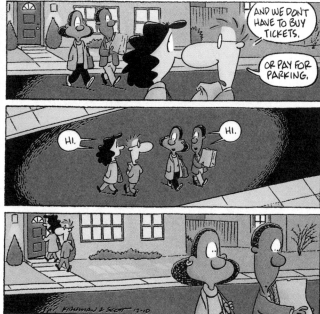

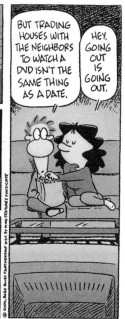

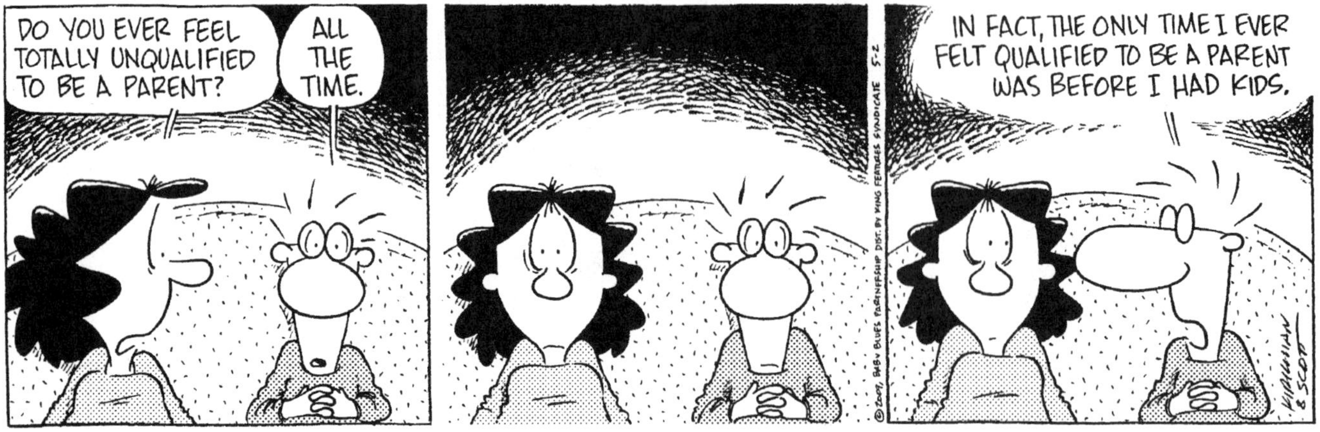
DO YOU EVER FEEL TOTALLY UNQUALIFIED TO BE A PARENT?
ALL THE TIME.
IN FACT, THE ONLY TIME I EVER FELT QUALIFIED TO BE A PARENT WAS BEFORE I HAD KIDS.
©2009, BABY BLUES PARTNERSHIP DIST. BY KING FEATURES SYNDICATE 5-2
KIRKMAN & SCOTT

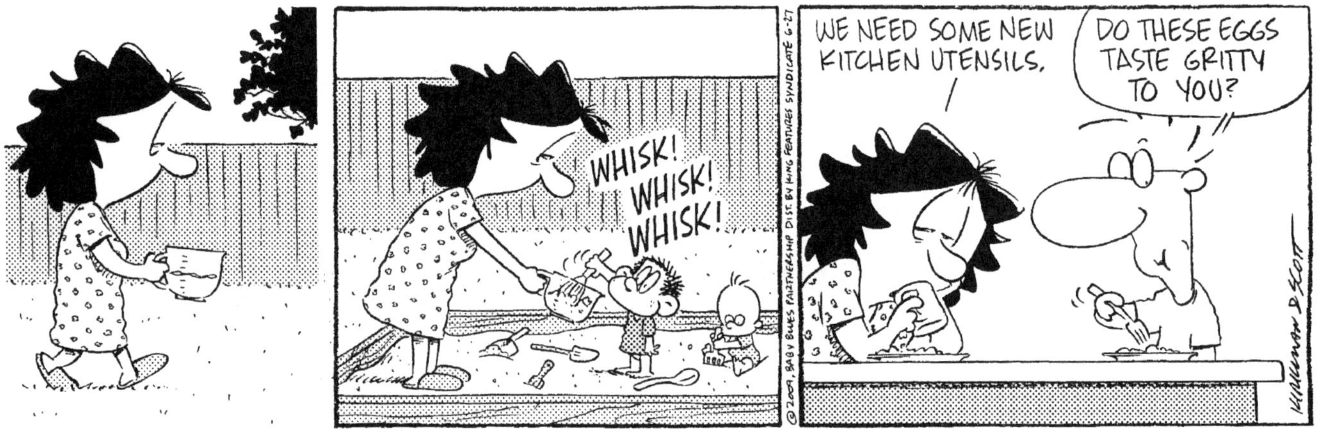
WHISK! WHISK! WHISK!
©2009, BABY BLUES PARTNERSHIP DIST. BY KING FEATURES SYNDICATE 6-27
WE NEED SOME NEW KITCHEN UTENSILS.
DO THESE EGGS TASTE GRITTY TO YOU?
KIRKMAN & SCOTT

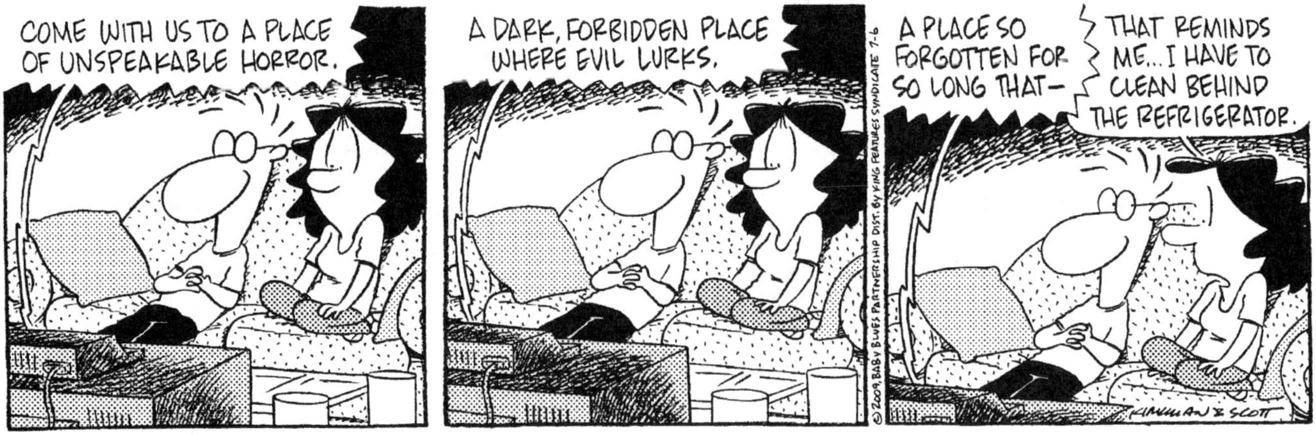
COME WITH US TO A PLACE OF UNSPEAKABLE HORROR.
A DARK, FORBIDDEN PLACE WHERE EVIL LURKS.
©2009, BABY BLUES PARTNERSHIP DIST. BY KING FEATURES SYNDICATE 7-6
A PLACE SO FORGOTTEN FOR SO LONG THAT—
THAT REMINDS ME... I HAVE TO CLEAN BEHIND THE REFRIGERATOR.
KIRKMAN & SCOTT

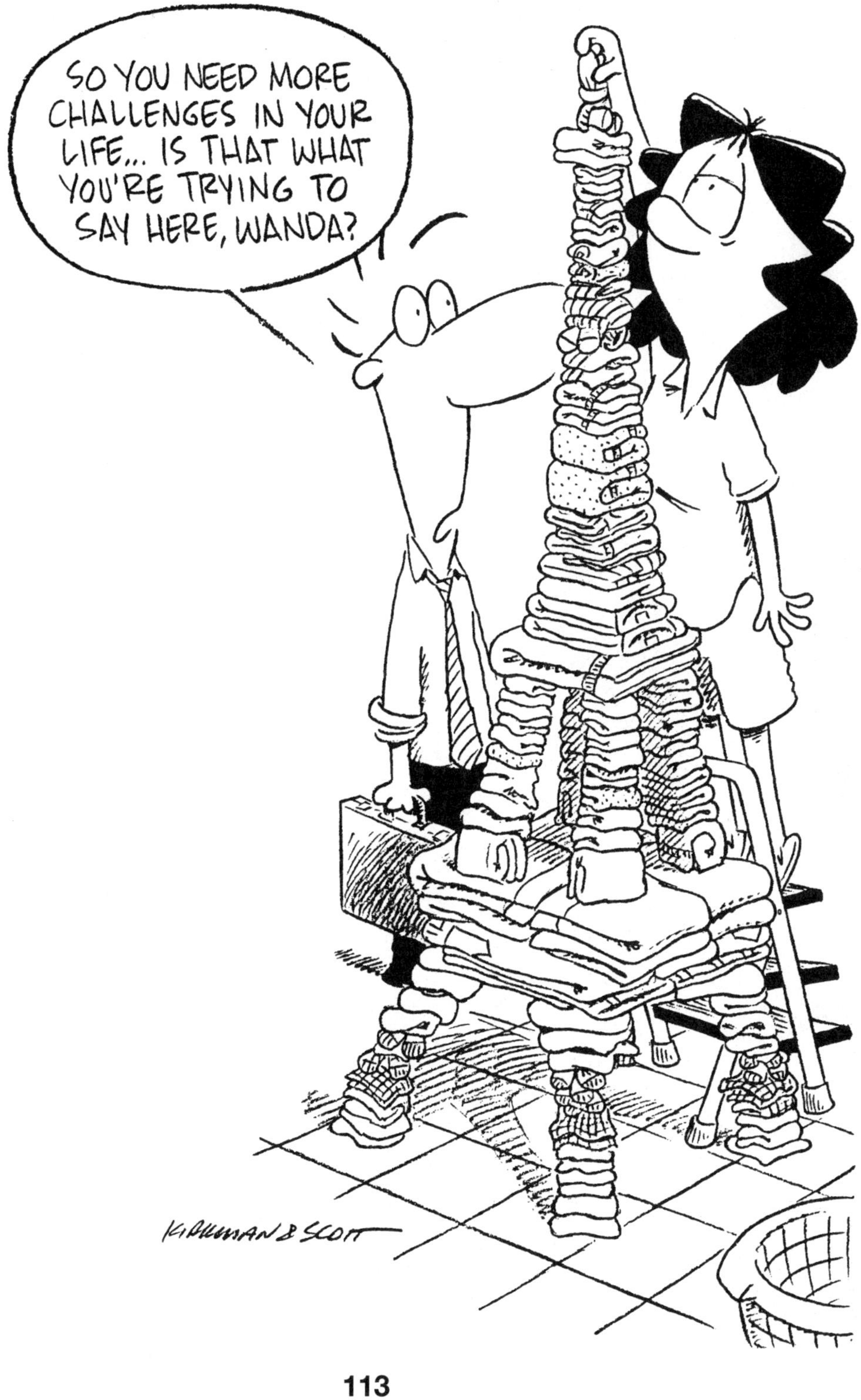
SO YOU NEED MORE CHALLENGES IN YOUR LIFE... IS THAT WHAT YOU'RE TRYING TO SAY HERE, WANDA?
KIRKMAN & SCOTT

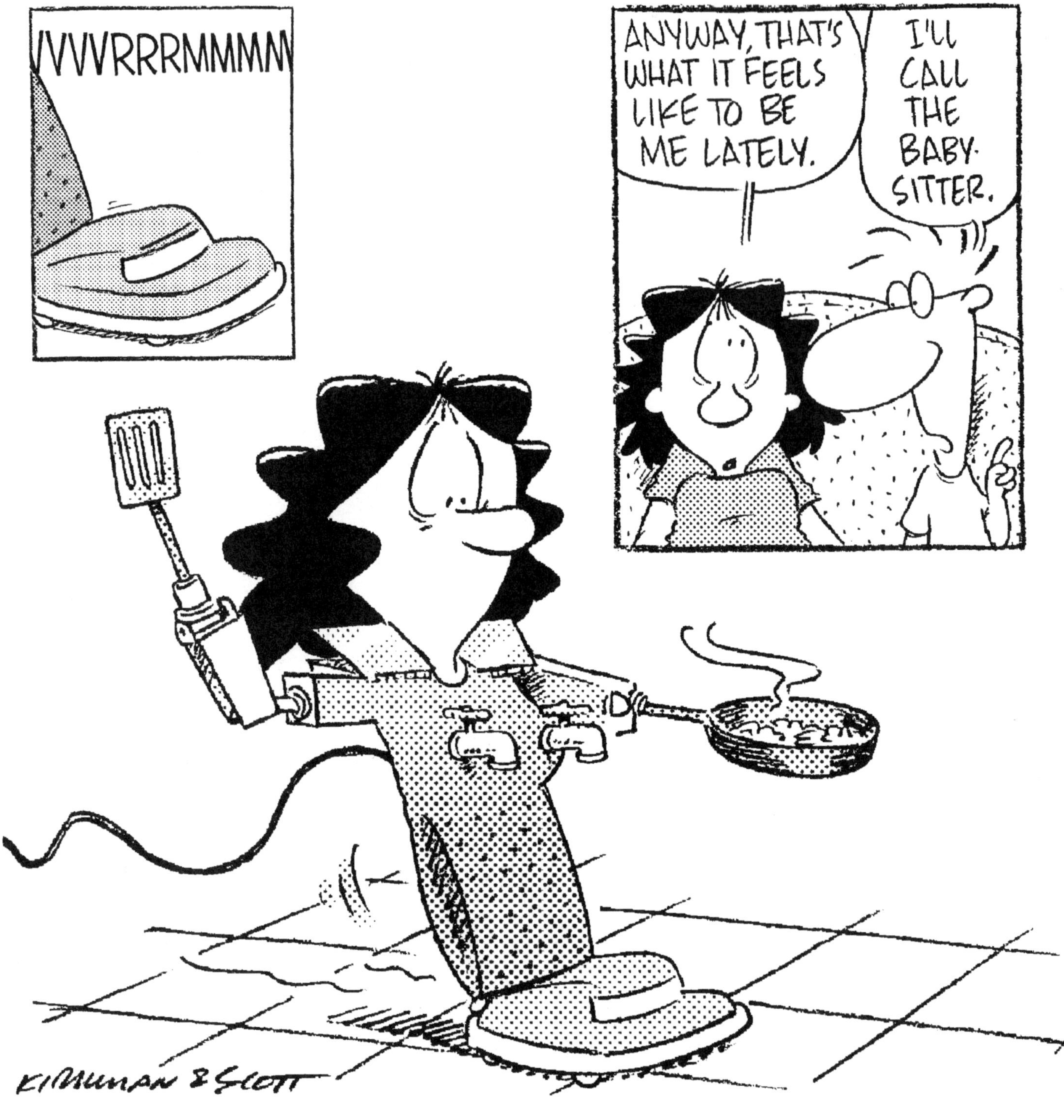
VVVVRRRMMMM
ANYWAY, THAT'S WHAT IT FEELS LIKE TO BE ME LATELY.
I'LL CALL THE BABY-SITTER.
KIRKMAN & SCOTT

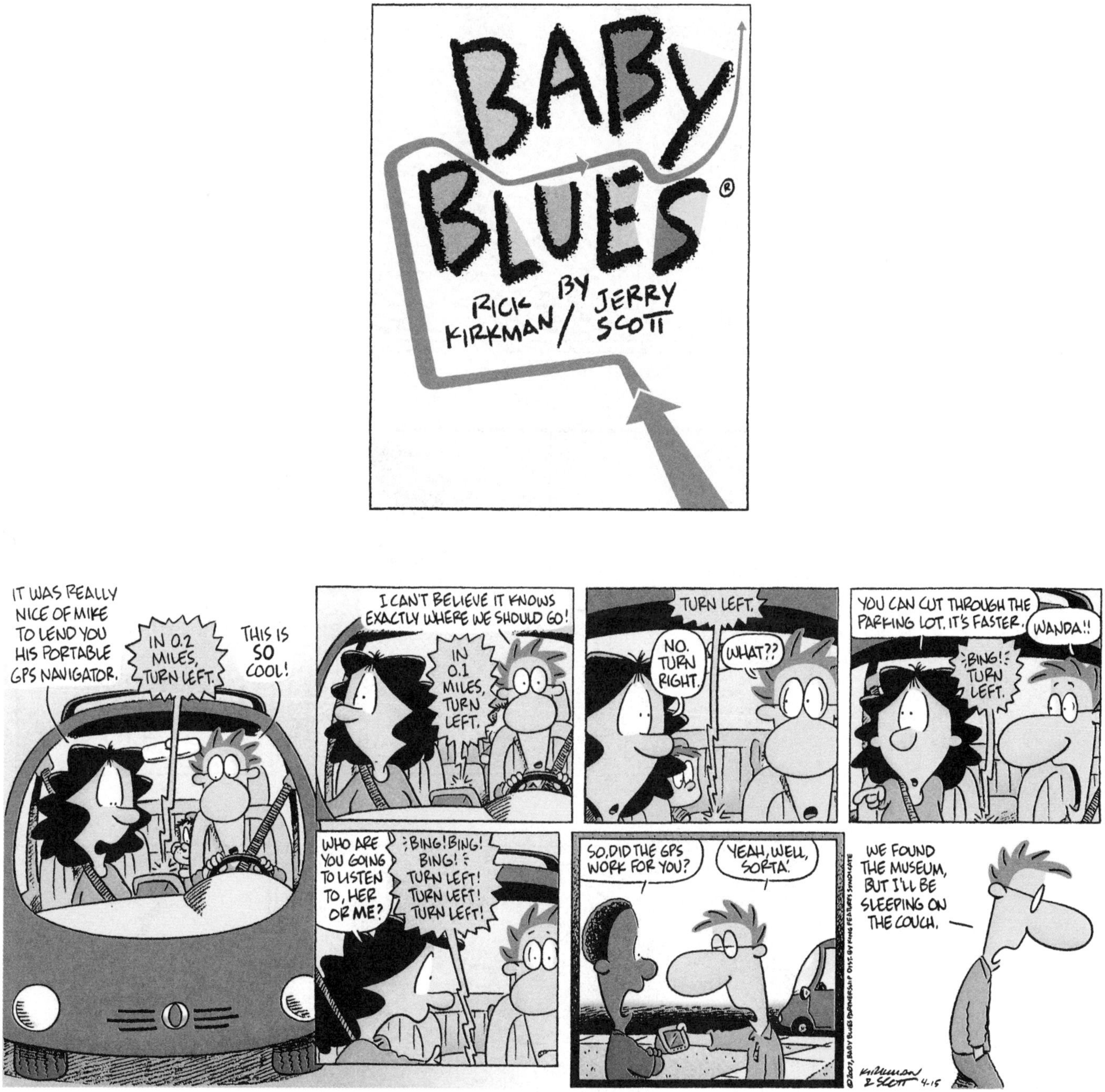
BABY BLUES®
BY RICK KIRKMAN / JERRY SCOTT
IT WAS REALLY NICE OF MIKE TO LEND YOU HIS PORTABLE GPS NAVIGATOR.
IN 0.2 MILES, TURN LEFT.
THIS IS SO COOL!
I CAN'T BELIEVE IT KNOWS EXACTLY WHERE WE SHOULD GO!
IN 0.1 MILES, TURN LEFT.
TURN LEFT.
NO. TURN RIGHT.
WHAT??
YOU CAN CUT THROUGH THE PARKING LOT. IT'S FASTER.
WANDA!!
BING! TURN LEFT.
WHO ARE YOU GOING TO LISTEN TO, HER OR ME?
BING! BING! BING! TURN LEFT! TURN LEFT! TURN LEFT!
SO, DID THE GPS WORK FOR YOU?
YEAH, WELL, SORTA.
WE FOUND THE MUSEUM, BUT I'LL BE SLEEPING ON THE COUCH.
©2007, BABY BLUES PARTNERSHIP DIST. BY KING FEATURES SYNDICATE
KIRKMAN & SCOTT 4-15

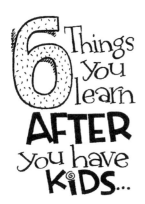

6 Things you learn AFTER you have KIDS...

YOU WANT SOME DESSERT NOW?
SURE.
KIRKMAN & SCOTT
©2009, BABY BLUES PARTNERSHIP DIST. BY KING FEATURES SYNDICATE 5-18

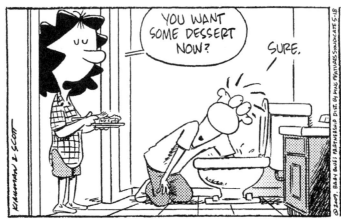

1.

Things you thought were really gross now barely qualify as yucky.

6 Things you learn AFTER you have KIDS...

KIRKMAN & SCOTT
©2009, BABY BLUES PARTNERSHIP DIST. BY KING FEATURES SYNDICATE 5-19

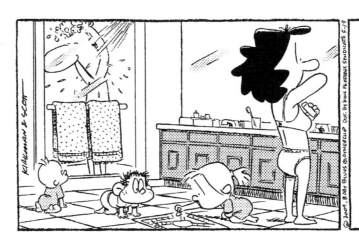

2.

The definition of privacy gets a lot looser.

6 Things you learn AFTER you have KIDS...

KIRKMAN & SCOTT
©2009, BABY BLUES PARTNERSHIP DIST. BY KING FEATURES SYNDICATE 5-20

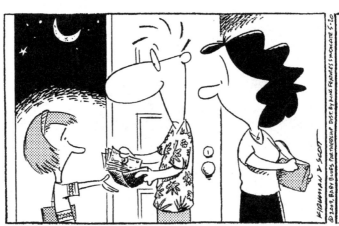

3.

Free time is anything but that.

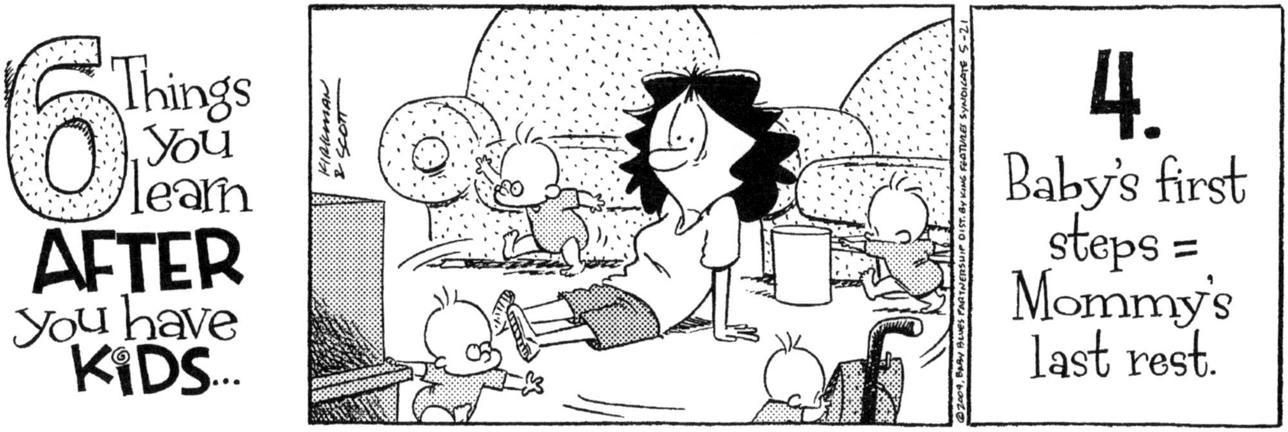
6 Things you learn AFTER you have KIDS...
4.
Baby's first steps = Mommy's last rest.

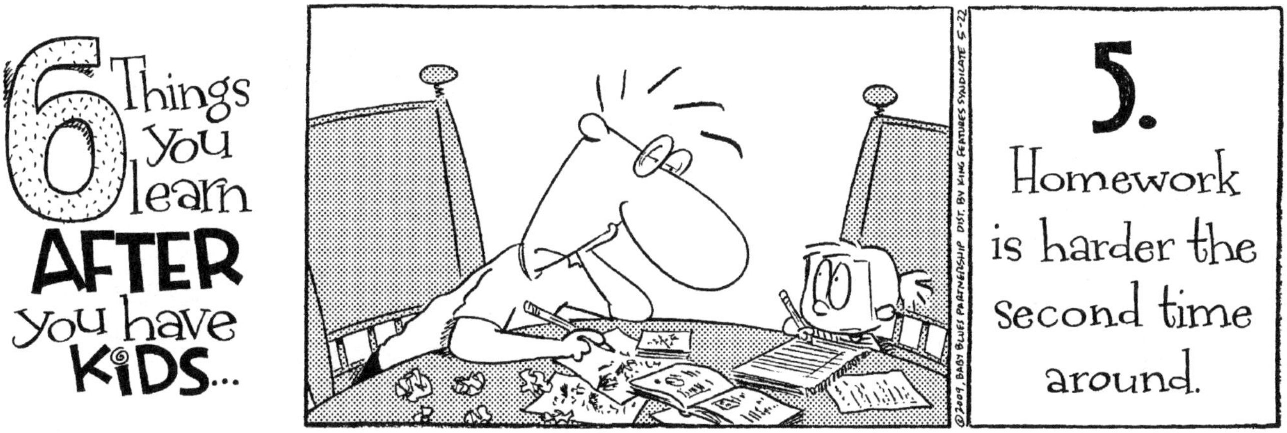
6 Things you learn AFTER you have KIDS...
5.
Homework is harder the second time around.

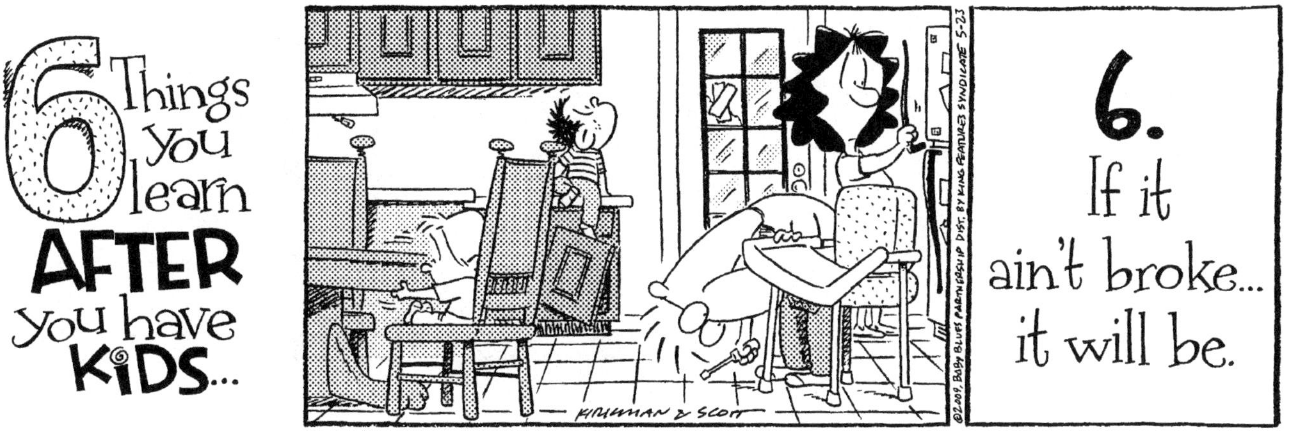
6 Things you learn AFTER you have KIDS...
6.
If it ain't broke... it will be.

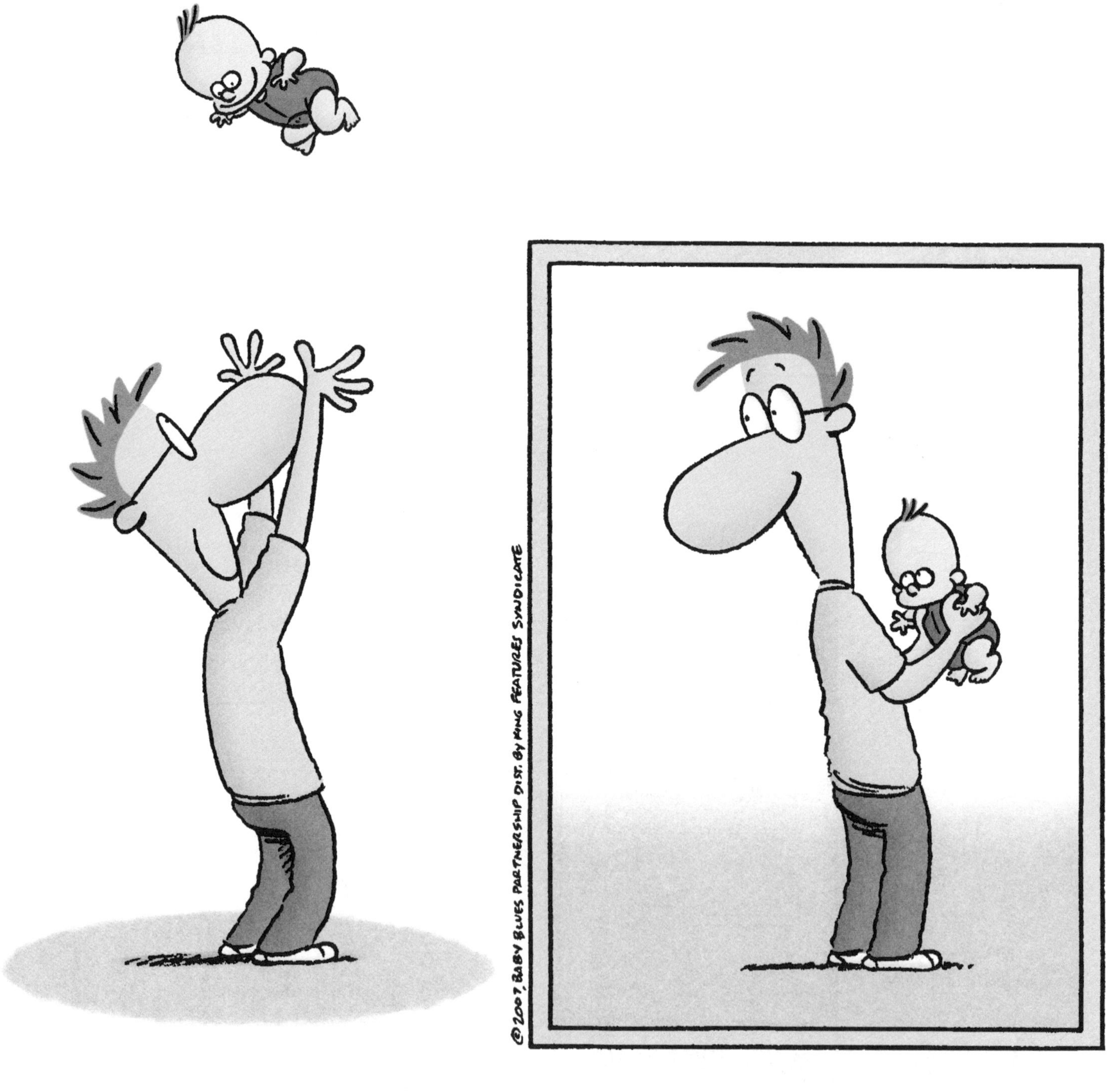
©2007, BABY BLUES PARTNERSHIP DIST. BY KING FEATURES SYNDICATE

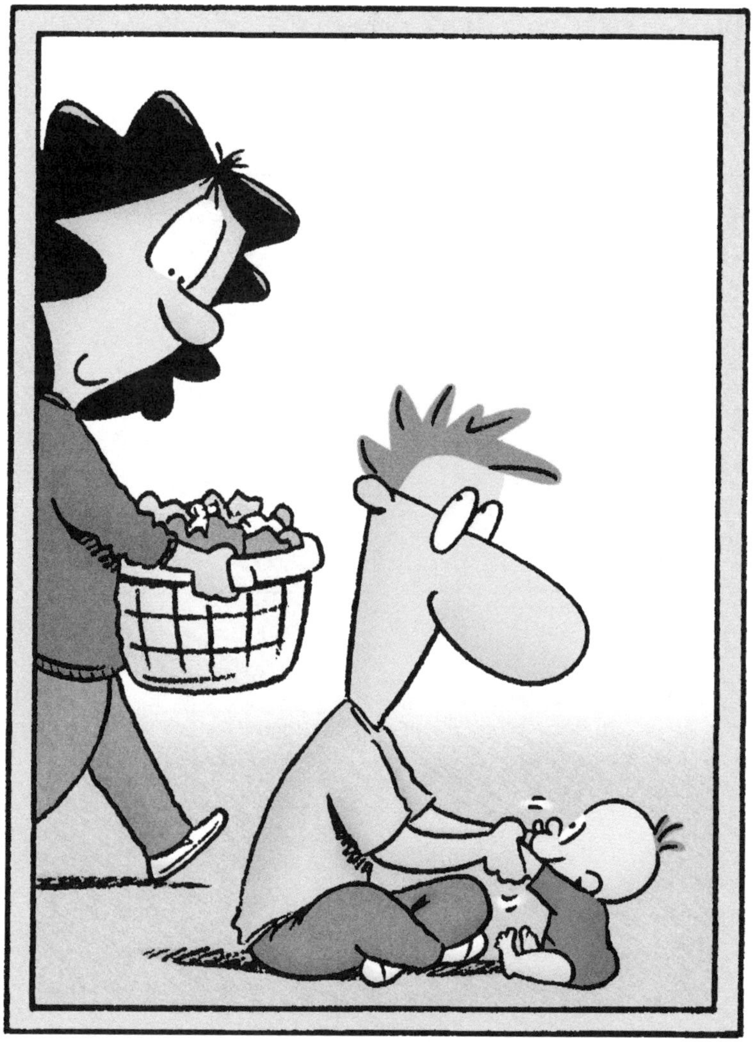

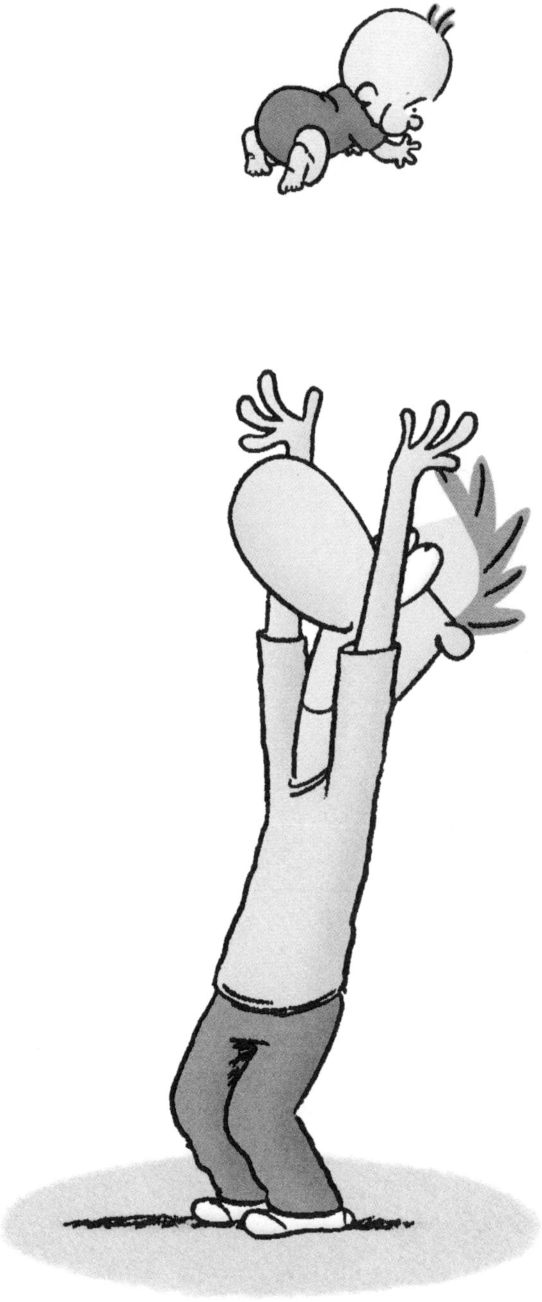

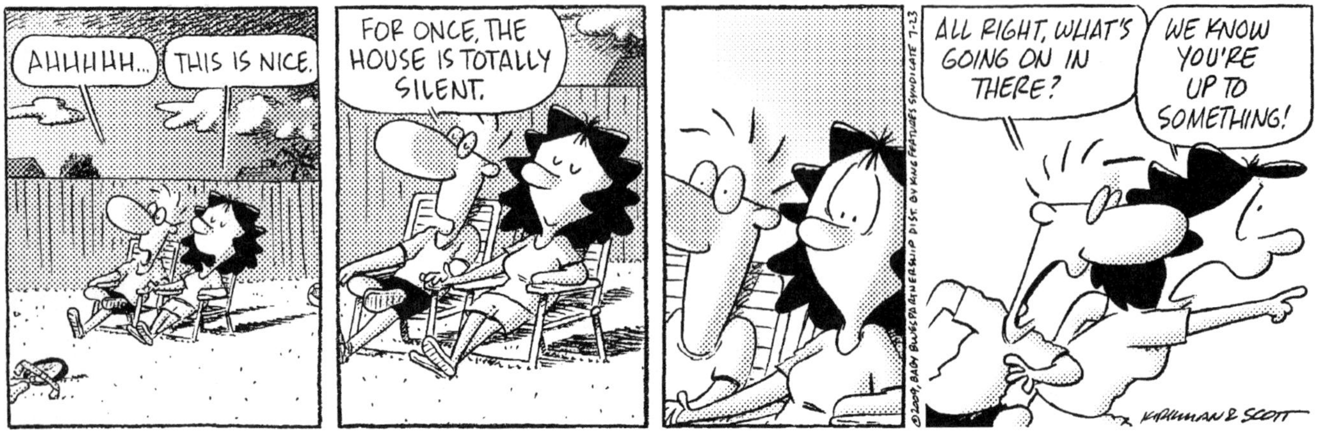
AHHHHH...
THIS IS NICE.
FOR ONCE, THE HOUSE IS TOTALLY SILENT.
ALL RIGHT, WHAT'S GOING ON IN THERE?
WE KNOW YOU'RE UP TO SOMETHING!
©2009, BABY BLUES PARTNERSHIP DIST. BY KING FEATURES SYNDICATE 7-23
KIRKMAN & SCOTT

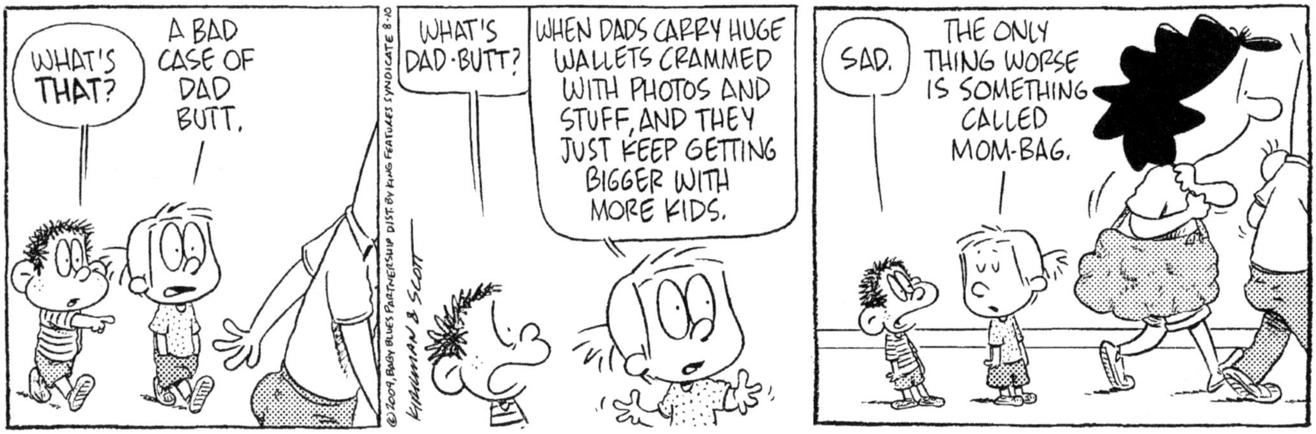
WHAT'S THAT?
A BAD CASE OF DAD BUTT.
©2009, BABY BLUES PARTNERSHIP DIST. BY KING FEATURES SYNDICATE 8-10
KIRKMAN & SCOTT
WHAT'S DAD-BUTT?
WHEN DADS CARRY HUGE WALLETS CRAMMED WITH PHOTOS AND STUFF, AND THEY JUST KEEP GETTING BIGGER WITH MORE KIDS.
SAD.
THE ONLY THING WORSE IS SOMETHING CALLED MOM-BAG.

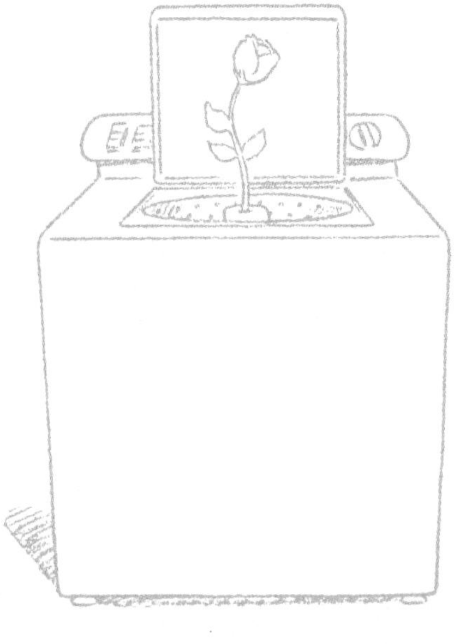

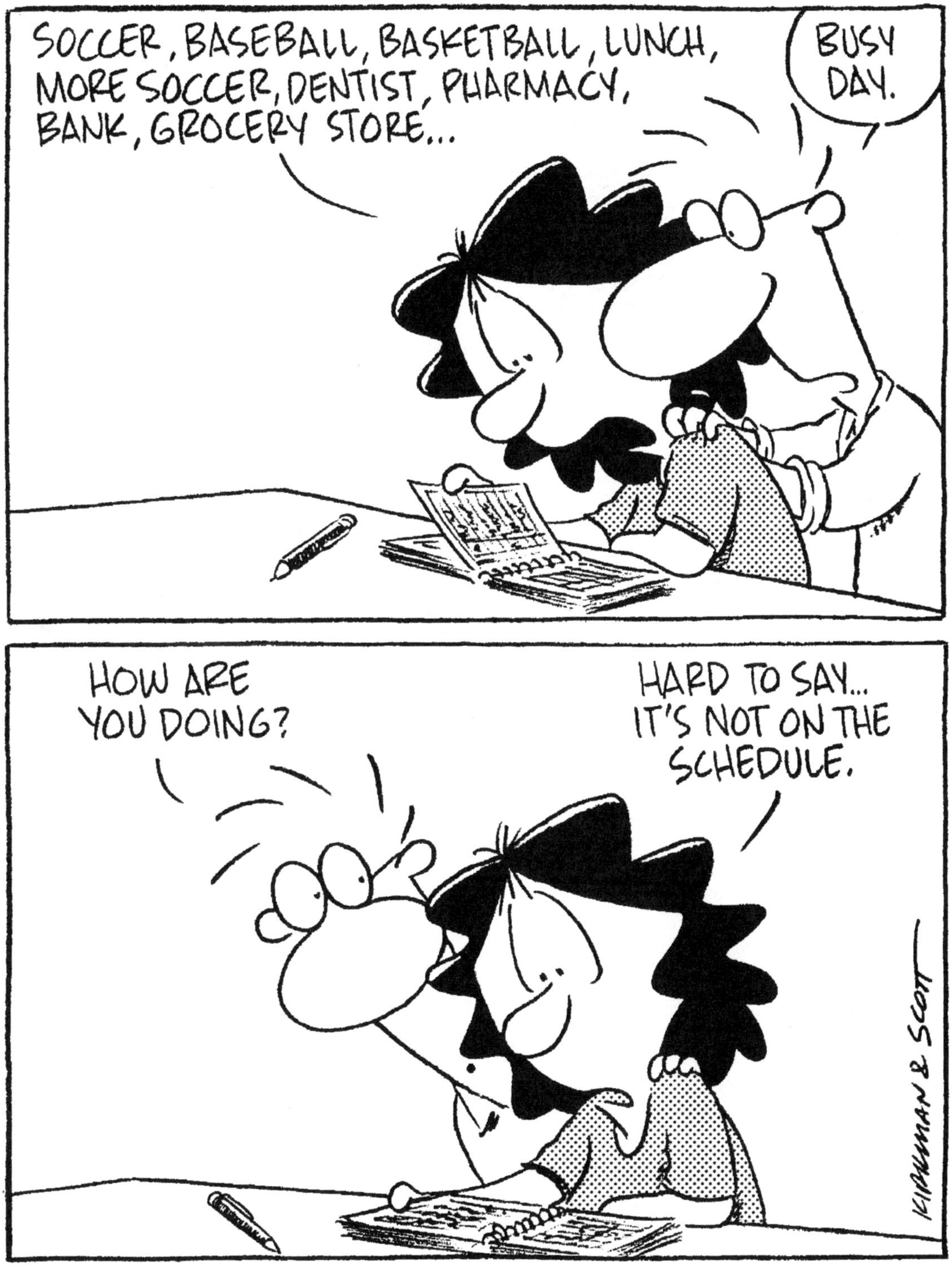
SOCCER, BASEBALL, BASKETBALL, LUNCH, MORE SOCCER, DENTIST, PHARMACY, BANK, GROCERY STORE...
BUSY DAY.
HOW ARE YOU DOING?
HARD TO SAY... IT'S NOT ON THE SCHEDULE.
KIRKMAN & SCOTT

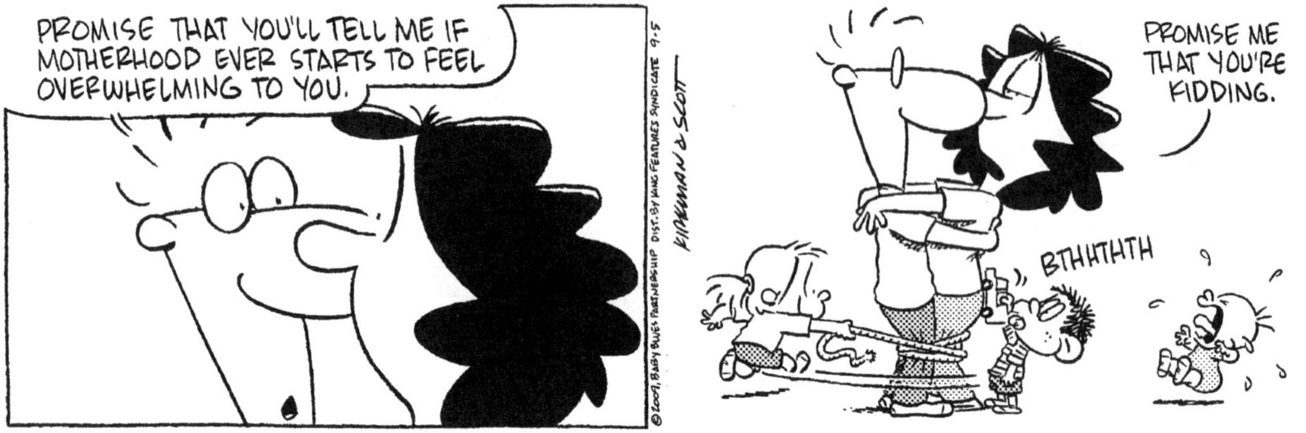
PROMISE THAT YOU'LL TELL ME IF MOTHERHOOD EVER STARTS TO FEEL OVERWHELMING TO YOU.
©2009, BABY BLUES PARTNERSHIP DIST. BY KING FEATURES SYNDICATE 9-5
KIRKMAN & SCOTT
PROMISE ME THAT YOU'RE KIDDING.
BTHHTHTH

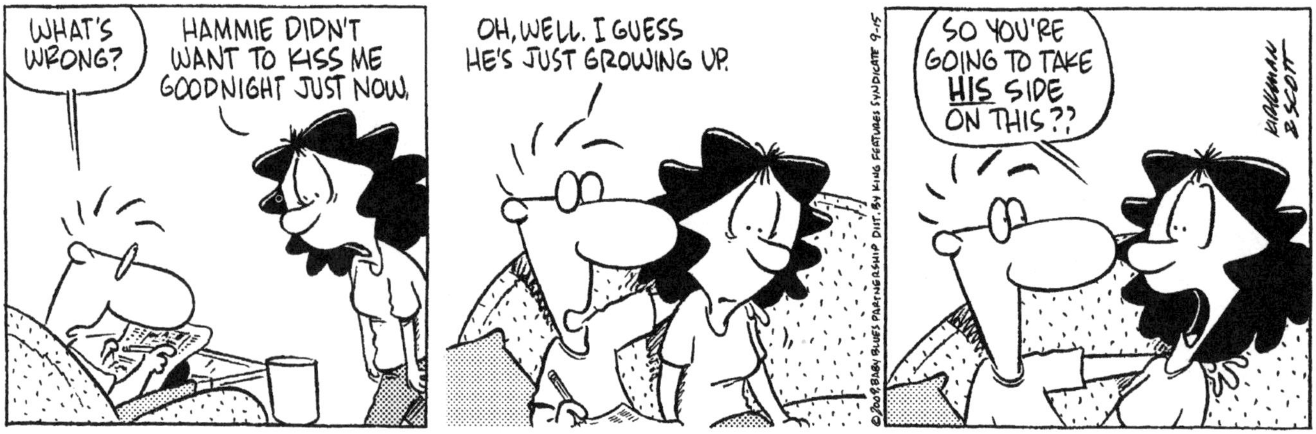
WHAT'S WRONG?
HAMMIE DIDN'T WANT TO KISS ME GOODNIGHT JUST NOW.
OH, WELL. I GUESS HE'S JUST GROWING UP.
©2008 BABY BLUES PARTNERSHIP DIST. BY KING FEATURES SYNDICATE 9-15
SO YOU'RE GOING TO TAKE HIS SIDE ON THIS??
KIRKMAN & SCOTT

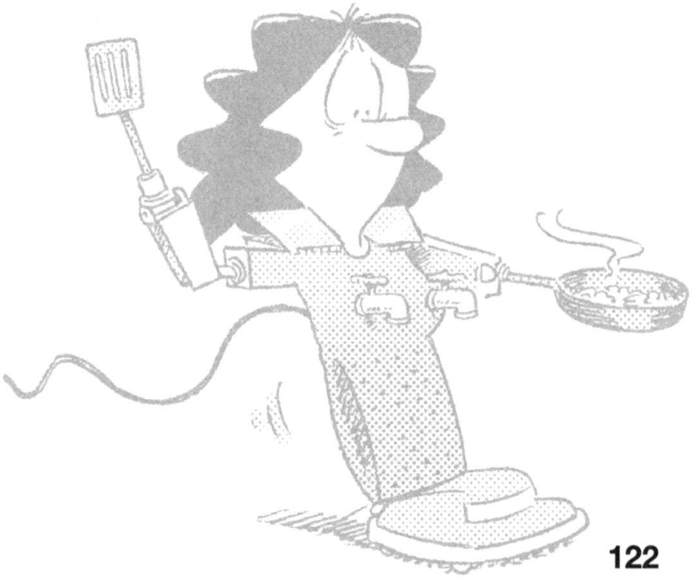

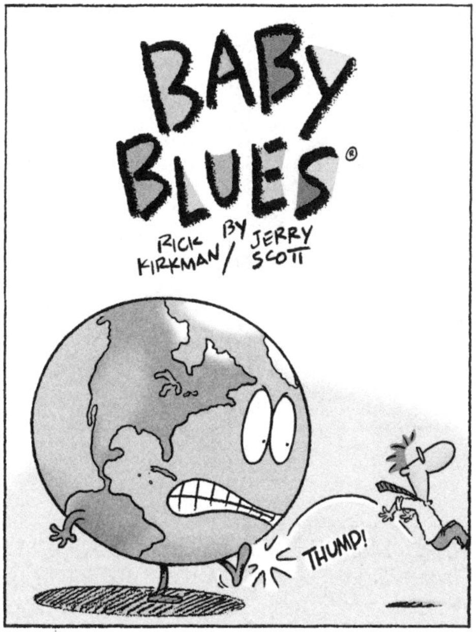
BABY BLUES®
RICK KIRKMAN / BY / JERRY SCOTT
THUMP!

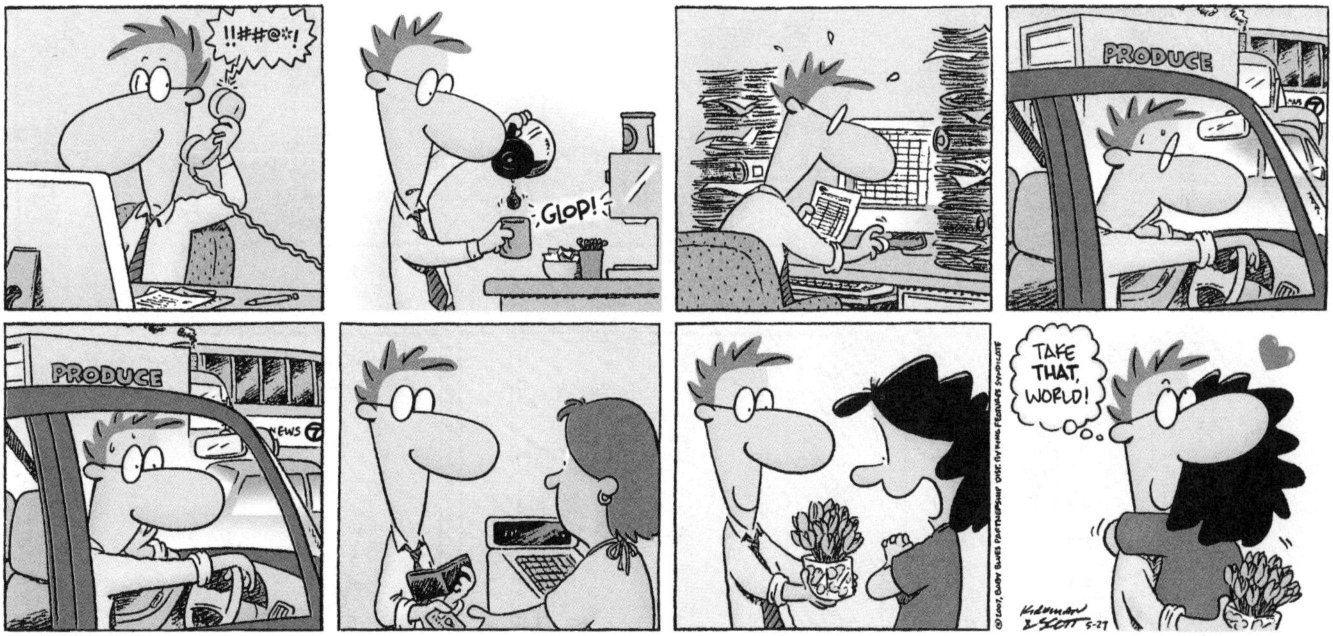
!!#@*!
GLOP!
PRODUCE
PRODUCE
NEWS 7
TAKE THAT, WORLD!
© 2007, BABY BLUES PARTNERSHIP DIST. BY KING FEATURES SYNDICATE
KIRKMAN & SCOTT 5-27

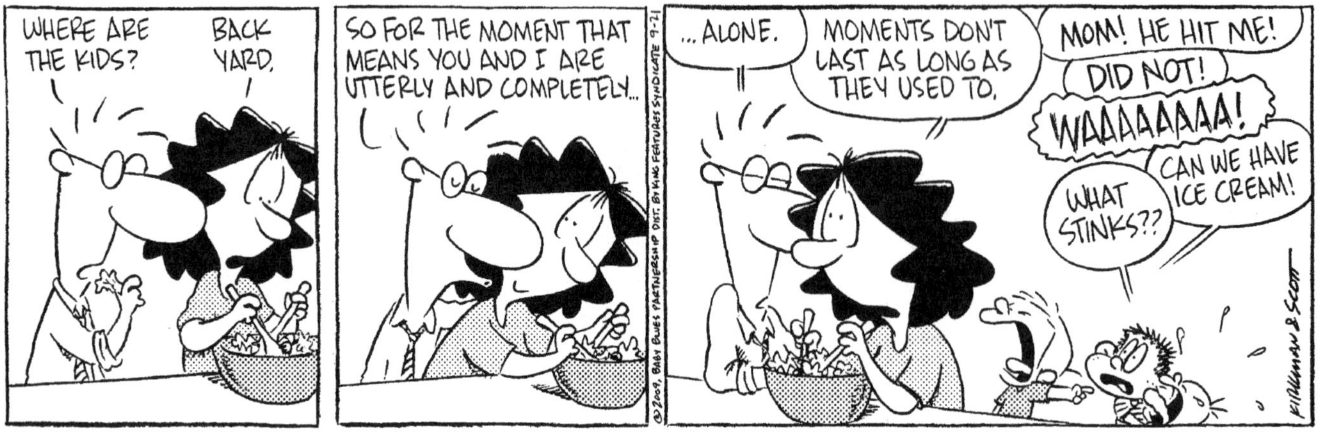
WHERE ARE THE KIDS?
BACK YARD.
SO FOR THE MOMENT THAT MEANS YOU AND I ARE UTTERLY AND COMPLETELY...
©2009, BABY BLUES PARTNERSHIP DIST. BY KING FEATURES SYNDICATE 9-21
...ALONE.
MOMENTS DON'T LAST AS LONG AS THEY USED TO.
MOM! HE HIT ME!
DID NOT!
WAAAAAAAA!
CAN WE HAVE ICE CREAM!
WHAT STINKS??
KIRKMAN & SCOTT

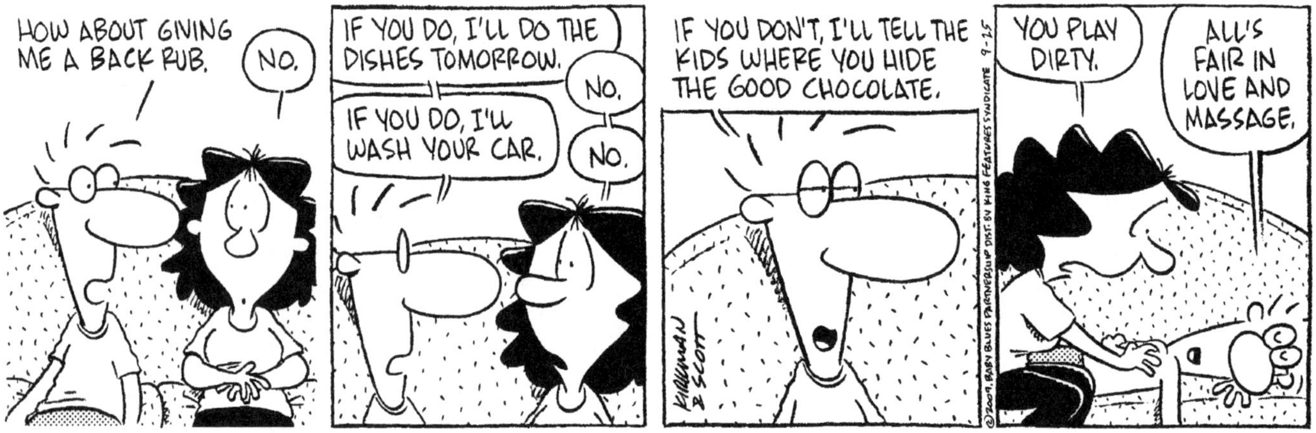
HOW ABOUT GIVING ME A BACK RUB.
NO.
IF YOU DO, I'LL DO THE DISHES TOMORROW.
NO.
IF YOU DO, I'LL WASH YOUR CAR.
NO.
IF YOU DON'T, I'LL TELL THE KIDS WHERE YOU HIDE THE GOOD CHOCOLATE.
KIRKMAN & SCOTT
©2009, BABY BLUES PARTNERSHIP DIST. BY KING FEATURES SYNDICATE 9-25
YOU PLAY DIRTY.
ALL'S FAIR IN LOVE AND MASSAGE.

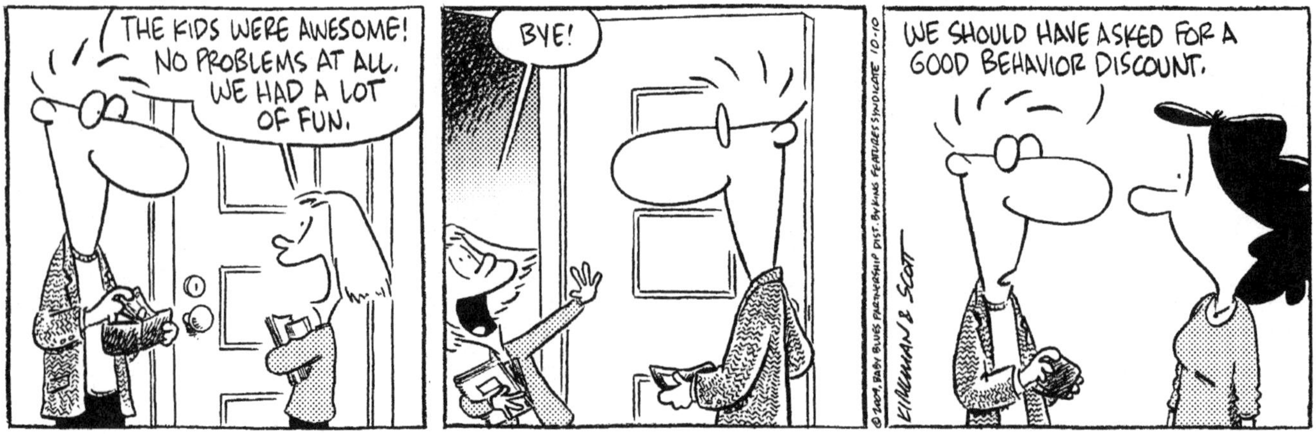
THE KIDS WERE AWESOME! NO PROBLEMS AT ALL. WE HAD A LOT OF FUN.
BYE!
©2009, BABY BLUES PARTNERSHIP DIST. BY KING FEATURES SYNDICATE 10-10
KIRKMAN & SCOTT
WE SHOULD HAVE ASKED FOR A GOOD BEHAVIOR DISCOUNT.

BABY BLUES®
BY RICK KIRKMAN / JERRY SCOTT

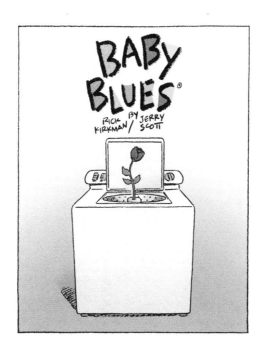

the NATURAL ORDER of THINGS-
Love
Lust
Bom-chicka-wacka
Bom-chicka-wacka
© 2008, Baby Blues Partnership Dist. by King Features Syndicate
Laundry
WHAT JUST HAPPENED HERE?
KIRKMAN & SCOTT
3-23

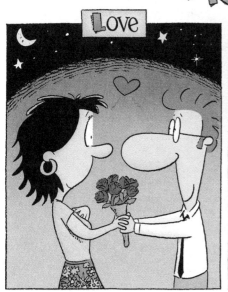

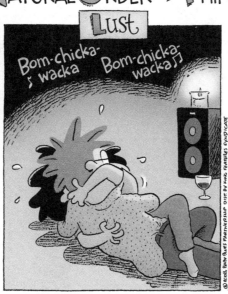

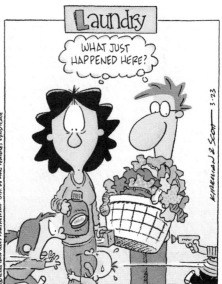

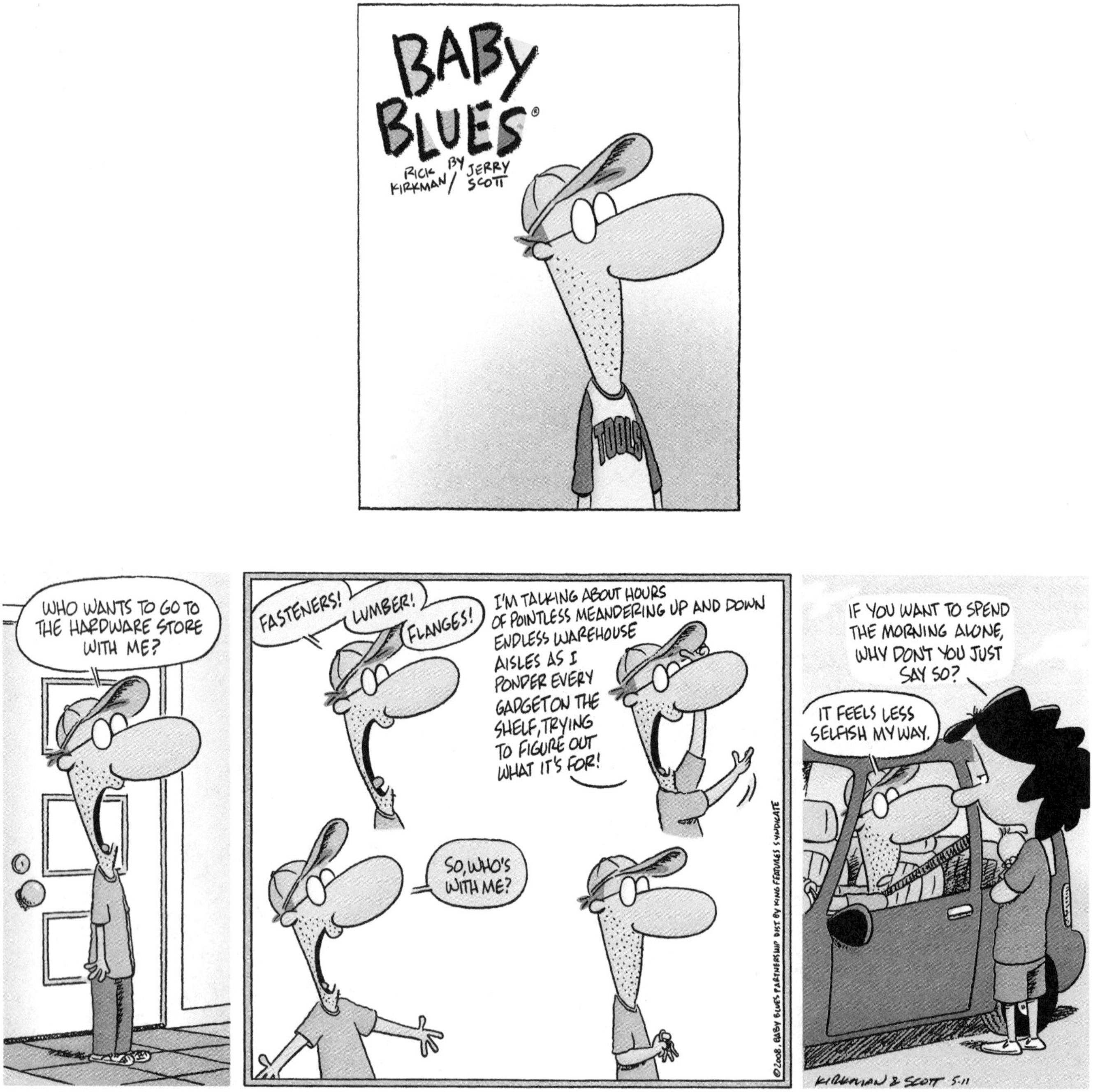
BABY BLUES®
BY RICK KIRKMAN / JERRY SCOTT
TOOLS
WHO WANTS TO GO TO THE HARDWARE STORE WITH ME?
FASTENERS!
LUMBER!
FLANGES!
I'M TALKING ABOUT HOURS OF POINTLESS MEANDERING UP AND DOWN ENDLESS WAREHOUSE AISLES AS I PONDER EVERY GADGET ON THE SHELF, TRYING TO FIGURE OUT WHAT IT'S FOR!
SO, WHO'S WITH ME?
©2008, BABY BLUES PARTNERSHIP DIST BY KING FEATURES SYNDICATE
IF YOU WANT TO SPEND THE MORNING ALONE, WHY DON'T YOU JUST SAY SO?
IT FEELS LESS SELFISH MY WAY.
KIRKMAN & SCOTT 5-11

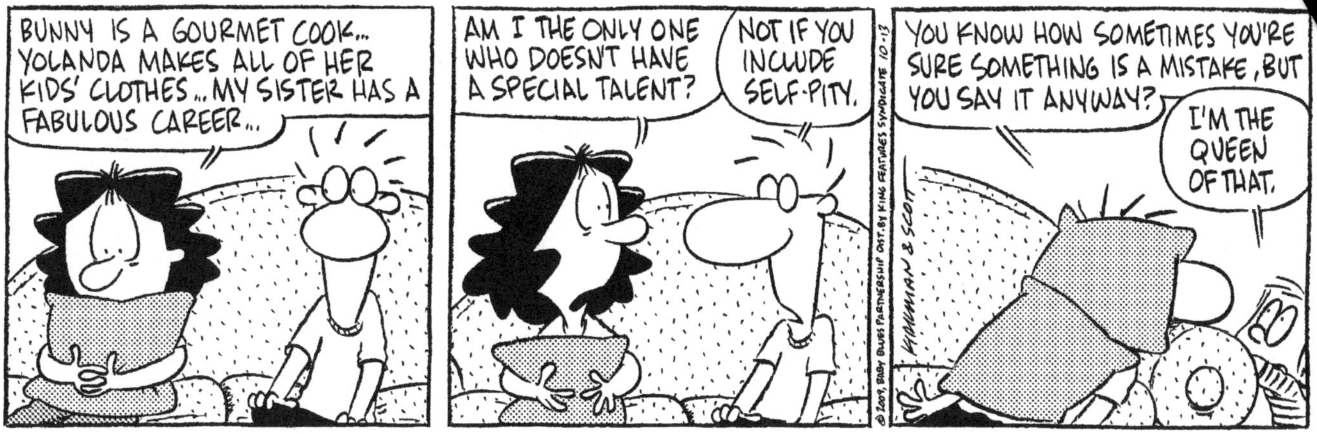
BUNNY IS A GOURMET COOK... YOLANDA MAKES ALL OF HER KIDS' CLOTHES... MY SISTER HAS A FABULOUS CAREER...
AM I THE ONLY ONE WHO DOESN'T HAVE A SPECIAL TALENT?
NOT IF YOU INCLUDE SELF-PITY.
YOU KNOW HOW SOMETIMES YOU'RE SURE SOMETHING IS A MISTAKE, BUT YOU SAY IT ANYWAY?
I'M THE QUEEN OF THAT.

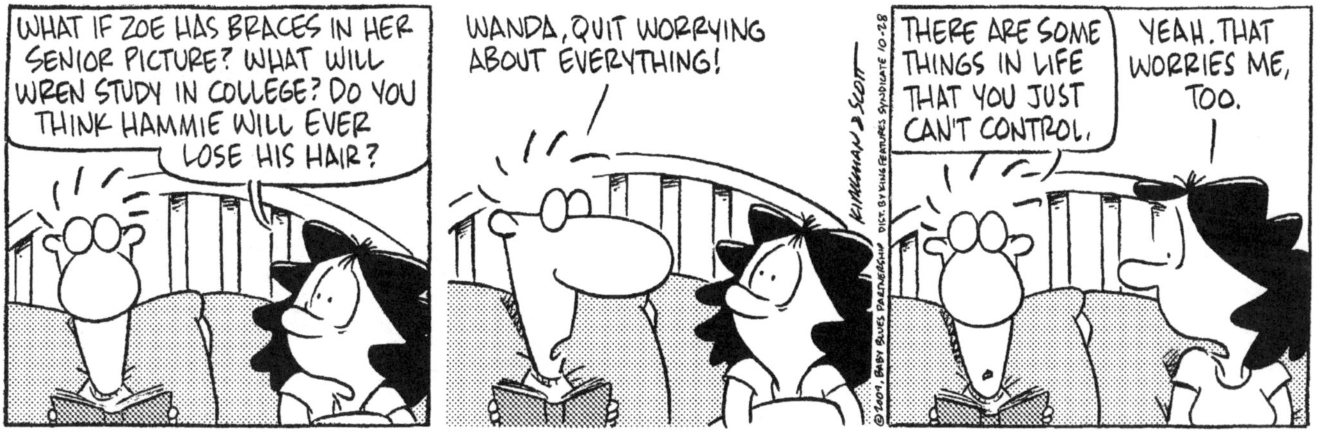
WHAT IF ZOE HAS BRACES IN HER SENIOR PICTURE? WHAT WILL WREN STUDY IN COLLEGE? DO YOU THINK HAMMIE WILL EVER LOSE HIS HAIR?
WANDA, QUIT WORRYING ABOUT EVERYTHING!
THERE ARE SOME THINGS IN LIFE THAT YOU JUST CAN'T CONTROL.
YEAH. THAT WORRIES ME, TOO.

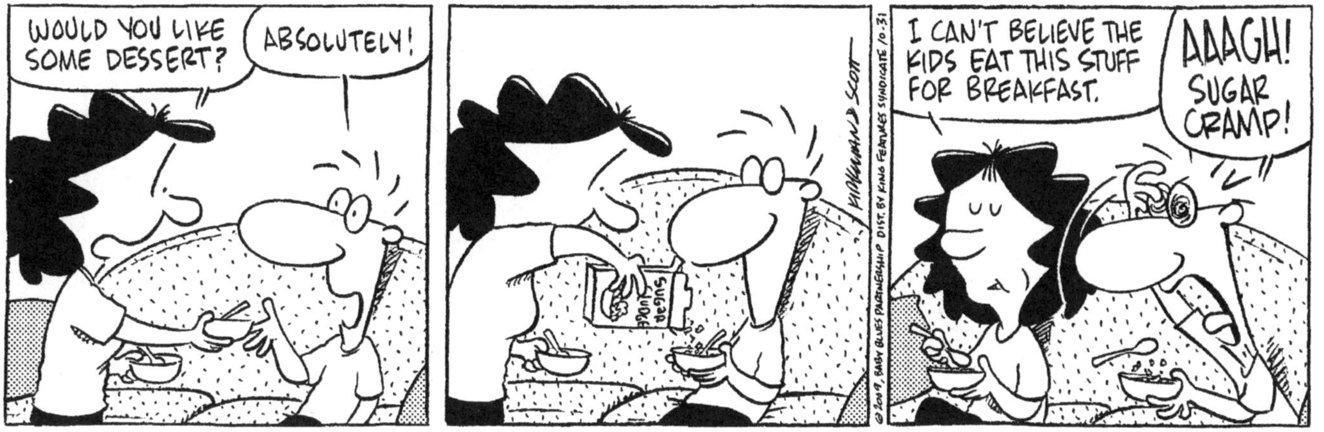
WOULD YOU LIKE SOME DESSERT?
ABSOLUTELY!
SUGAR
I CAN'T BELIEVE THE KIDS EAT THIS STUFF FOR BREAKFAST.
AAAGH! SUGAR CRAMP!

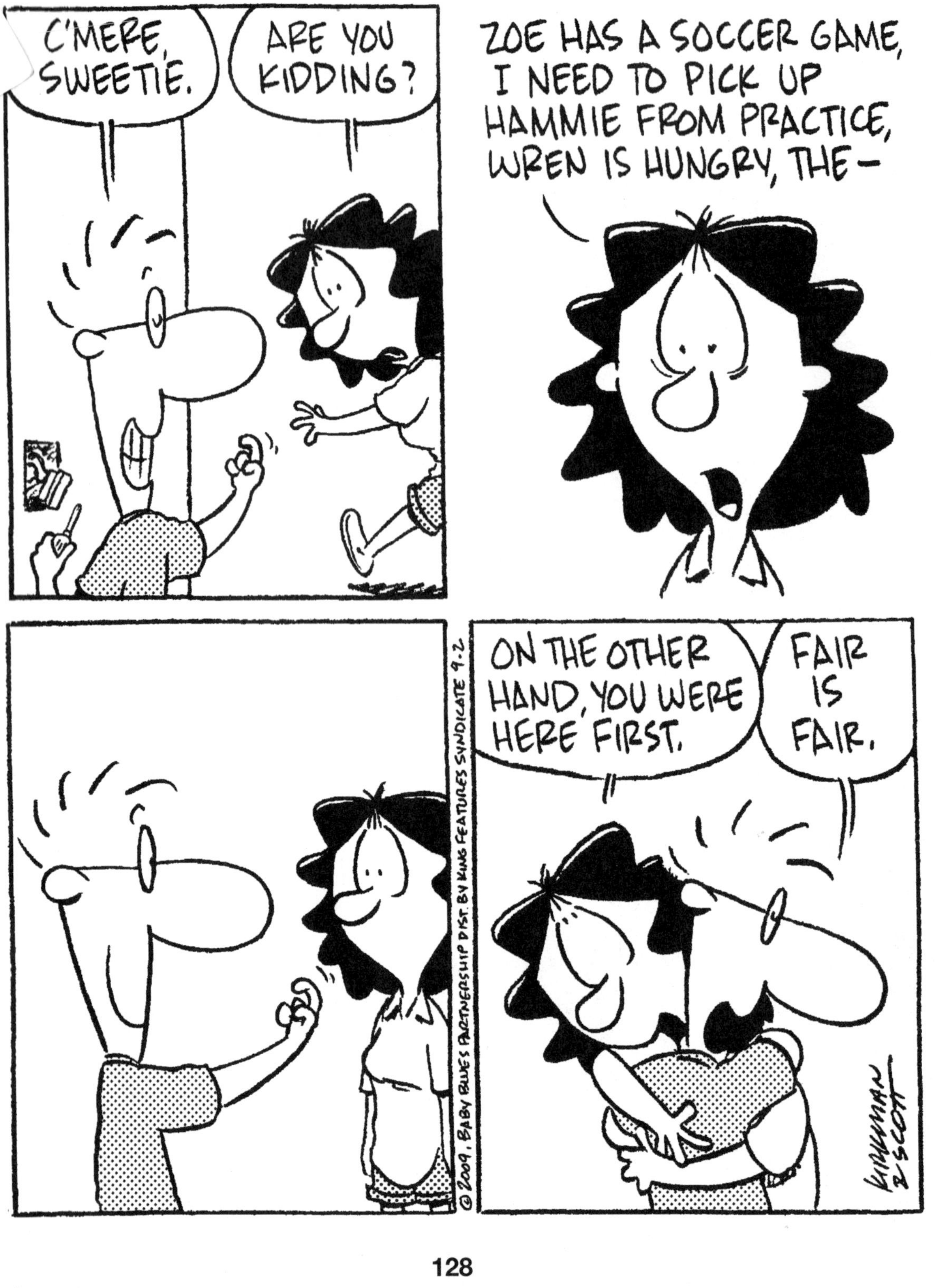
C'MERE, SWEETIE.
ARE YOU KIDDING?
ZOE HAS A SOCCER GAME, I NEED TO PICK UP HAMMIE FROM PRACTICE, WREN IS HUNGRY, THE-
© 2009, BABY BLUES PARTNERSHIP DIST. BY KING FEATURES SYNDICATE 9.2
ON THE OTHER HAND, YOU WERE HERE FIRST.
FAIR IS FAIR.
KIRKMAN & SCOTT